VICTORIAN JEWELLERY

VICTORIAN JEWELLERY

by Margaret Flower

WITH A FOREWORD BY MARGARET J. BIGGS
AND A CHAPTER ON COLLECTING BY
DORIS LANGLEY MOORE

NEW AND REVISED EDITION

SOUTH BRUNSWICK AND NEW YORK:
A. S. BARNES AND COMPANY

© 1951 and new material © Margaret Flower 1967
Library of Congress Catalogue Card Number: 72-6463

A. S. Barnes and Co., Inc.
Cranbury, New Jersey 08512

ISBN 0-498-01265-4
Printed in the United States of America

NEW AND REVISED EDITION

1973

FOREWORD

by MARGARET J. BIGGS

I feel very honoured and flattered to have been asked by Mrs Flower to write a few words of introduction for her book. Having been in the Jewellery Trade all my life, I am naturally very interested in this subject, not only from the point of view of the intrinsic value of jewellery as seen by the average male jeweller, but also of its feminine appeal and how it has always been, and is now, complementary to the fashions of the day.

This book is unique in many ways. It is the first to be written in our language on Victorian jewellery and so will fill the gap on the shelf of reference books used by jewellers. Having read this book, and being a past Chairman of the National Association of Goldsmiths and engaged myself in selling jewellery, I can truly say, on behalf of my colleagues, that it will be invaluable to us. We thank Mrs Flower for having spent so much time and trouble in collecting all this information and condensing it into such absorbing, and at the same time, instructional reading.

It certainly must have been very difficult work, because Mrs Flower had not had any previous training in the jewellery trade. It is only because she is so deeply interested in Victorian jewellery that she has accomplished so much. For this very reason, she has approached her subject from an entirely different angle from other textbooks. Perhaps it is not true to call it a textbook, it is more an intriguing historical account of Victorian jewellery and fashions, and how they influenced each other and in turn were both dictated by the standard of living and economic state of the period.

The Victorian era was one of peace and development. The Industrial Revolution brought new prosperity and wealth to thousands, which enabled them to give more extravagant gifts to their women folk. The opening of the gold mines in California and Australia and the discovery of diamonds in South Africa gave added scope to the designers and manufacturers of jewellery. There was more jewellery produced in these years than at any other time before, and each piece the work of a skilled craftsman, designed to suit the particular fashions of each era—the grand romantic period of the crinoline, the more demure mid-Victorian styles, the gorgeous, gay nineties, each called for a different design in jewellery to enhance it. The latter part of the century saw the start of mass-produced jewellery to meet the needs of the middle class.

v

The average man or woman in the street knows little about the way a piece of jewellery is made, how to assess its value or how to distinguish one precious stone from another or from an imitation, but he or she is always interested to hear of the history behind jewels. For this reason, *Victorian Jewellery* must prove to be one of the most fascinating books of its kind.

Mrs Flower shows us how the changes in dress and hair styles altered the kind of jewellery worn, and so, by comparing one fashion with another and by reference to the many beautiful illustrations Mrs Flower has collected, one can easily ascertain the approximate date of a piece of jewellery. This is an important point and of great use to the jeweller, as Victorian jewels are the antiques of tomorrow.

I hope I have now made you thoroughly interested in this most rewarding subject, so that you are impatient to delve into the study of *Victorian Jewellery*.

CONTENTS

COLOUR PLATES

MONOCHROME ILLUSTRATIONS

ix

NECKLACES, NECKLETS AND CHAINS

PENDANTS AND LOCKETS

CORSAGE ORNAMENTS

BROOCHES

BANGLES AND BRACELETS

* By gracious permission of H.M. The Queen.

RINGS

MISCELLANEOUS

* By gracious permission of H.M. The Queen

ACKNOWLEDGEMENTS

I should like to express my very grateful thanks to all those who have helped me in the preparation of this book. First among these comes Mrs DORIS LANGLEY MOORE, who suggested to me some years ago that such a book as this was needed and urged me to put it together. She has been unfailingly encouraging and helpful while I have been at work on it. She has allowed me to make unlimited use of her excellent library of women's magazines and fashion-plates. All the quotations from fashion magazines and all the reproductions of fashion-plates in this book come from works in her possession. She has kindly allowed a large number of her fine pieces of jewellery to be photographed, as the reader will easily see from looking through the illustrations.* Mrs Moore is well known as an authority on women's costume, and her knowledge in the field of jewellery is equally extensive. For what I have learned through her expert criticism and advice, I can never be sufficiently grateful.

Miss MARGARET J. BIGGS, whose knowledge and experience of jewellery is apparent from the fact that she is the first woman ever chosen to be Chairman of the National Association of Goldsmiths, has done me the kindness of reading the manuscript before publication. Miss Biggs has also supplied some of the most interesting illustrations.

In my search for examples of jewellery to be photographed, I have met in nearly every case with courtesy and consideration. I am particularly honoured by the gracious permission of HIS MAJESTY THE KING to reproduce photographs of some of Queen Victoria's jewellery in the Royal Library at Windsor.

Among those who have given me advice and encouragement, I should like particularly to thank:

Mr G. F. ANDREWS, of the National Association of Goldsmiths
Mrs C. R. ASHBEE
Mr LIONEL C. T. BOX, of The *Watchmaker, Jeweller and Silversmith*
Mr A. E. BOYLES, of The Goldsmiths & Silversmiths Company Ltd
Mr COLLINS, of Sotheby's
Mrs MONA CURRAN, of the National Jewellers' Association
Mr DAWKINS, of Sotheby's
Mr F. FURNESS, of Messrs Bracher & Sydenham
Mr L. F. GOODFORD

Mr W. H. Traies Green, of Messrs Harvey & Gore
Mr John Hayward, of the Victoria & Albert Museum
Miss Hilford
Mr Martin Holmes, of the London Museum
Mr James Laver, of the Victoria & Albert Museum
Sir Owen Morshead, k.c.v.o., d.s.o., m.c.
Mr C. C. Oman, of the Victoria & Albert Museum
Mr Mosheh Oved, of Cameo Corner
Messrs S. J. Phillips
Messrs R. Pringle
Mr Norman Reid, of the Tate Gallery
Mr Frank Schwickerath
Miss Scott-Elliot
Mr Edward H. Smith, of Christies
The Staff of the London Library

I am very grateful indeed to my friends and acquaintances who generously lent me their Victorian jewellery so that it could be photographed, and to Mr Morgan, of R. B. Fleming & Co, who took nearly all the photographs and whose patience and interest seemed to be endless.

Finally I want to thank my husband, who first woke my interest in Victorian Jewellery, and whose taste, knowledge and encouragement have made this book possible.

M. F.
1951

* Note: The jewellery which belonged to Mrs Doris Langley Moore when this book first appeared belongs now to her daughter, Mrs James Walker, whose name appears instead of Mrs Langley Moore's in the present edition.

M. F.
1972

ON COLLECTING JEWELLERY

by DORIS LANGLEY MOORE

WHETHER stolen jewels are sweeter than those which are come by honestly we must leave it to some candid burglar to inform us: so far as my own knowledge goes, there are none so delectable as those we have acquired through being early in the field. Collectors of Victorian jewellery who launched out in that epoch of reaction when the word 'Victorian' applied to any decorative object was a term of contempt have been able, during the past decade or two, to enjoy a double pleasure. Not only their taste but even their wisdom has been vindicated. They see their treasures both admired and valued.

Though late Victorian design remains (for the time being) in the trough where all discarded fashions must lie for a more or less measurable number of years, the products of the early and middle periods are mounting to the crest of the wave, and those who had their family jewels reset in the style of the nineteen-twenties or destroyed merely for the price of the materials have cause to regret their short-sightedness.

I recollect going into the shop of a Harrogate jeweller many years ago and finding him with a pile, a rich mound, of nineteenth-century trinkets which he was preparing to send away for breaking up. I picked out a number of interesting pieces and begged him to preserve them, but the market for gold was higher than the market for craftsmanship, and he had already made his bargain. This was but one of his monthly consignments to the dealers in precious metals who, working both through local tradesmen and a widespread system of house-to-house canvassing, succeeded in demolishing tens of thousands of specimens not inferior to those illustrated in this book. Similar holocausts have been offered periodically throughout history, and even the masterpieces of Cellini have not been spared.

Between the vicissitudes of fashion and the exactions of war, jewellery of what Mrs Flower defines as the primary kind has but a meagre chance of surviving long in its original form, and it is not surprising that we see only occasionally, and then for the most part in museums, the exquisitely wrought 'toys' of the later Renaissance, the splendid diamond parures of the eighteenth century, and those fine examples of the goldsmith's skill which are characteristic of the French Empire and the English Regency.

Fortunately, the Victorians used, beside precious stones and metals, an immense variety of materials which offer few temptations to the breaker-up, and it is still possible to make a good collection without a very long purse—though the palmy days are undoubtedly over.

When I first began to spend my pocket money on what was then regarded as a slightly ludicrous hobby, earrings of inlaid tortoiseshell or carved ivory were generally to be found in the jewellers' ten-shilling trays; combs pavé-set with coral or turquoise seldom cost more than about a pound each; and it seemed an extravagance to buy the parure of seed pearls shown here in Fig. 6 for twelve guineas. To be able to look back on an early start is a lasting satisfaction, but one not unqualified by twinges of shame for the mistakes of ignorance and misjudgment, and it is from the memory of these not less than of happy finds and successful machinations that I venture to write a sort of footnote to this work intended to be of service to the collectors of a younger generation.

With such a book as this to consult—immeasurably surpassing the few scattered chapters and magazine articles which have hitherto provided all the accessible data—ignorance will very easily and agreeably be overcome, so my few counsels are of a general character and directed principally against misjudgment.

The first will be in the nature of a paradox. If you desire your collection to appreciate in value never be tempted to regard your buying as an investment. Such an outlook in anyone but a highly experienced tradesman is all but certain to lead to follies. It is difficult to ignore the monetary aspects, for the very simple reason that hardly any of us can afford to, but the best collections have always borne a strong imprint of the taste of the collector and the worst are those on which money has been spent in the hope of a rising market.

It seems to have been decreed by the rather malicious gods who preside over the destinies of things made to please the eye that those who, pretending to be amateurs, are secretly speculators shall sooner or later be exposed as laughing-stocks. Either they are deluded in their choice, like the magnates who 'invested' two thousand pounds a time in Marcus Stones and Alma Tademas when almost any work of the Impressionists could have been had for a tiny fraction of that sum, or else some social upheaval or new invention brings about a change in standards.

The discovery of apparently inexhaustible diamond mines at Kimberley in the mid-Victorian period diminished the price of diamonds bought when those stones were of a much greater rarity, while the adaption of new methods of cutting which strikingly heightened the brilliance of the gems reduced the worth—commercially speaking—of rose-cut diamonds set in the eighteenth century.

In the long run the best reason for buying a jewel, as for buying any other object, is that its intrinsic qualities make a genuine appeal to the purchaser, and thus it will still have its charm even though its intrinsic value should fluctuate.

To the young collector who would like to be guided by his, or more probably her, own taste but feels some lack of confidence in its promptings, I should say that the three attributes to look for are good workmanship, soundness of the materials used, and well-defined style.

The pendulum of fashion may eclipse the merit of a fine piece of workmanship but only for a limited span: sooner or later, unless it has been wasted on a thoroughly bad design, it will command respect. Beautiful design, on the other hand, cannot redeem bad workmanship. A crude machine-stamped copy of some brooch or bracelet originally produced by an expert craftsman will be a trumpery thing, however elegant the creation that inspired it.

As for the materials, they need not be precious, but they should be respectable of their kind. Pinchbeck is better than rolled gold with its thin glitter wearing away to show the base metal beneath. Good specimens of semi-precious stones are superior to precious ones of poor colour or in a damaged state. Such at least is my opinion.

When I speak of a well-defined style, I mean that a jewel is likely to be more interesting and consequently better worth possessing if it is frankly of its period and not endeavouring to be artistic by some impossible timeless standard. There are really no timeless standards. Great masterpieces may just as readily be dated from stylistic evidence as the works of minor artists, and something meretricious always hangs about the productions of those who seek to raise the level by turning their backs upon their own age. A designer, of course, may well, like Giuliano and Castellani, revive ideas from so remote a past that it has all the attractions of novelty, but if he is truly creative he cannot help bringing to his work something expressive of himself and his time, so that his pieces are as easy to 'place' as if he had deliberately made them so. I am always chary of buying jewellery of a vague and indeterminate type.

Speaking then as one who has been, so far as her very modest means would permit, an indefatigable collector, I should reply to the question,

'What to collect?' that it is rewarding to buy well-wrought pieces of honest quality, whether precious or semi-precious or of materials in themselves valueless, such as hair or potter's clay, and that such pieces, however outmoded, should be clearly representative of a mode.

The next question is obviously 'Where and how to collect?' and the only valid answer seems to be, 'Anywhere and by every method that the law allows'. From the stalls of street markets to the most select antiquarian jewellers' shops, from the private transaction with a friend to the public transaction with an auctioneer, from the lucky dip of an advertisement in a newspaper to the sensitive feelers thrown out for a particular birthday, Christmas, or wedding gift, all roads may lead to acquisitions that will be treasured just as all may lead to the most absurd disillusionments.

It is a mistake to think that bargains are not to be had from dealers who specialize in a carefully selected stock, and an even greater mistake to suppose that bargains abound in the junk shops. But the greatest mistake of all is to imagine that a good collection can be made up of bargains. Most things have some sort of market price and few are disposed of for less by those whose lives are spent in buying and selling.

Certainly it is known to happen that an inexpert dealer in an out-of-the-way place will fail to recognize a good piece for what it is. Equally there are occasions when, in some shop where everything appears luxurious and costly, you are suddenly given the opportunity of buying a desirable item at a very low price. It may spring from the wish to reward or to secure a regular customer—and there is much to be said for being a regular customer even in a small way—or perhaps the object concerned is one which is so trifling compared with those the firm usually handles that they can afford to take a narrow margin of profit on it. (Only thus can I account for having been able to buy the Nineties brooch shown in Fig. 86b from one of the best-known diamond merchants in London for one-fifth of the valuation placed on it by another firm a few days later; while by a similar lucky stroke my favourite ring was the unwanted part of a lot just brought from the auction room by a dealer in a particularly benevolent frame of mind.)

Yet on the whole it must be admitted as quite improbable that a notable collection of any type could be amassed, like that of Cousin Pons, on the strength of enthusiasm alone unsupported by an adequate income. Bargains are delightful, but it will generally be found in real life that, if some things are acquired cheaply, others, because we are drawn towards them, we buy too dear.

Where the lay purchaser is concerned, I should recommend auction sales for their quiet but deeply stirring excitements rather than for their prospects of enrichment. Unless you bid for secondary jewellery that has become unfashionable and are prepared to wait twenty or thirty years till it swings back into vogue—a gamble that might not come off—the chances of doing better than the dealers are peculiar rather than extensive, though it is amusing to try.

An acquaintance of mine with a shrewd eye noticed in one sale some years ago a displeasing photograph of a Turkish gentleman in a frame studded all over with pieces of glass which were set in a kind of greyish cement. Not having attended the pre-view, he was unable to examine it closely, but knowing something of Turkish ways, he decided to venture thirty shillings. The prize was what he had scarcely dared to hope. Both by dirty and dingy setting and their excessive profusion, a quantity of large and fine rose diamonds had succeeded in passing themselves off as coarse paste. It would be unwise, however, to regard such an instance as typical.

Since the imposition of a massive purchase tax on new jewellery, there has been a steep rise in the prices of second-hand pieces, at least in English salerooms. Yet there is always one cheering possibility. Some item may be put up which is in a different category from that which has attracted the dealers to the sale. Thus, on an occasion when important precious stones were being auctioned, a pair of handsome paste girandole earrings of the eighteenth century fetched a mere song which I, so to speak, was fortunate enough to sing. But then I have committed follies under the hypnotic influence of the auctioneer's eye which I could hardly recount to my best friend, and which have effectually cancelled out all my little victories.

In making private transactions, you will find your friends quite as much disposed to overvalue as to undervalue their possessions, and the negotiations can sometimes be embarrassing; while newspaper advertisements, though they produce many interesting results, involve a weariful amount of correspondence, much of which is likely to prove futile. Except for the collector whose hobby is a passion, the shop remains the happiest hunting ground. If you are good at resisting the wrong temptations and succumbing to the right ones, the shops will yield you entertainment even in the dullest and seediest districts, or through the longest hours to be whiled away in a town at a railway junction. Browsing among the shops and markets of a strange city with a little valid currency to spare is surely to be classed high among the enjoyments of life.

Let us suppose then that, by any or all of the means I have set out, you are getting together a selection of Victorian pieces worth preserving, the final question is, 'How to preserve them?'

The three cardinal rules are: Keep them neatly arranged in a suitable case and do not let sets become divided. Never leave damage unrepaired. Let things remain as far as possible in their original state.

It is almost incomprehensible that any woman who loves to wear jewels, even of the humbler kind, can be content to keep them in an old cigar box or else lying loose in the drawer of a toilet table, delicate chains knotted up in bracelets and pendants, soft materials scratched and brittle ones chipped. Worse still, as you endeavour to sort out the tangle, you will probably be regaled with some such running commentary as this:

'There used to be a brooch to match that necklace, but I had it made into a clip for a hat I was fond of, and it must have fallen out somewhere or other . . . That earring's odd, I'm afraid. I was going to take it to the jeweller to see if he could find a brooch in the same style, and I put it in a used envelope and I think it was accidentally thrown away . . . Oh, don't look at my poor bracelet. You'd hardly believe how nice it was before it lost its stones. I must really have it repaired some time, and there's a broken locket too that ought to be attended to.'

This same jumble of trinkets which you turn over so doubtfully, surprised to find a single choice item, might have made a beautiful and enviable array if properly looked after and presented with a touch of showmanship. Stones would not fall out without being at once replaced: indeed, they would perhaps not fall out at all since the settings would be frequently examined. Broken specimens would not be mixed up with sound ones giving a shabby look to all that is seen. Good spacing on a padded background would minimize the risk of damage and enhance the attractiveness of the display. Earrings and brooches would not have been severed from matching pieces, thus ruining parures and demi-parures. (By a mysterious law of providence a set of jewels, like a set of volumes, is all but impossible to reunite once it has been split up. As for an odd earring, it is little better than an odd glove.)

The sort of jewel case you will require depends, naturally, on the scale of your collection. It is well not to invest too soon in the luxury of a handsome leather one divided into compartments because you may rapidly outgrow it. Victorian jewellery needs a roomy container. In the early stages, home-made pads of velvet can be used to line any box or boxes of appropriate size and little velvet cushions can separate the layers. A small Wellington chest with lined drawers is an excellent cabinet for ornaments of the larger type—combs, diadems, heavy Sixties and Seventies chains, silver belts and chatelaines—and, if it can be securely locked, is more baffling to thieves than an easily portable case. That is to say—more baffling to casual thieves, for it takes a great deal to frustrate a planned burglary.

How far it is legitimate to alter and adapt well-made period jewels is a topic open to controversy. I have been guilty of having earrings shortened when long ones went out of fashion during the nineteen-thirties, but in all save two regrettable instances, I kept the portions not in use and have since had them restored. It is not, however, the sort of practice to be commended, for the chances of losing or mislaying the sections which have been removed are considerable.

It is perhaps a little pedantic to object to the replacement of hooks by screw fittings, but the conversion certainly affects the character of the jewels, and if you are going to collect extensively, it would be as well to have your ears pierced. Not only will you then be enabled to wear quite heavy earrings without discomfort, but you will find the risk of losing them substantially reduced. The modern method of ear-piercing is a great improvement on the old, and if, as is said, the practice is a relic of barbarism, it seems to me about the least odious of all the relics of barbarism we cling to.

The actual remodelling of old jewellery is always to be deplored, except when the original was itself of bad workmanship or wholly insipid design. I have caused a plain diamond stud to be reset as a ring without a qualm, but I am not so sure whether I was right to have a typical early Victorian necklace shortened to provide earrings—though it is true that the length was awkward and earrings of the period are so rare that there was little hope of finding any to go with it. (I pause to wonder incidentally how those necklaces about eighteen inches long which always lie so snugly on the shoulders in fashion plates—see, for instance, Fig. 1—were really kept in position. My own experience has been that, instead of giving a round effect as intended, they fall untidily forward, and I can only suppose that, since they could not have been glued to the skin, they must have been perpetually readjusted with a self-conscious gesture.)

I have never myself—alas!—had to deal with the problem of what to do with a diamond tiara which is only wearable on such occasions as we seldom nowadays see, but if I were consulted I should say even in that extreme case: 'Do not break up such a piece! If it cannot be made reasonably useful as a collarette or bracelet without spoiling the design, then wait patiently until grandeur again becomes fashionable. And if that should never be, you will still have done well to preserve what must assuredly come to be regarded as a rich and rare example of a bygone mode.'

A harrowing tiara story was once told me by my jeweller while I was waiting for some rings to be cleaned. A friend of his who owned a small shop was offered a capacious chocolate box full of oddments of old-fashioned paste, loose synthetic pearls, and the battered silver stoppers of lost scent bottles. He bought it for the apparently talismanic sum of thirty shillings. When he came to look over its contents more closely a few days later, he noticed among the glitter of artificial gems a brilliance more convincing. Mixed up with the beads and buckles were several fragments which were, to his professional eye, plainly the remnants of a Victorian tiara that had been broken up.

Being honest and also anxious to avoid trouble, he consulted the police. He summed up the woman who had sold him the box as an old servant who was disposing of some small perquisite—decidely not stolen goods or she would have known better than to part with them for so low a price. The police made efforts to trace her, but her description was commonplace, she had left no clue, and after some months the jeweller was informed that he was free to consider himself the owner of his purchase. He sold the diamonds later for a thousand pounds, and it was always his opinion that they had been the property of a woman who had died and on whose death they had descended, unrecognized for what they were, to her maid or nurse. Only by some such theory could one account for a transaction which was never followed up by any attempt to recover the property.

The moral is—keep your tiara intact, or at least make sure that your diamonds are not allowed to stray into a company of trash.

It is a literal fact that, through a combination of ignorance and carelessness, some of the greatest treasures now seen in art galleries or cherished by private collectors have lain under an eclipse for generations on end, lost to the families that should have benefited from them . . . a point which I will illustrate with one last cautionary story. It happened to a very near friend of mine and I know it to be true.

This lady at an early age acquired a wealthy mother-in-law who owned a quantity of Victorian jewellery which was regarded in the family as irredeemably out-of-date and unattractive. On the rare occasions when any of it came to light, it was always spoken of deprecatingly as something which could not exactly be thrown away, but which no one need pretend to like.

My youthful and inexperienced friend therefore placed no great value on the gifts that were from time to time handed her, generally with some half-apologetic little speech.

One Christmas she received with only a very muted flourish a necklace seemingly of garnets, a stone highly esteemed by the Victorians and consequently out of favour with their immediate successors. My friend was pleased with it, however, in a mild sort of way and took it to London on her next visit. When about to return to the distant Northern town where she lived, she found herself rather short of cash. Engine trouble soon after the beginning of the journey compelled her to spend at a garage the very small amount she had with her, and, having lost a good deal of time, she decided to call on the first pawnbroker she could find and pledge her garnets, which were handy, for a couple of pounds.

It may be hard for those who are prudent and methodical to believe, but the scatterbrained heroine of this story delayed redeeming her pledge until she had lost the pawn-ticket. She had forgotten the pawnbroker's name, and in any case to redeem the necklace without the ticket would, it appeared, be a boring and troublesome process which its value hardly seemed to warrant. Lazily, without a word to anyone, she let the matter drop.

At least eighteen months later, her mother-in-law said to her: 'I notice you never wear my grandmother's rubies'. And as my friend gazed back, uncomprehending, she added, 'Of course, the setting isn't the sort of thing anyone likes nowadays but they're very good stones, you know. I hope you've got them properly insured'.

The unlucky culprit, without making any confession, took the first opportunity of going to London, but among the miles of unfamiliar streets through which she had driven with more than one wrong turning on her way to the Great North Road, she was quite unsuccessful in finding the pawnbroker's shop; and it is highly improbable that, even if she had done so, she could have recovered the jewels so foolishly squandered. Her only clear memory of a transaction which she had regarded at the time as altogether unimportant was that the man behind the counter had asked her sharply and somewhat insultingly as she thought: 'Are you sure that this article is your own property?'

Though this is an exceptionally egregious instance, multitudes of errors have been made similar in kind and differing only in degree. And the démodé jewellery of the present century has even less chance of surviving for the collectors of the future than the once-despised adornments of the Victorians, for this is an age of shortages. People no longer put aside for a lifetime things they have ceased to use. The materials have now become too precious to be thus conserved, and space in the rabbit warrens where so many of us now live is more precious still. Even an aigrette, a bangle, a vanity case, a jewelled mount for a handbag, are considered to take up too much room. There will be little, it seems, to remember our mothers by.

The true collector is essentially a preserver and I am wholly at a loss to see why so many of the few who figure in novels are portrayed as cold, frivolous, or even villainous. A man in a book has only to handle a finely chased snuff-box with affectionate fingers, a woman's eyes have only to light up at the sight of a splendid gem, and we are meant to know that here is a base character. In real life we should instantly warm to such sensitive and appreciative qualities.

Collectors tend to fall into two categories—the virtuosi and the historians or amassers of documentary evidence. The virtuoso desires only what is choice and excellent of its kind, he prefers perfection to plenty, he enriches museums with what are known as 'museum pieces'. The historian on the other hand seeks what is representative and typical irrespective of beauty or rarity. He builds up with a large variety of specimens the portrait of a period—an aim which could never be accomplished by concentrating only on what was made for the connoisseur. Both approaches have something to recommend them. To advise which line the eager beginner should follow would be a futility, for each is a matter of temperament in the most fundamental sense.

Whatever course may be taken, the young enthusiast who is equipped with this superb text-book may be congratulated on having adopted a hobby so rich in possibilities that it may be guaranteed to provide entertainment, excitement, and a firm assurance against boredom as long as there remains a peril to be avoided or a prize to be won.

I
INTRODUCTION

INTRODUCTION

JEWELLERY, like every form of decoration, reflects the taste and circumstances of its period. The reign of Queen Victoria was an age of increasing prosperity with a firm belief in progress: it was accordingly to be expected that during such a time a great quantity of jewellery should be made and worn, that jewellery should, as never before, be subject to rapid changes in fashion, and that the consequent variety of styles should appeal to a competitive society in which new wealthy families were constantly arising—all convinced that the latest thing must be the best. The astonishing range of quality, from the finest examples of the goldsmith's art to the cheapest products of the machine, was equally natural during a period when expert craftsmanship and mass-production were alike causes for gratification and wonder. There was nothing, the Victorians thought, which their artisans were not capable of producing.

The Victorians liked jewellery; they were pleased to see it and delighted in wearing it. They believed, in their exuberance, that if a thing was good, you could not have too much of it. Gold and precious stones were good, and when they were chased, polished and transformed into ornaments which were, in their way, works of art, they were even better. No one seems to have feared that the display of a great deal of portable wealth might arouse resentment in the underprivileged; no long or costly wars raised the threat of sumptuary laws over them, nor was taxation so great as to curtail their expenditure on jewels.

The Queen herself was fond of jewellery and encouraged others to wear it, by her example and by her numerous gifts of brooches, bracelets and necklaces. When the Queen wrote to Florence Nightingale in 1856, praising her work in the Crimean War, she sent with the letter a brooch, of which the form and emblems were symbolical of Miss Nightingale's 'great and blessed work'.[1] The silver necklace which the Queen gave to Jenny Lind is shown in Fig. 76. The pendant in Fig. 80c, with an inscription commemorating the death of the Queen's half-sister, is one of many such jewels sent by the Queen to her family circle on these sad occasions. (The Princess of Wales also gave jewels as presents to her friends, one of which is in Fig. 89b.) In her many portraits Queen Victoria usually wears several pieces of jewellery in the latest fashion. An advertisement of Sully's portrait painted in 1839 describes her as 'ascending the throne of the House of Lords in the robes and jewels of

[1] Hector Bolitho: *The Reign of Queen Victoria*. London, 1949.

[3]

state'. In less formal poses she is usually shown wearing several jewelled bracelets. Engravings of these portraits found their way into homes throughout the country, and it was natural that the Queen's subjects should be influenced by what they saw her wear. The rich and the well-to-do were thus able to give considerable satisfaction to themselves and pleasure to others by the confident display of sumptuous ornaments.

Part of the excitement of the many great occasions so beloved of this age lay in the certainty of seeing magnificent jewels. Mrs Ruskin in her long letters to her mother about parties in London always took care to describe the jewellery which she saw. At a party at Lansdowne House, Lady Shelburne wore 'a beautiful necklace of large pearls and handsome bracelets, one of the fashionable shape, in gold and stones'.[1] The two princesses of Saxe-Weimar on another occasion 'were dressed in deep mourning with large jet ornaments on their necks'.[2] The villagers in Mrs Gaskell's *Wives and Daughters* looked forward with delight to the appearance of a duchess at their Charity Ball. But when she appeared on the night without her jewels there was intense disappointment and they thought her a very poor sort of duchess. At fashionable weddings the present which excited the greatest interest among the guests was the *corbeille*, or casket of jewels given by the bridegroom to the bride. And for those who could not attend the ceremony there was always a detailed description of the *corbeille* in the ladies' magazines, with engraved reproductions of the most splendid pieces.[3]

The function of exhibiting the family's prosperity was handed over to the female early in the nineteenth century. Voluntary discipline in men's clothes had been introduced by Beau Brummell, who insisted that a gentleman could wear nothing other than a plain blue coat, and this began a fashion which

[1] Adm. Sir William Milburne James: *Order of Release*, 1947. Letter dated 1 June 1848.

[2] Ibid. Letter dated 1 July 1848.

[3] For example, from the *World of Fashion*, 1838: 'We have recently seen in a *corbeille de mariage*, an *aigrette d'esprit* mounted in a kind of *crep* which was in the form of a tulip, enveloping the beards of the feather in its leaves; the mounting composed of a quantity of small coloured stones mingled with diamonds has a dazzling effect at the foot of that light and graceful feather, which is to be placed on one side of the head'.

And from the *Queen*, 1890: 'The *corbeille* of Mlle de Pourtalès included a *rivière* of diamonds with two ends, which crossed over, and at the ends were two very large diamonds, ten other equally large diamonds were mounted on invisible wire, and fell on the neck, without any apparent support'.

The *Queen* of 1890 also describes and illustrates the half-hoop bracelet of Golconda diamonds and two pear-shaped Ceylon sapphires, the diamond 24-point flaming stars, the pearl and brilliant rosebud brooch, and other presents given by Henry M. Stanley to Dorothy Tennant on their marriage on 12 July of that year.

degenerated easily into the sombre anonymous costume affected by men of the industrial revolution as being expressive of their solidarity and serious purpose. Successful business men loaded their wives with jewels as a means of showing off their newly acquired wealth. Mr Merdle in *Little Dorrit* owed a great part of his reputation for soundness in the City to the splendid jewels displayed on his wife's handsome bosom. In those days a merchant's wife longed for a fine parure as her modern counterpart covets a mink coat—as an assurance that her husband has arrived. The ladies were perfectly content with this arrangement. Their duty was to be decorative rather than active members of society.

Thus until near the end of the century jewellery was regarded as an essential part of the dress of women of the upper and middle classes. Tennyson's miller's daughter wore a jewel that trembled in her ear, and a necklace that rose and fell on her bosom all day long. The impoverished Nell l'Estrange, in Rhoda Broughton's *Cometh Up as a Flower*, put on her best ornaments—a pair of wooden bead bracelets—when she went to meet her sweetheart. Victorian fiction is filled with reference to necklaces, earrings and bracelets; sometimes, as in *The Moonstone* and *The Eustace Diamonds* jewels form the subject of a book. They figure largely in Charlotte Yonge's novels. In *The Daisy Chain* the pearl hoop which Alan Ernescliffe gave as a betrothal ring to Margaret May has an important place, for after his death in the Pacific the ring is set round a chalice in the church which he endowed—a symbol of human love thus continuing as a symbol of divine love; and, on a slightly lower level, in *Heartsease*, Arthur Martindale chooses a blue locket, set with a diamond fly, as a peace-offering to his wife.

Not until the eighties, with the advent of University education and agitation for the vote, did women begin to wonder if such display was proper. 'Tell me, please, is it vulgar to wear jewellery?' wrote one young lady, who signed herself Lucilia, to the *Ladies' Treasury* in 1886. She was assured that it was not vulgar except at unsuitable times, but her letter must have been prompted by definite moral or social qualms. In the same year the *Ladies' Treasury* praised a French princess for receiving her guests in plain white, 'without a single gem, whether in her hair or on her neck', so that her humblest visitor might feel at ease. Such consideration and such praise would have been out of place in the fifties.

Writers of books on beauty and etiquette had much advice to give on the wearing of jewellery. Coral, ivory and semi-precious materials were, they considered, suitable for morning wear, but gold and precious stones were to be reserved for more formal dress.[1] The grandest ornaments were naturally to be kept for an appearance at Court or for a great Ball. Young ladies were advised against wearing precious stones. In 1837 Mrs Walker wrote 'Flowers decorate the system of life, which is exuberant only in the young; jewels decorate the system of mind, which excels in the old'. That is to say that flowers may be thrown over the person generally, while jewels are usually attached to an organ of sense or intellect. 'Young ladies should never wear rings on their fingers, unless they desire to seem older' was another of Mrs Walker's precepts; and again: 'Long brilliant earrings are becoming to noble and grave features'. The ladies who might have read Mrs Walker's book can be seen in Finden's *Portraits of the Female Aristocracy at the Court of Queen Victoria:* they apparently obeyed her directions, for the unmarried ones are seldom to be seen wearing more than a fine chain, while those who were married were decked in splendid ornaments.[2] Mrs Haweis, writing in 1889, urged moderation in the use of jewellery: 'How seldom one sees a woman use jewels properly! She either obliterates her eyes and complexion by too much dazzle, wearing brilliants as big as pigeons' eggs . . . or she goes to the other extreme and wears none, looking as if she had been disturbed at her toilet by burglars, or rifled by her creditors just before dinner'.

Besides the experts on beauty, who wished jewellery to improve the appearance of the wearer, and the experts on etiquette, who wished it to be worn at the proper time and place, there were the fashion writers who prescribed the ornaments required for each toilette, and described the latest novelties to be found in the shops.[3] Another important function of the fashion writers was to describe the jewels worn by the leaders of society. The spirit

[1] 'In promenade or carriage dress jewels are out of place. Nothing should be worn round the neck but a plain or watered ribbon, about half an inch broad, or a chain of silver or gold, as a guard to suspend the watch, or eyeglass if the wearer be shortsighted, for wearing an eyeglass without occasion for it is a piece of impertinent affectation.
'The ball dress requires a union of beauty, elegance, lightness and magnificence. All the resources of the toilet must be lavished upon it. No trivial embroidery or ornaments of gold or silver must glitter there: their place is supplied with pearls, diamonds and other jewels.'
Mrs Walker: *Female Beauty*, 1837.

[2] Yet in the sixties and seventies young girls wore earrings, necklaces and bracelets, often made of expensive materials. Diamonds, however, remained the prerogative of the married woman.

[3] The fashion magazines are the richest source of information about changes of fashion in jewellery. They tell us, for instance, that hair-work was considered to be in execrable taste in 1838, yet was highly prized in 1853; that necklaces with pendent medallions were much worn in the late sixties; that lockets in many patterns were popular in the seventies; that silver was the favourite metal of the eighties; and that moonstones, opals and turquoises were fashionable in the nineties.

of emulation in Victorian women was strong. Having read the fashion writers to discover what was new, correct and socially acceptable, the wealthier women bought jewelled ornaments as nearly as possible like those of the aristocracy, and the poorer ones found adequate substitutes—first in pinchbeck and paste, and later in machine-stamped jewellery.

Mr Quentin Bell has pointed out that fashionable changes take place only in a society which itself is changing and in which more than one class can afford the luxury of sumptuous dress. These conditions were fulfilled in Victorian England, and consequently new styles of jewellery were quickly adopted by the upper and middle classes alike. As a result, the productions of this era may be divided, for purposes of discussion, into two classes: primary jewellery, constructed of precious stones and precious metals; and secondary, comprising all semi-precious ornaments. Jewellery made entirely of gold belongs sometimes to one class and sometimes to the other, according to the fineness of the design and the quality of the workmanship.

Primary jewellery was intended for wear on state occasions and for the public appearances of royalty; it tends—perhaps in consequence—to be conservative in design and international in character. It was made to last, and for that reason designs which are *outré* or purely local in their style are unsuitable to it. Primary jewellery was, and still is, distinguished by excellence of material and proficiency of workmanship. The care taken in choosing the stones and in designing the mount makes the production of a piece of primary jewellery a long affair, and the number of pieces existing at any one time is never very great. Of those which survive intact in their original setting the number is even smaller: the quality of the stones being so high, people who inherit these pieces show a regrettable tendency to have the valuable gems reset in the latest fashion of their own day. In consequence primary specimens of this Victorian art are not abundant.

Secondary jewellery in its original state, however, survives in great quantities. This is the type of ornament which displays most clearly the wide variations of style and range of materials used by the Victorians in their jewellery.

The first group of secondary jewellery is that which is simply a less expensive imitation of primary jewellery; it follows the same designs but uses garnets for rubies, chrysolites for emeralds, paste for diamonds, and so on. Inexpensive materials, such as coral, ivory and jet, come into this class; so also do many ornaments made of gold or silver without stones of any sort. A great deal of this jewellery is well made and very desirable. On the other hand, the later Victorian machine-stamped pieces, which come at the bottom of the scale, have little to recommend them but their curiosity.

Next there is the jewellery of novelty, equivalent to the costume jewellery of today, which showed its wearer to be not necessarily wealthy but up to the minute. This was the type of ornament which obviously went most quickly in and out of fashion. For example, in the sixties flies under crystal were popular; in the seventies earrings in the shape of hammers, tongs or ladders were affected; while demi-parures of locomotives were worn in the eighties.

The strings of beads, the lockets and tiny earrings worn by young girls and children may be regarded as a third group of secondary jewellery.

Folk jewellery in traditional designs was another type of ornament which was very popular with the Victorians; the fashion was largely brought about by the Queen's fondness for Scotland. The Edinburgh firms which specialized in silver brooches in the form of shields or claymores set with cairngorms sold them in large numbers to English visitors. Mrs Ruskin wrote to her mother, from her honeymoon trip in Scotland, that John thought of sending for Peter McAlpin to see if he had any pearls or cairngorms, but was told that he would have none at that season (Spring, 1848). The jewellery of Ireland was also popular. Copies of ancient Irish brooches appeared in nearly every exhibition of importance, and carved ornaments of bog-oak, set with Irish pearls, were much admired.

A further group of secondary jewellery, showing in its origins some influence of folk design, may be called the Arts and Crafts type. This originated in the distaste which the Pre-Raphaelites felt for everything connected with industrialism, and it can be seen represented in the paintings of Rossetti.[1] It was self-consciously archaic, seeking its inspiration in primitive patterns. It was usually the work of amateurs, and hence lacked the professional's precision and finish; for this reason, if for no other, it was not popular, and few women wore it who were not in some way connected with the Pre-Raphaelite circle. But in its unconventional design it opened the way for the jewellery of the *Art Nouveau* school which took the artistic world by storm in the nineties. As the name of their movement implied, the designers of this school wished to break away from every convention and produce something entirely new—in fact, they did create much that had not been seen before.

---

[1] Sir Sydney Cockerell tells me that the actual ornaments which Rossetti used as models were old trinkets (one of them a seventeenth-century Italian crystal heart, being in Sir Sydney's possession), but Rossetti represented them in the manner of the jewellery to which I am now referring.

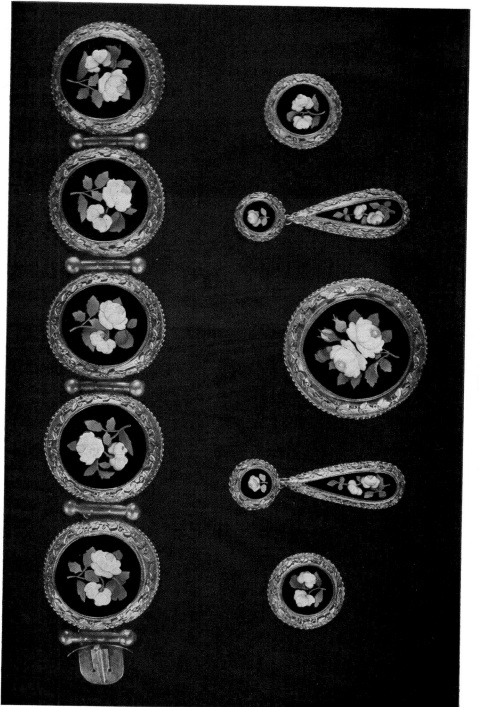

PLATE I

Parure of inlaid work, sometimes called Florentine Mosaic, set in gold

The medallions are of black marble inlaid with roses and leaves in pink and green
marble. Each medallion is set in a gold frame ornamented with a garland of vine-leaves
in appliqué. Italian, 1845 – 50.

(Mrs Charles Ede)

Their work had a profound effect on style in ornament which, beginning in the secondary group, had by the end of the century spread upwards and changed the appearance of primary jewellery to an equal degree.

So far, all the types and styles mentioned have belonged to the jewellery of display: equally important in the nineteenth century was the jewellery of sentiment. Locks of hair from the heads of relatives or sweethearts were shaped into pictures set in gold, or woven into strands from which bracelets, brooches or earrings were made.[1] Long after ornaments made entirely of hair had gone out of fashion, most gold brooches and pendants still had a little glass box at the back in which a lock of hair could be kept. Lockets, invented to enclose locks of hair or portraits, are naturally important in the jewellery of sentiment.

Miniatures were much used as clasps for bracelets or as centres for brooches. The Queen liked to wear a bracelet which was made up of linked miniatures of all her children, and the bridesmaids of Princess Alexandra gave her a bracelet containing miniatures, on her marriage to the Prince of Wales.[2] Towards the end of the century it became fashionable for engaged couples to exchange miniatures. The girl's portrait, framed in pearls, was worn by the man, attached to his watch-chain. The man's miniature, framed in diamonds and pearls, was worn as a locket by the girl.

Occasions as well as persons were commemorated in jewellery. Brooches sometimes consisted simply of a name or a date in gold; bridegrooms often gave the bridesmaids brooches bearing the date of the ceremony or the name of the bride. Exhibitions also produced a crop of sentimental jewellery, like the Trocadero bracelet of 1878, described on page 138. Souvenirs of travel to bring back memories of happy days in Switzerland or Italy added a foreign flavour: suites of lava from Pompeii, shell cameos and mosaics from Naples and carved ivory from Switzerland were brought home in large quantities.

But by far the largest part of the jewellery of sentiment was that devoted to mourning. Victorian matrons often had to spend several years in full or half mourning, and on many occasions mourning had to be worn by the ladies of the Court. At these times the only permissible jewellery was jet.[3] The jet industry at Whitby, which flourished throughout the century, turned out brooches, necklaces, earrings and bracelets in vast numbers to satisfy this constant market. And when the prescribed period for wearing

[1] Figs. 31b, 42b and 44a, b and c.
[2] Fig. 85.
[3] Fig. 1.

black was past, the memory of the departed could still be enshrined in one of the brooches, rings or lockets which had space within them for a lock of hair.

Fashions in jewellery of all types were closely related to changes in hair-dressing and clothes: particularly in the kind of ornament preferred from time to time as interest shifted from one part of the body to another. For instance, in the late thirties the head and neck were centres of interest; and the brow, framed by smooth hair drawn down from a central parting, was set off by a pendent jewel or *ferronnière*; the chignon, built up in fancy shapes, was pierced by arrows and daggers; the open necks of the dresses revealed small lockets or decorative necklets; the flat broad shoulders allowed plenty of space for long earrings.

Clothes in the forties were demure and covered nearly all of the body during the day: there were no open necks for necklaces, and since the ears were always covered—either by hair or by close-fitting bonnets—earrings went out of fashion. At the high necks or on the low evening *décolletages* brooches were worn; they were sometimes rather large, often with pendants, as if to make up for the lack of any other jewels.[1] In the forties the centre of interest was unquestionably the hand: rings were fashionable, and large bracelets with pendants, which made the hands of their wearers appear attractively small.

In the fifties clothes were rich and elegant. That prosperous and optimistic decade brought back into favour many forms of ornament which had not been seen for years. The hair, rising slightly from its centre parting, made a good setting for a diadem. The lobes of the ears had appeared once more and earrings were worn again, though they were generally small ones. Large brooches were pinned at the throat during the day, while at night elaborate necklaces reappeared. Bracelets, single or in pairs, were highly fashionable.[2]

The dashing styles and strong colours of the sixties, notable for Garibaldi shirts and bright red stockings, had their counterpart in the massive and brilliantly-coloured jewellery. Necklaces, brooches and bracelets were heavy and elaborate; gold-topped combs of solid appearance held up the large chignons; earrings were long and fringed. When towards the end of the decade—about 1867—the necks of day dresses began to open a little, lockets at once reappeared to fill the opening; they were larger than the lockets of the thirties.

Dress in the seventies was remarkable for its ruching, bows, braid and

[1] Fig. 4.
[2] Fig. 5.

polonaises.[1] The jewellery too became elaborate. Gold fringes on earrings and pendants grew longer. The patterns engraved on lockets increased in their intricacy. Every bit of gold surface on settings was decorated. The facets of stones were set with tiny motifs, and the heads carved on cameos were *habillés* with earrings or necklaces of tiny brilliants.

When the Æsthetic reaction set in about 1880 and dresses were for a short time straight and simple, jewellery went through the same phase: a plain string of amber beads was the only acceptable ornament. Apart from the Æsthetic movement, the sumptuous, formal clothes of this decade, with their cuirass bodices and forbidding bustles, brought with them heavy chains for day wear and diamond stars for the evening; plain gold bangles were worn on the wrists and small neat earrings in the ears.[2]

The nineties were intensely feminine, bringing fashions which emphasized the curves of the figure, with lace on the bosom and on the abundant, rustling petticoats. The jewellery worn with these delicate creations was smaller and lighter than before. Bracelets and rings were narrower; pins replaced heavy brooches; earrings, except for the tiniest studs, disappeared. The hair was swept up into a top-knot on which might be placed a small jewelled ornament.[3] Diamonds were preferred to all other stones. Small diamond stars of flowers or animals were dotted about on the evening coiffure or on the shoulders, so that the general effect was one of small scintillating points distributed haphazardly about the person.[4]

These are some of the changes in the general character of jewellery which accompanied changing fashions in dress. But it would not be true to imagine that jewellery altered with the same rapidity as costume. The details of dress in the nineteenth century changed so quickly and so markedly that any specimen can be ascribed to a particular year with a fair degree of certainty; but in the case of jewellery the general style can be seen to have changed only every five or ten years; so that it is difficult to date a piece more closely than within a decade. Sometimes there is information which tells us when a particular style came into fashion, but it is hard to say when it ceased to be made and worn. Serpent rings, for instance, were never completely out of

[1] Fig. 50.
[2] Fig. 51.
[3] Fig. 96.
[4] 'Fancy jewels are more fashionable than ever; pins and brooches of all styles—flowers birds, emblems, animal's heads, beetles, dragon-flies, etc. It is the fashion to stick pins, the head of which is a jewel, here, there, and everywhere—in the hair, in the draperies of the bodice, in folds of lace or bows of ribbon, and even in bonnets and hats.' The *Young Ladies' Journal*, January 1890.

fashion during the century. Plain gold bangles enjoyed a vogue which lasted for at least forty years. Curb chain bracelets were popular for many years, and are being made today. On the other hand *ferronnières* and Benoîton chains had a short life and can be dated with some accuracy. The durability of jewellery and the sentimental value often attached to individual pieces act as a brake on the spirit of emulation and slow down the speed of changes in fashion.

II
THE EARLY VICTORIAN
OR
ROMANTIC PERIOD
1837-1860

The
EARLY VICTORIAN
or Romantic Period
(1837-60)

QUEEN VICTORIA came to the throne during the full flowering of the Romantic movement. The interest in the Middle Ages, which had increased since the days of Chatterton's forgeries and Macpherson's *Ossian*, through the horrifying tales of Monk Lewis and Mrs Anne Radcliffe, had found its culmination in the medieval romances of Scott.[1] In France, too, the cult of the *moyen âge* was apparent in Victor Hugo's *Notre Dame de Paris*, Mérimée's *Charles IX*, and Vigny's *Cinq-Mars*. But this nostalgia for the Middle Ages was not confined to fiction; it spread through every form of art and craft. Ruskin and Pugin successfully proclaimed the superiority of the Gothic to the Classical in architecture. In 1834 Tudor Gothic was chosen as the style for the new Houses of Parliament. 1839 saw the famous Eglinton Tournament, which reproduced as exactly as possible a tournament of the Middle Ages. In 1840 the Oxford Society for the study of Gothic architecture was founded.

The past of England, which had formerly been the concern of dilettantes and scholars, now became a subject of enthusiastic general study. Organized parties inspected churches and abbeys, learning to distinguish between Gothic and Norman. The same parties re-read the ballads, and developed a keen eye for the picturesque, the principles of which were so admirably set

[1] Scott's reference to opals as being unlucky, in *Anne of Geierstein* (1829), caused those beautiful stones to go out of favour for nearly thirty years, according to Harry Emanuel, in *Diamonds and Precious Stones* (1865).

out for them in the publications of Gilpin. In such magazines as the *Art Journal* (founded in 1839 as the *Art Union Journal*) they read articles on painting and sculpture, ancient costume or medieval buildings. This eagerness for information was not limited to the arts: young women studied geology, zoology and botany, and on their walks took with them sketchbooks and hammers. The general increase of interest in the arts and sciences culminated and found supreme satisfaction in the Great Exhibition of 1851: a display of manufactured marvels which induced a mood of happiness and complacency that lasted throughout the prosperous fifties. The jewellery trade flourished. The discovery of gold in California in 1849 and in Australia in 1851, gave it a great impetus, and the general prosperity produced a multitude of buyers.

The patrons for whom the jewellers worked at the beginning of the new Queen's reign tried enthusiastically to evoke the past in their dress. They wore their hair *à la reine Blanche* (see right-hand figure in Fig. 3), or *à l'Agnes Sorel*, and stuck jewelled arrows and daggers into these historical coiffures.[1] They put *cordelières*—long beaded girdles thought to be medieval, round their waists, often with chatelaines attached. But the supreme example of their enthusiasm for the past was the *ferronnière*, characteristic of the years 1830 to 1845. This was an ornament (shown in Fig. 2) composed of a chain or cord encircling the crown of the head, with a single jewel depending from it, hanging in the centre of the forehead. The name came from the portrait by Leonardo, in the Louvre, which at one time was called 'La Belle Ferronière'. The lady of the portrait, once thought to be the *ferronnière*, or blacksmith's wife, who captivated François I, wears a black cord round her head, supporting a diamond on her forehead. Early Victorian ladies wore *ferronnières* at all times of the day, with hats and without, as a tribute to the Renaissance.

The jewellers drew the inspiration for their pieces chiefly from the Renaissance, the Middle Ages and the natural world. They adapted these themes to suit their fancy, but—except for traditional Scottish and Irish pieces, and a few Assyrian jewels—they did not copy ancient jewels exactly. (This development was left for the mid-Victorian craftsman.)

Foremost among the Romantic designers was François-Desiré Froment-

---

[1] 'The forms of our *bijous* are now entirely borrowed from the style of the Middle Ages; massive gold pins, with the heads richly chased, or composed of coloured gems set in small flowers, *couronnes* or *guirlandes* of gold and diamonds, or else of gold set with coloured gems. All our ornaments, in short, are *moyen âge* . . . .'
World of Fashion, January 1839.

Meurice,[1] of Paris. According to Eugène Fontenay, it was this great jeweller who first conceived the idea of putting medieval motifs into jewellery and so paved the way for a freedom of style unknown before. He opened the door to fantasy and originality, using human figures, or motifs from heraldry or architecture as he pleased (see Figs. 25b and 46b). This free style is apparent in nearly everything produced between 1840 and 1860. Angels, or knights and their ladies, appear combined with decorative patterns drawn from furniture or ceramics, in borders of foliage or strapwork. The productions of Froment-Meurice were much admired at the Great Exhibition, particularly a Gothic bracelet with scenes from the life of Saint Louis (shown in Fig. 40a). Another Parisian jeweller whom the English admired was Rudolphi who, himself a Dane, carried on the Paris business of the German Wagner, one of the jewellers interested in reviving the arts of working in enamel and niello. Rudolphi's style can be seen in the silver brooch in the form of an angel, reproduced in Fig. 29d.

The influence of the French designers naturally spread to England. Robert Phillips, the most renowned of the English mid-century designers, was certainly affected by their work, as shown by the bracelet in Fig. 40d. Pugin's medieval jewellery in the ecclesiastical style,[2] though owing nothing to the French, also showed the tendency to return to the Middle Ages.

A development of the free tendencies initiated by Froment-Meurice was the jewellery designed in imitation of wood. Gold, ivory and tortoiseshell were carved into twisting branches, forming bracelets.[3] Rings and brooches were composed of ivy leaves and tendrils or of bunches of grapes among their leaves as in Figs. 24 and 28d. Earrings were made of tiny gold leaves and curling stems encircling a bud or berry which was a precious stone, a style shown in Fig. 18c.

Another motif from the natural world which was extremely popular with the Romantics was the serpent. Queen Victoria wore a serpent bracelet at her first council meeting,[4] and her betrothal ring was a serpent studded with emeralds. Though serpents have been used for rings and bracelets since the days of the Romans, and continued to be used throughout the nineteenth century, these early-Victorian serpents are particularly charming. Their scales, of links as in the necklace in Fig. 14b, or of chased gold as in

[1] 1802–55. One of Froment-Meurice's engravers was Barye, later famous as an animal sculptor and the master of Rodin.
[2] See Fig. 20.
[3] See Fig. 39b.
[4] See Fig. 34a.

Fig. 10c, are usually beautifully executed, and the heads, of enamel and gems, are brilliant and arresting.

Two other influences on the jewellery of this period may be mentioned: North African and Assyrian. The war of the French against Abd-el-Kader in the early forties turned the eyes of the world to Algeria, and when that country became French territory tremendous interest was shown in its arts and crafts. French jewellers designed bracelets and brooches inspired by Moorish pieces, decorated with arabesques, and having numerous curiously-shaped pendants. The Algerian knot became a favourite shape for a brooch, and the *peigne d'Alger* was fashionable in the hair.

As for Assyria, Layard's *Nineveh and its Remains* appeared in 1848, with reproductions of the treasures found in excavating that city. Jewellers lost no time in making bracelets and earrings based on Assyrian patterns. One of the bracelets appears at the top of Fig. 24. The lotus flower, as a popular motif, had arrived, and was to stay for about forty years. This enthusiasm for Assyrian ornaments foreshadowed the passion for archæological jewellery which was to come some ten or fifteen years later.

In looking at the jewellery of the early Victorians, it is impossible not to be struck by the great use made of coral. This material became fashionable just after the marriage in 1845 of the Duchesse d'Aumale and a Prince of the Two Sicilies who presented his bride with some exquisite coral ornaments in her *corbeille*. It remained very popular until about 1865. George Augustus Sala, writing in 1867 when the vogue had somewhat declined, says that a few years before, people had gone about 'bedizened with twisted sticks of seeming red sealing-wax; and coral earrings had an unpleasant resemblance to fragments of ginger or orris-root, or even the domestic forked radish, smeared with red ochre'. The coral he describes was worn in its natural, or branch form—as the Italians wear it to ward off the evil eye or *jettatura*, and as the Romans hung it on their children's necks to preserve them from danger. But even more prized were ornaments of finely carved coral, in the shape of crosses, roses, hands, cameos and the like. Beads of polished coral were seen in great number. English children wore them, and English babies used coral rattles and teething-rings. The colours most esteemed were dark red and pale pink.

Much of the coral jewellery worn by the Victorians came from Naples or Genoa, but one English jeweller was famous for his work in coral. This was Robert Phillips (*d.* 1881) of Cockspur Street, already mentioned in connexion with Gothic jewellery, whose displays of carved coral at exhibitions through-

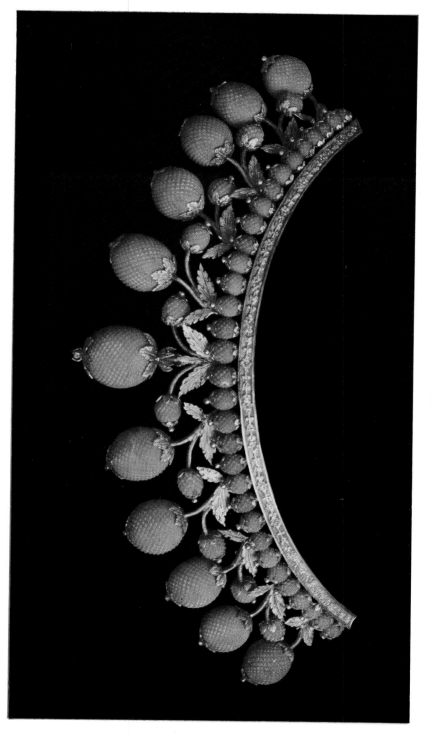

PLATE II

Diadem of gold and coral

Each of the berry-shaped pieces of coral is finely carved, and
the gold, of various colours, is chased to resemble leaves. *c.* 1837.

(*The Author*)

out Europe never failed to win high praise. In 1870 Phillips received a decoration from the King of Italy in recognition of all he had done to develop the coral trade of Naples.

These early years of Queen Victoria were the last in which extensive use was made of seed-pearls,[1] so popular for parures in the late eighteenth century. They were used by the Victorians to make parures in floral patterns,[2] and were usually found as an embellishment with the Prince of Wales's feathers in hair, or with hair landscapes. They were often used in the late thirties to encircle coloured stones.

Precious stones, but particularly diamonds, were sometimes mounted in a rain. This meant that each stone fell from a central piece on a thin, mobile stalk of its own. Or they were mounted in a waterfall, which consisted of jointed bands or ropes of diamonds, falling straight down, side by side.

For ornaments designed to give a more massive effect large cabochon stones were used, sometimes in conjunction with rains or waterfalls, as in the corsage ornament in Fig. 25d, and sometimes simply framed with pearls or diamonds. The taste for cabochon stones, according to Fontenay, is one of the few fashions which originated in England and was adopted later in France.

Turning to the secondary jewellery of the Romantic period, we can observe many pieces of Mediterranean origin. Travel was becoming very much easier, now that it was no longer necessary to go in one's own travelling-carriage; and increased numbers of families took holiday trips abroad, bringing back with them a great deal of jewellery from the Continent. In 1855 Thomas Cook arranged a 31/- trip from Leicester to Calais and back, for those who wished to visit the Paris Exposition; and in the following year he arranged a great circular tour on the Continent. These early Cook's tourists returned with souvenirs, carved ivory from Dieppe—which was the centre of that trade—and mosaics, lava, or cameos from Italy.

The mosaics, like those in Fig. 8, usually showed temples, fountains, and other pieces of classical architecture, but sometimes birds or classical portraits. The lava, or Pompeiian jewellery, was carved *en cameo*, usually with classical heads. The cameos, more numerous and more popular, must be dealt with separately.

---

[1] Tiny pearls, of less than a quarter-grain in size, coming chiefly from China and Madras. Chinese seed-pearls have such minute holes that they must be strung on horse-hair—preferably white horse-hair, pulled from a living horse. All seed-pearl work is applied to a foundation of pierced mother-of-pearl.

[2] See Fig. 6.

Cameos are of two kinds; the first being gem cameos, in which a design is cut in relief on a stone, and the second being their imitations, carved on shells,[1] or cut or moulded in glass or paste. They have had three periods of great popularity—in classical times, in the Renaissance, and in the late eighteenth and nineteenth centuries. Queen Victoria was fond of cameo jewellery and her approval helped to preserve its popularity during her reign.

The onyx, sardonyx and agate, with their layers of different colours, have always been the stones most favoured for cameos. But in the fifties cameos cut in coral and in black onyx by Isler of Rome were considered extremely fine.

The manufacture of shell cameos, the *Art Journal* of 1854 tells us, is said to be of Sicilian origin, and has been carried on at Rome since about 1805. However, in about 1830 an Italian began the carving of shell cameos in Paris, 'and at the present time a much larger number of shell cameos are made in Paris than in Italy. The Roman artists have attained perfection in this beautiful art'. But English artists had begun to try their hand at cameos. Among the exhibitors of shell cameos at the 1851 Exhibition, we find not only Savalini and Salvator Passamonti of Rome, but Mr Brett of Tysoe Street, Wilmington Square. Fourteen years later a young English artist, Mr Ronca, created an agreeable sensation by exhibiting at the Royal Academy three cameos carved by him: 'a bust of the late Prince Consort, a remarkably beautiful head of a young girl, and the helmeted head of Geraint, from Tennyson's *Idylls of the King*'. From this we see that the nineteenth-century carvers did not limit themselves to classical subjects—indeed, portraits of Victorian statesmen and court beauties were as much admired as Greek deities and nymphs, and scenes from such popular painters as Horace Vernet were in demand when engraved on cameos.

The eighteenth-century imitation cameos in blue and white composition made by Wedgwood and in moulded glass paste by James Tassie had their Victorian counterparts in 'the beautiful opaque cameos, incrusted in transparent glass, manufactured by Mr Apsley Pellatt'.

Scotland, a favourite resort for those in search of the picturesque, contributed its quota to the store of regional jewellery. The Queen's love for Scotland and everything Scottish was well known. The Royal children wore tartan, and at the State Ball given at Buckingham Palace to celebrate the

---

[1] The shells chiefly used are the red and white Bull's Mouth, the pink and white Queen's Conch and the brown and white Black Helmet.

Dishonest dealers in the seventies used to cut out the relief portion of shell cameos and attach them to a base of agate, thus producing a cameo apparently engraved on a stone.

opening of the Great Exhibition all the guests were required to wear Stuart costume. Scottish jewellery of silver, set with pebbles[1] and cairngorms was accordingly highly fashionable. Miss Yonge, who was always interested in jewellery, describes in *The Daisy Chain* (1856) a brooch sent to Ethel May by Norman Ogilvie—one of the round Bruce brooches, of dark pebble, with a silver fern-leaf lying across it, and with dots of small cairngorm stones. The shape was his family badge, and no gift could have had greater sentimental value.

Scientifically-minded young women bought brooches set with the marbles of Devonshire found on the coast near Torquay, or rings of fluor-spar from the Blue John mine in the Peak district. Most interesting of all was the jewellery composed of the fossils known as ammonites or snakestones. These fossils, looking like small coiled snakes, were characteristic of the Whitby district, and were mounted in gold or silver as brooches or earrings (see Fig. 18b). A commentator writing in 1856 says that they were eagerly sought by the curious, 'forming at the same time, most elegant ornaments, and instructive examples of one of the forms of life which had existence upon this world ere yet man had being'.

The jewellery of sentiment flourished during the Romantic Period. The finest hair brooches and earrings ever made belong to the forties and fifties, and so do the most exquisite pictures in hair. They were made by amateurs and professionals alike;[2] in fact, young ladies were urged to learn the art, in order to guard against dishonest tradesmen who might substitute the hair of a stranger for that of a departed friend. Armed with a fitted box containing tweezers, knife, curling-iron, gum and a porcelain palette, the Victorian lady could weave hair into basket patterns or construct a landscape with weeping willows or make a design of a nosegay or the Prince of Wales's feathers. Professional workers in hair could produce most elegant pictures for decorating a drawing-room. A *tour-de-force* which drew a crowd of sightseers at the Paris Exposition of 1855 was a full-length, life-size portrait of Queen Victoria made entirely of human hair. As an example of what was considered the height of achievement in this medium, here is a note from *La Belle Assemblée* of 1858:

The sentimental jewellery of Limonnier is of another character from what all the world is acquainted with, and which gives the locket, or brooch, or ring, in which

---

[1] Scotch pebbles were usually pieces of agate, quarried near Perth. They were frequently cut and mounted at Oberstein in Germany. (Harry Emanuel, *op. cit.*).

[2] For full details on working in hair, see *The Lock of Hair* by Alexanna Speight, London, 1871.

some beloved tress or precious curl is enshrined, the appearance of having been designed from a mortuary tablet. Have we not all met ladies wearing as a brooch, by way of loving remembrance, a tomb between two willow trees formed of the hair of the individual for whom their crape was worn, and which from its very nature must be laid aside with it? Our artist converts the relic into an ornament for all times and places—expands it into a broad ribbon as a bracelet and fastens it with a forget-me-not in turquoises and brilliants; weaves it into chains for the neck, the *flacon*, or the fan; makes it into a medallion, or leaves and flowers; and of these last the most beautiful specimens I have seen have been formed of the saintly white hair of age. This he converts into orange-flowers, white roses, chrysanthemums and, most charming of all, clusters of lily-of-the-valley.

The Crimean War and the Indian Mutiny unhappily caused many women to wear such jewellery of remembrance. Those who did not wear hair jewellery wore jet.

This material is a kind of lignite or anthracite—in other words, a sort of harder coal.[1] The jet found along the Yorkshire coast at Whitby is said to be the finest in the world. It has greater tenacity and elasticity than other sorts, and will take a fine polish and retain it for years. Spanish jet, from Galicia, is softer and when ground to a fine edge will not keep it. Accordingly, Whitby jet was used for pieces which were to be carved and polished, and the cheaper Spanish jet was largely employed for the making of beads.

The modern jet industry began at Whitby in about 1800, when John Carter, an innkeeper, and Robert Jefferson, a painter, hacked some necklaces and crosses from jet with files and knives. They sold one of these pieces for a guinea and so were encouraged to continue. Soon after, a naval pensioner suggested that they turn their beads on a lathe, with the result that the first jet workshop was started at Carter's house, in the years 1808–10. In 1850 there were fifty workshops and in 1873, two hundred. In 1853 the industry amounted to £20,000 annually and in 1870 to £84,000. Visitors to Whitby complained that the town had an excessively mournful aspect, as every window was filled with a sombre display of jet jewellery.

Jet was worn as court mourning for William IV,[2] and again, for many years after the death of the Prince Consort, ladies presented to the Queen were requested to wear no other jewellery.

Not all the jet sold as Whitby jet came from Whitby; and some so-called jet ornaments were not jet at all. The very fine, sharp-edged ornaments

[1] The prehistoric Britons used jet to make ornaments. Gaius Julius Solinus, in the third century mentions the abundance of jet to be found in Britain. Caedmon, the monk of Whitby, in the seventh century alludes to it.
[2] See Fig. 1.

called French jet are actually black glass (see Figs. 63b and 84)—a quite different substance, though equally attractive.

One more material belonging to this period was porcelain. Parian—a statuary porcelain sometimes called Carreran—was the favourite sort. Its chief use was for figures reproduced from sculptures, but it was also employed to make chessmen, vases, salt cellars, candlesticks and preserved-meat pots. For a short time, about 1850, Parian bracelet clasps and brooches were greatly admired. The material was easily moulded into bouquets and other floral designs, resembling carved ivory but at a third of the cost. Mrs Mary Brougham of Burslem was the most successful manufacturer of Parian jewellery. Unfortunately it proved so fragile that extremely few examples have lasted until today. Engravings of Parian jewellery can be seen in Figs. 29b and 43d.

Belleek porcelain, with its pearly lustre, was also made into brooches, one of which is shown in Fig. 33c.

The mounts of inexpensive stones were often made of pinchbeck, an alloy closely resembling gold, which had been the invention of Christopher Pinchbeck (1670–1732), a watchmaker of Fleet Street. The formula, kept a closely guarded secret, is said to have been 83 parts copper to 17 parts zinc.

But after 1854, gold of low carat standard gradually took the place of pinchbeck. In that year, the use of 15-, 12-, and 9-carat gold was made legal in order to meet foreign competition.

Gilt articles were usually mercury-gilt at this time, but electro-gilt articles were shown as early as the Paris Exhibition of 1844.

Summing up the jewellery of the Romantic Period, it was very much what one would have expected to please an enthusiastic, optimistic and enquiring public. Most jewels were elegant compositions, with equal import-ance given to the setting and the stones. The workmanship was imaginative rather than precise, and gave to these pieces a charm lacking in the more exact work of the mid-Victorians. Gold was the most generally used mate-rial; and it was engraved, pierced or woven, and decorated with enamel to make a worthy setting for a few fine stones.[1] The primary jewellery was rich, graceful and elaborate; and the secondary jewellery, in most cases carefully executed in less expensive materials, was not without merit.

[1] A commentator in the *Art Journal Catalogue* of the 1851 Exhibition remarks that 'the taste for floral ornament in jewellery has been very prevalent of late; and it is a good and a happy taste, inasmuch as the brilliant colouring of an enamelled leaf or floret is an excellent foil to a sparkling stone'.

III
THE MID-VICTORIAN
OR
GRAND PERIOD
1860-1885

The
MID-VICTORIAN
or Grand Period
(1860-85)

Most of us when we speak of Victorian jewellery, have in mind the large, imposing, highly-coloured pieces worn during the sixties and seventies. The change which came over jewellery about 1860, transforming it from something imaginative and delicate into something much bolder, corresponded with the change which was taking place in the position of women. The early Victorian woman had been considered a fragile flower whose rôle in life was to be decorative and who must be protected against the harsh realities of existence; but the mid-Victorian woman was emerging into the fields of business and politics. Women were entering into competition with men as clerks, factory inspectors and teachers. They were learning how to combine and agitate in order to remedy abuses like the Contagious Diseases Act,[1] and they were fighting hard to secure the right to vote. In order to compete with men on a more equal footing, they were demanding admission to the Universities, and in 1873—a landmark in the education of women—three young women passed the Cambridge Tripos.

Women also had more money. In 1870 they managed to gain the right to keep as their own the money which they earned themselves.

It was such women as these who wore, boldly and joyfully, the new and

---

[1] This Act, passed in 1864, provided for the compulsory medical examination of prostitutes. But it meant that sometimes innocent women could be picked up by special police and taken off for examination. Mrs Josephine Butler and other women agitated for its repeal, which took place in 1886.

flamboyant jewellery of the Grand Period. They wore a great deal of it, too[1] —earrings invariably, brooches and bracelets usually, and necklaces by night and lockets by day.

Several things are to be noted about this jewellery. In primary jewellery, we find most notably the influence of Greek and Etruscan ornament, and the tendency to reproduce rather than to create designs. Later, about 1880, we find the colours fading and the colourless stones like diamonds and pearls replacing the bright stones and enamels of the sixties. In secondary jewellery we find a tremendous increase in the amount of imitation jewellery worn. This accompanied the birth of what we today call costume jewellery—which is bought to be worn for only a short time. It was the result of a great appetite for novelty; and as more and more curious bits of cheap jewellery were produced, so the appetite grew. One of the novelties which came to stay—for thirty or forty years—was sporting jewellery.

Let us turn now to the most important new development in the jewellery of this period—the fashion for 'Etruscan' pieces, and to a lesser degree for pieces inspired by Greek and Renaissance jewels. It has always been the case that a people preoccupied with new developments in science, education, economics and industry have little energy left for creating new forms in art, and this was certainly so with the mid-Victorians. However, just at this time a talented family in Italy had re-discovered the technique for reproducing ancient goldsmiths' work, and their products appeared in England when popular taste was so ready to receive them that they took the fashionable world by storm.

This Italian family, called Castellani—with Froment-Meurice, the greatest name among nineteenth century jewellers—began their activities in 1814, when Fortunato Pio, the father, started a business in Rome. At first he simply imitated the jewellery of France and England. But on seeing some Etruscan jewels which had been recently discovered, he was fired with enthusiasm for reviving classical jewellery. The delicacy of the workmanship in the Etruscan ornaments appeared to be beyond the powers of nineteenth-century craftsmen, especially the application of minute grains of gold as decoration. But Castellani was not to be deterred, and eventually in a remote village of the Umbrian marches, St. Angelo in Vado, he found craftsmen who still used some of the processes of the Etruscans. He brought work-

[1] At a fashionable dinner, Madame Max Goesler wore, according to Anthony Trollope, 'a short chain of Roman gold with a ruby pendant. And she had rubies in her ears, and a ruby brooch, and rubies in the bracelets on her arms'. *Phineas Finn*, 1869.

men from St. Angelo in Vado to Rome where they taught others and where they made some remarkably successful imitations of Etruscan jewels. Castellani introduced these to the public under the name of 'Italian Archæological Jewellery'.[1] In doing all this, his motives appear to have been as much æsthetic as commercial, for he was intensely eager to cultivate in the public a purer taste in jewellery.

During the unsettled years from 1848 to 1858, nothing was done at the Castellani workshop in Rome. Fortunato Pio had retired in 1851, and left the business to his son Augusto, a brilliant craftsman. After 1858, Augusto Castellani resumed the reproduction of Greek and Etruscan jewellery: in addition to these he reproduced Renaissance and Scandinavian jewels. The other son, Alessandro, amassed a remarkable collection of antique jewellery, which can be seen at the British Museum, to which Alessandro was attached in his later life.

As the jewels of the Castellanis became known abroad, jewellers of other countries began to make pieces in the same manner: Fontenay in France, Robert Phillips and John Brogden in England, and Carlo Giuliano,[2] who came from Naples to settle in London, through the friendly offices of Robert Phillips, and whose workmanship was thought to surpass even Castellani's.[3]

A representative of the *Art Journal*, visiting Robert Phillips's establishment in Cockspur Street, singled out for praise a reproduction of an antique necklace in the Museo Borbonico at Naples 'with its pendent reticulation of masks and acorns and floral drops'. Phillips had also copied in gold a curious iron fibula representing a five-horse chariot.

These accurate reproductions from the ancient world had a tremendous appeal for mid-Victorian women, who were seriously bent on improving themselves. Ornaments of this sort gave pleasure, I believe, as much for their *accuracy* as for their beauty. Yet today it is not hard to distinguish Victorian classical jewellery from its originals. The nineteenth-century artists were so accomplished technically that their productions have a regularity and finish which real classical jewellery lacks.

[1] See Augusto Castellani: *Antique Jewellery and Its Revival*. London. 1862.

[2] Giuliano, the father, carried to great perfection the arts of filigree, granulation and enamelling. His business was situated at 115 Piccadilly. During the eighties, his sons Federico and Fernando opened a shop in Howland Street, where they worked in the same style as their father.

[3] Examples of Castellani's work are shown in Plate VII, Fig. c, and in Figs. 60b, 74, 92c.
Examples of Giuliano's in Plate VI, Plate VII, Fig. b, Plate IX, Figs. b and c, Plate X, and in Figs. 65a, b, c, 75, 77a, 78a, b, 81b, d, 90c, 93d and 98b.
Examples of Brogden's in Plate V and in Figs. 79c, 91a, 92b.

As time passed, the interest of the fashionable world in Etruscan and Greek reproduction spread to the less wealthy, and motifs from the antique —amphorae, masks, lotus-flowers, sphinxes and the like—appeared in the work of lesser craftsmen. The circular-shield shape replaced the oval as the fashionable form for brooches, and small grains and tiny wires of gold became the accepted form of decoration for settings.

Reproductions of ancient jewels were not made from classical examples alone. While Castellani and Phillips preferred Etruscan and Greek models, they both tried their hands at reproducing the silver work of the Scandinavian peoples. Froment-Meurice's son carried on the tradition of fine craftsmanship inherited from his father, but he preferred to make jewels in the style of the Renaissance. John Brogden's work was often inspired by the art of Egypt or Abyssinia. Moorish, Turkish and Chinese pieces were also made. And from 1876, when the Queen assumed the title of Empress of India, Indian jewellery and its imitations became fashionable (see Figs. 81b and 104b). The liking for Scottish jewellery continued, and the Edinburgh firms which specialized in it were praised for the examples which they sent to all the International Exhibitions.

Alessandro Castellani's summing-up of the British jewellery shown at the Paris Exhibition of 1878 gives a general view of the situation at that time. He observed three distinct schools in the goldsmiths' art in England. First, there was the Scottish, inspired by the traditional jewellery of the Anglo-Saxons and Celts, and like the ancient jewels except for the substitution of hard stones for vitreous pastes. Next came the school, exemplified by Mortimer, which made sumptuous jewels of massive gold, with or without gems, designed with geometric precision. The third, in which John Brogden was outstanding, was founded on the Italians' researches into ancient jewellery.

Gold, during this period, took on a new appearance. From the early seventies to the end of the eighties it had a soft look, rather resembling the skin of a peach. This was called 'bloom', and it was produced by a process called 'colouring' which meant dipping the article into a boiling mixture of muriatic acid, saltpetre, salt and water. The acid in the mixture removed all the alloy from the surface of the article, and left a thin film of pure gold dotted with innumerable tiny holes. We can see today many demi-parures of 'coloured' gold; those shown in Figs. 59b and c are made of it.

The mid-seventies, as mentioned before, brought in the fashion for colourless stones. More pieces were set with diamonds alone than had previously

PLATE III

Fig. a. Bracelet of gold, pearls, diamonds and dark-blue enamel
c. 1845.   (*The Author*)

Fig. b. Croix à la Jeannette in garnets and rose diamonds
The cross and the slide in the form of a heart are on a gold chain. *c.* 1838.
(*Cameo Corner*)

been the case. By the eighties, diamond jewellery was considered in far better taste than the brightly-coloured jewellery of the sixties. And by the nineties, colour had gone quite out of fashion. Two reasons can be suggested for this: first, the discovery of diamonds in South Africa in 1867 made these stones more plentiful and cheaper; secondly, the growing use of electric light with its hard brilliance may have caused the elaborate jewels of many colours to look too garish. When the Savoy Theatre opened in 1881—the first theatre to be lit throughout by electricity—it is possible that the ladies of the audience who wore diamonds made a better appearance than those who wore other jewels. We find, too, that settings gradually became less elaborate. Enamelling and engraving around stones gave place to settings which were nearly invisible, and all the attention was focused on the actual gem. The jewellers who followed the great men of the sixties became more interested in setting diamonds. Massin at the Paris Exhibition of 1878 showed jewels in which tiny diamonds were set in a pattern so fine that it might have been taken for lace.

Electricity had another part to play in the history of jewellery, though rather a transient one. Visitors to the Paris Exhibition of 1867 were interested to see the new 'Electric Jewels'—ornaments for the hair which were kept constantly in motion by a Voltaic battery worn down the back inside the dress. One of these electric jewels was a diamond skull which made grimaces, and another was a rabbit which beat a drum.

Equally new, but more pleasing, was the fashion, which first became general in the sixties, for setting small stones into large ones. Small diamond stars would be set into the large amethysts of a necklace, as in Plate IV, or tiny flowers into earrings as in Fig. 59a. Pearl stars and flowers set into carbuncles made charming ornaments, as we see in Fig. 64f. Workmanship in the jeweller's craft had never been better, though designing perhaps left something to be desired; and as though to show off their skill, craftsmen delighted in producing cameos *habillés*, with a necklace and earrings of tiny brilliants set into the head carved in the stone.

Turning to secondary jewellery, if in the middle sixties a lady could not pay the high prices demanded for the best jewellery, she could buy a handsome suite of a brooch, earrings and a necklace with three pendants, the base of which was an imitation substance called Abyssinian gold. 'The design is Grecian and is executed in blue-and-white enamel and pearls . . . The earrings and pendants are finished off with long fringes of gold, and the fineness and elasticity of the collar is wonderful; fine chains connect the three pendants.' Edwin Streeter of Conduit Street offered suites of machine-made jewellery—bracelet, brooch and earrings—for ten guineas. You could have a Grecian pattern with a raised ornament in the centre, or a pattern of twisted gold round a centre either chased, or bearing the head of the sacred ram.

By the eighties, these gorgeous suites were no longer in demand. Silver was the popular metal, and heavy necklaces were made of it. Queen Victoria chose one of these as a present for Jenny Lind.[1] A silver chain and heavy engraved locket, as shown in Figs. 55b and 77b, were the most fashionable ornaments for everyday wear. Silver brooches, engraved by hand, or more often stamped out by machinery, bore names, dates, monograms, or mottos, such as Mizpah ('I will watch over thee').

As the taste for highly-coloured jewellery declined, so jet and ivory sprang into favour. They were made into ornaments of a heavy appearance. Jet or ivory neck-chains had enormous links. Large jet serpents encircled the arm, and were worn all through the day, even when bathing in the sea during the summer holidays. Polished balls of jet made necklaces, earrings or bracelets—a fashion sponsored by Adelina Patti who is shown in Fig. 55a, wearing a typical set of these ornaments.

'Scotch jewellery as well as Scotch costume is *de rigueur*' said the *Englishwoman's Domestic Magazine* in 1867, 'and the badges of the different clans are worn as brooches, earrings, buckles, and as the centre of shoe rosettes.'

Pinchbeck had disappeared, replaced by gold of low-carat quality or by new alloys (which have not lasted so well). Other types of jewellery which had disappeared were those made of seed-pearls and hair. Machine-made goods were so cheap and so pretty that the more expensive products of painstaking craftsmen found no buyers. Besides, seed-pearls were too delicate in appearance. Pearls now must be large, and in long strings, so as to encircle the neck several times (see Fig. 49). Hair no longer composed earrings or bracelets, but was relegated to a small box on the underside of a brooch or pendant.

The case of piqué is interesting. Piqué is tortoiseshell (or sometimes ivory) inlaid with tiny dots or lines of gold or silver. The French Huguenots brought the craft with them to England when they came here for refuge in the seventeenth century, and made many beautiful piqué snuff-boxes, needle-cases,

[1] See Fig. 76.

and small decorative articles. This material was fashionable for brooches, buttons and earrings during the sixties (see Fig. 66), when it was still worked by hand. But mass-production of piqué began in Birmingham in 1872 and after that, the beautiful hand-produced articles were no longer made. The new makers specialized in crosses, inlaid with geometrical patterns. These chaste designs—chiefly waves and meanders—were considered to be a great improvement on the 'ultra-naturalesque' details which had formerly been used for this sort of ornament.

By this time, Birmingham, always a centre for the manufacture of trinkets and 'toys', had become important in the trade as a source of jewellery designs. The Birmingham manufacturers produced patterns from which the London retailer chose those he preferred. The retailer kept the exclusive right to the patterns he had bought, and the Birmingham producer received no credit whatever. Photography began to play its part in the jewellery trade. In 1879, photographic patterns of lockets, brooches, bracelets, and so on, began to be used, so that it was no longer necessary to send articles on approval to country buyers.

The jewellery produced by machine—much of it in Birmingham—became so popular that in 1879 Mrs Haweis lamented that 'many a woman imagines that her friends will have a higher opinion of her wealth and wisdom by being able to count twenty machine-made lockets and chains in her jewel-case, than if they never see her wearing anything but one diamond brooch, or one really fine cameo, or one priceless ring'. She also complained that machine-made jewellery had increased the ignorant and mistaken craze for 'sets' and 'pairs'.

Let us now look at some of the novelties produced during this period.

The most transient was the Benoîton chain, worn during the years 1865–70. This belongs really more to a discussion of costume than of jewellery, for it was a chain worn in a particular way. It hung from the bonnet over the bosom, instead of simply encircling the neck. The composition of the chain mattered not at all; it could be of gold, silver, filigree, pearls, or jet, but it *must* hang from the bonnet. The name comes from a play of Sardou's, *La Famille Benoîton*, first produced in 1865, dealing with a *nouveau-riche* family notable for their dashing toilettes.

More remarkable was the vogue for insects. Mr William d'Arfey in *Curious Relations* mentions that in the late sixties 'Bonnets and veils were covered with every kind of beetle; that at least was the beginning of the mode, but it soon extended itself from rose-beetles with their bronze and green carapaces to stag beetles . . . Parasols were liberally sprinkled with ticks, with grasshoppers, with woodlice. Veils were sown with earwigs, with cockchafers, with hornets. Tulle scarves and veilings sometimes had on them artificial bed-bugs . . .' These insects appeared on necklaces, bracelets and earrings, as well as on veils and parasols (see Figs. 58 and 72). Flies of gold, coloured with enamel, were set under crystal to form jewels. Butterflies, dragonflies and beetles in gems were worn as brooches and shoulder knots. Bees, too, were fashionable, some people thought because they were the emblem of young Prince Victor Bonaparte, who was a great favourite in Paris society.

'We do not require to go to the Zoological Gardens to see strange animals', said a writer in the *Ladies' Treasury* in 1884. Anything in the animal or vegetable kingdom was thought a fit motif for jewellery: dogs, horses, lions, roses, pansies, violets. Still more extreme novelties were coal scuttles, tongs, hammers, ladders, trowels, and even locomotives. Nothing was too unusual for the ladies of this period to wear on their necks or in their ears.

Elaine de Marsay, writing in the *Queen*, 3 January 1880, is full of enthusiasm for the latest novelties: 'Enamelled flowers, especially violets; a large gold walnut, studded with pearls; a spray of eglantine, with silver and gold foliage; a pea pod half opened disclosing pearls for peas; an enamelled fan; a Delft plate with a gold spoon in it'.

Among the new styles of the period were those derived from sport. Horseshoe brooches first appeared in the sixties, and Napoleon III bought one while visiting England, so introducing sporting jewellery into France. Messrs. Hancock & Co were early in the field with their gold suite—a necklet, bracelet and earrings—constructed of miniature saddles and bridles, whips, bits, spurs, stirrups, horseshoes and portions of horse-harness. The critic from the *Art Journal*, who saw this suite exhibited in 1872, was roused to protest: 'A more outrageous instance of misapplied ingenuity and skill it is impossible to conceive, and that any woman would condescend to wear such abominations is more inconceivable still'. But such pieces took the public fancy. During the eighties, nearly every young woman wore a horseshoe brooch, and in the nineties, sporting jewellery occupied a large place in every jeweller's catalogue.

Only one point remains to be mentioned—the short but intense fashion for amber necklaces, which lasted from about 1878 to about 1883. The vogue was a part of the Æsthetic Movement, which caused young ladies to sigh for the Middle Ages, to wear straight gowns when the fashion was for ruffles and curves, to trim their collars with old yellowed bits of lace, and, as a crowning touch, to wear a long string of amber beads.

Except for these æsthetic ladies, the Renaissance of wonder was over, and the jewellery, of these middle years of the nineteenth century, from Castellani's down to the machine-stamped Mizpah pins, was forthright, assertive and solid.

IV
THE LATE VICTORIAN
OR
ÆSTHETIC PERIOD
1885-1901

The
LATE VICTORIAN
or Aesthetic Period
(1885 - 1901)

THE ÆSTHETIC PERIOD in jewellery came at a time of reaction against what had gone before. 'It is certain,' said Aymer Vallance in 1902, 'that, thirty years since, it was quite impossible to procure jewellery in the design and composition of which there entered any artistic taste whatever. Such simply did not exist. Whereas now there is a widespread, though unhappily not universal, movement amongst us for the design and production of jewellery on true æsthetic principles.' The late Victorians looked with horror at the complacency of their parents, and with distaste at their fashions and furnishings. They wanted a complete break with tradition. In their eagerness to escape from everything conventional they became romantic in a new way.

They turned with gratitude to Morris, who had tried to keep the spirit of the Middle Ages alive in a period of industrialism, and were fired with enthusiasm for the beliefs and the paintings of the Pre-Raphaelites. Rossetti stood so high in public esteem that six of his paintings, sold in 1886, realized £10,000. As a result of Pre-Raphaelite influence and Morris's example, a band of craftsmen in 1884 formed the Art Workers' Guild, and a group of young artists, led by Walter Crane, formed a body which in 1886 became the Arts and Crafts Exhibition Society. These two groups tried to interest the public in the new work that was being done by artists and craftsmen. They publicized the simpler new patterns in furniture, the new fabrics of Crane and Morris, and the new style in book illustration represented by Ricketts and Beardsley. Gradually they effected a revolution in public taste.

In this changing world women were still trying to improve their position. They continued to work actively in politics; in 1885 they founded the Primrose League and in 1886 the Women's Liberal Federation—the two first women's party organizations. They redoubled their efforts to secure the right to vote. Those who were interested in Socialism joined the Fabian Society, which had been founded in 1884. Young women, insisting on greater personal freedom, left their parents' homes and claimed the right to lead their own lives. These young people, who went to college, played hockey and took long bicycle rides into the country, were worlds away from the sentimental young ladies of the forties.

Among fashionable women the break with tradition took the form of a certain daring or naughtiness in behaviour. Those who were less courageous contented themselves with appearing to be frivolous or roguish. To be modern, or *fin de siècle*—and that was the general desire—it was helpful to give an impression of slight perversity.

The jewellery worn during these years shows, as we should expect, considerable difference from the style of the Grand Period. Aside from the revolution in taste, there was a change in the attitude of women towards the wearing of jewellery. Very little jewellery was worn during the day. In the eighties, to wear diamonds in the daytime was the height of bad taste.[1] It may be that a growing sense of social responsibility made women shrink from too much display, or simply that the designs of their hats and gowns were unsuited to extra ornamentation. At any rate, so little jewellery was worn between 1887 and 1890 that the Jewellers' Association became alarmed and appealed to the Princess of Wales for help.[2] She kindly consented to inspect some of their samples, and bought a few pieces which she wore on important occasions. But in spite of the example of the Princess of Wales and her sympathy with the jewellers, comparatively little jewellery was worn—except at great balls, at Court, or at the opera—during the nineties.

'Taste for jewellery seems to be a thing quite of the past with our *élégantes*, especially that for necklaces', said the *Young Ladies' Journal* in 1893. 'Brooches are extremely small, eardrops of the simplest description, and as for bracelets they have almost completely disappeared. A tiny watch concealed in the neck, from which depends a short gold chain, finished with a

[1] At balls they were still worn, in profusion, as in Fig. 95.
[2] J. C. Roche: *History of the Birmingham Jewellery and Allied Trades.* 1927.

plain or jewelled ball, and diamonds closely fixed to the ear, are all the jewels a lady wears in the daytime. For evening-dress very few ornaments are worn. Diamonds are mounted very lightly in graceful devices, but beyond this, scarcely any precious stones grace the neck or head-dress; nor are flowers in demand either; bows of ribbon and light aigrettes are the style of parure most in vogue.' Matching sets of jewellery were still made, but the leaders of fashion thought them vulgar. Etruscan jewellery, with its fine grain and wire decoration, though it still figured in jewellers' catalogues to please patrons with conservative tastes, was no longer much admired. As for hair jewellery, the women of the Æsthetic Period considered it hideous. And as for silver, a character in *The Spoils of Poynton* (1897) remarks that nothing is now more vulgar than the wearing of silver jewellery, so popular fifteen years before.

The new generation of designers, appalled like their patrons by what seemed to them the lack of artistic taste shown by their predecessors and by the slavish reproduction of historic styles, determined to produce jewellery on true æsthetic principles. Their designs were original, and showed the freedom of treatment which seems to accompany any break with tradition. In this they were like the Romantic designers of the forties and fifties. Soft curves replaced the lines and angles of the Grand Period. The jewellery of the forties and fifties had shown curves also, but the new ones were different, being often irregular and broken, and not usually symmetrical.[1] The curves were reproduced from natural forms. Such natural shapes as roses or butter-flies,[2] which have been constantly used for personal ornament, assumed a new realistic appearance. The colours, too, when used, were softer and more natural, being modelled on the delicate shades of pale flowers or sea shells. Polished stones were preferred to facetted stones,[3] and amethysts, emeralds and opals were cut *en cabochon*.

The pioneer among the English designers of the period was C. R. Ashbee.[4] In the middle eighties, his interest in the Arts and Crafts movement, of which he was a leader, led him to try his hand at designing jewellery. His designs were carried out by craftsmen at Essex House in London, and at Campden in Gloucestershire. Ashbee had very much at heart the abolition of the commercial system in all its aspects, and the commercial jewellery produced at Birmingham, with its harsh angularities, repelled him. He

[1] See Fig. 108d.
[2] See Fig. 111a.
[3] See Fig. 98b.
[4] Ashbee's work is shown in Figs. 105a, b, 106a, 108a, c, 110a, b, d and 118a and b.

valued spontaneity of treatment above all things, deploring any regard for the monetary value of an ornament. 'The treatment of stones in metal', he wrote, 'should be a matter of personal taste, of character.'[1] His own taste was for rose topaz with grey gold, and amethysts with silver—and the silver should be dull, not highly polished. He was equally happy with designs taken from flowers and with abstract patterns. The new jewellery of Ashbee was so much admired in artistic circles that other artists and craftsmen were encouraged to follow his example. Among them were Nelson and Edith Dawson, Arthur J. Gaskin and his wife, Fred Robinson, and George J. Frampton, who took up enamel work in order to provide his wife with jewellery of which both of them could thoroughly approve. Henry Wilson, author of *Silverwork and Jewellery*, 1912, and Master of the Art-Workers' Guild in 1917, also began work in this period.

In France, where the new decorative style was known as *Art Nouveau*, a genius was soon to arrive on the scene. This was René Lalique, whose jewels had an immense success at the Paris Salon of 1895. Lalique, who was as great a figure in the jewellery design of his period as Froment-Meurice and Castellani had been in theirs, was responsible for introducing a number of new motifs into personal ornaments. Female heads with long waving hair and such humble plants as nasturtiums and morning-glories appear often in his designs. His flowing line and his taste in the juxtaposition of softly-coloured stones and delicate enamels made his work superior to that of most other designers. His pieces were sought after, not only by the French, but by the English, who saw in them the culmination of all the doctrines of the Pre-Raphaelites and of the Arts and Crafts group. Lalique's fame helped the *Art Nouveau* style to spread to many countries, and his influence was noticeable for twenty years or more.

Not unlike the new jewellery was the jewellery of India, which fascinated the amateurs of the arts when it was shown at the Exhibition at South Kensington in 1886. The irregularly-shaped stones and the lack of mechanical precision in these jewels appealed instantly to the public, tired of ornate, geometrical pieces. Mrs Haweis in 1889 declared that she loved the natural spontaneous variety in Indian jewellery—'Such spirit and fancy, and such a wholesome, happy element of *truth* behind the fancy, the pearls simply transfixed, the fastenings decorated but never concealed . . . no mechanical packing, no casting'. So began a fashion for wearing jewels from India,[2]

[1] The *Art Journal*, 1894.
[2] As in Fig. 104b.

which, unlike the jewels of the Greeks and Etruscans, were apparently not imitated by English craftsmen.

The jewellery of the Arts and Crafts movement and the *Art Nouveau* designers of France comprises the first sort of primary jewellery during the Æsthetic Period. Though the stones used in it were not always precious, and the monetary value of the pieces was not great, it must be considered primary jewellery because of the artistic value of the compositions as a whole.

The other sort of primary jewellery was the more conventional type composed of precious stones, particularly diamonds. In this jewellery, the emphasis had passed completely from the setting to the stone—from the harmonious ensemble to the single fine specimen. The *bijoutier*, the specialist in gold and enamel work, had almost vanished from the picture, and the *joaillier*, the specialist in mounting precious stones, had supplanted him. Public interest in gems was growing. The sales of diamonds and other gems in Birmingham were twenty times greater in 1886 than in 1865.[1] The first scientific handbook on gems, by A. H. Church, appeared in 1882. It now seemed important to have good specimens of precious stones, and to try to get genuine stones instead of the synthetic ones which were being manufactured with increasing success. A single beautiful stone was the ornament which the majority of women would have chosen during the nineties. And the stone should, if possible, be a diamond. The preference for diamonds, which was first noticeable in the late seventies, had now arrived at its peak. Diamond tiaras, diamond *rivières* and diamond bracelets were the choice of fashionable women for splendid occasions. The only stones considered acceptable for use in combination with diamonds were the nearly colourless pearls, opals and moonstones.[2] Diamonds were now often mounted in silver, but backed by gold to give stability.

This jewellery, though more conservative than the *Art Nouveau* sort, did not go untouched by the change in taste. It had an appearance of greater fragility than the jewellery of the Romantic and the Grand periods. The settings of stones were nearly invisible, and any pieces of metal which had to be seen were made as small as possible. Bracelets were of thin gold wire, with a diamond motif attached at one spot.[3] The shanks of rings grew extremely

[1] J. C. Roche, *op. cit.*

[2] It was not until the Boer War, at the end of the century, had cut off the supply of South African diamonds that coloured stones like peridots, topazes, tourmalines and zircons came into more general use.

[3] Fig. 116.

narrow. Very small brooches, called lace brooches, in the shape of jewelled butterflies, insects, shamrocks and the like, were attached in numbers to the bonnet strings or scarf.[1] The bar brooch arrived—a single narrow bar of gold with a small motif set on the edge. Neck chains were of spidery fineness. Tiny horseshoes, crescents, stars and knots decorated these delicate ornaments. But the favourite shape was the curved and romantic heart—double or single, surmounted by a true lovers' knot. Diamond, pearl or moonstone hearts are, more often than not, relics of the nineties.[2]

The secondary jewellery[3] showed the same fondness for the heart, and the same appearance of fragility. Thin gold wires formed small open-work pendants. The curb-chain, always popular as a bracelet, was reduced to half its former size. Some of the ornaments were so small and insignificant that they seem to have been hardly worth wearing. But they were new—and accordingly irresistible.

An enormous number of new motifs were introduced to satisfy the demand for jewellery of novelty, and they could not be too fanciful. Jewelled lizards, owls and frogs belong to this period. So do such whimsical pieces as a diamond chicken just emerged from an enamel egg; the 'Honeymoon' brooch, formed of a bee and a crescent moon; and the diamond 'Merry Thought' brooch. Many of these new motifs were in the form of small lace-brooches, or on the new bar brooch. Some were set on safety-pins or on the lace-pins which were shaped like men's tie-pins, but shorter. They served to attach the fashionable 'Baby' shoulder-bows on to the sleeves of evening gowns, or simply to glitter in the frills of lace at the neck of the new tea-gowns.

'Large ribbons or scarfs are much worn with low-necked evening dresses', said the *Ladies' Treasury* in 1884: 'They are fixed to the shoulder by a flower, or a butterfly, or a jewelled arrow. This fashion made its appearance last winter at the Italian Opera House in Paris, when a large bright-coloured ribbon was worn across the bodice, like the Queen of England wears the Order of the Garter. Young ladies wear tulle or gauze. Some ladies—a very

---

[1] Fig. 112.

[2] In 1895. 'Heart-shaped ornaments are still favourites, and the pretty moonstones and aquamarines, set around with small diamonds, are still very much in favour.' *Young Ladies' Journal.*

[3] The mass-production of secondary jewellery had increased enormously. J. M. O'Fallon in the *Art Journal* of 1894 states that in Birmingham, cups to take different sized stones and pastes were stamped out by the thousand gross at the press. Brooch backs and fronts were also produced in great numbers.

few—wear rows of diamonds, pearls, and precious stones in this way'. And a few months later: 'A brooch is worn on the point of the waist in front . . . Clasps and insects are worn on the shoulders; and pins in the hair. Dog-collars in shape continue to be worn round the neck'.

The dog-collar[1] which was a band of wide ribbon, or several rows of pearls held in place by upright strips of gold or silver, encircled the necks of fashionable women throughout most of this period. And as the dog-collar encompassed the neck, so wide metal belts, or ribbon belts with large clasps encircled the slender waists.

The outline of the *fin de siècle* woman resembled that of a butterfly: a slender body, with enormous wings formed by the spreading shoulders of the dress, and a small head, with a top-knot, from which a slender aigrette or comb rose like the butterfly's antennae.

A short fashion, beginning in 1885, was for jewellery made of the caps covering the escapement wheels of old verge watches.[2] These caps, all of them skilfully chased and all different, were joined by links to form necklets and bracelets, or set as the bezels of rings. By 1889, Mrs Haweis was con-demning this jewellery as showing the very worst taste. 'The people who now destroy old watches to make this horrid use of the pierced cocks', she wrote, 'are the same who a few years ago destroyed medieval books to torture the wrought clasps into the ugliest of belts, and wore the furry feet of grouse as brooches'.

A revival of ornaments with Egyptian motifs, in turquoise and oxidized silver, came about through the great success of Bernhardt in *Cléopatre*, in 1890. In this play she wore a number of handsome turquoise ornaments, and the public followed where she led.

Sporting jewellery was as popular in the nineties as sentimental jewellery had been in the fifties. Golf-clubs in gold, embellished with pearl golf-balls, were the newest thing. For hunting enthusiasts there were horns, hounds, and game-birds in gold or diamonds. But the favourite pattern for brooch, bracelet or pin was a fox-head looking through a horse-shoe. The roguish, frivolous tendencies of this period appear in the fashion for combining horse-shoes and riding-crops with bows of ribbon.[3]

The jewellery of this period presents an appearance that can hardly be called Victorian. It seems to show a complete break with what had gone

[1] See Figs. 102 and 103a and b.
[2] See Fig. 106b.
[3] For sporting jewellery, see Fig. 113.

before, and it certainly represents the beginning of Edwardian jewellery. But the *Art Nouveau* style springs from the Romantic young men of 1848 who founded the Pre-Raphaelite brotherhood; and the conventional jewellery with its emphasis on large stones in invisible settings springs just as surely from that spirit of emulation and optimism—the desire to have the best that money can buy—which flowered in the 1851 Exhibition. The break is not quite so great as it appears.

V

EARLY VICTORIAN JEWELLERY

1837-1860

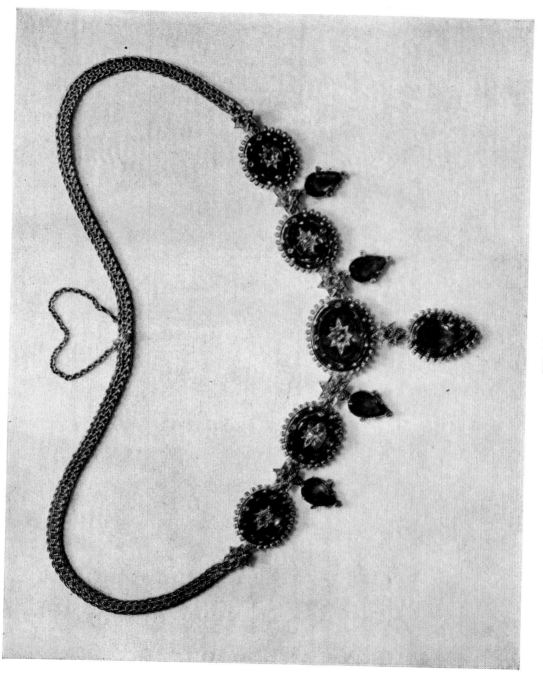

PLATE IV

Necklet in gold, amethysts and diamonds
The large stones are framed in green and white enamel. *c.* 1870.

(*Mrs H. O. Leighton*)

1. *Parures*

1837–50.   Worn only with ball dress.
1850–1860. Worn with ball dress and sometimes during the day.

Cameos, shell or gem.   [1837]
Coloured stones set in gold, or encircled with seed-pearls (as the set in *Fig.* 14a).
Turquoises in flexible gold settings (*Fig.* 9).
Seed-pearls (*Fig.* 6).
Beads of gold, silver or glass (*Fig.* 7a).
Roman pearls.[1] 'Pearls are much in request with muslin robes, and it matters
  little whether they are mock or real.' *World of Fashion.* 1838.

Turquoise and diamonds.   [1840]
Rubies and diamonds.
Silver filigree.
In 1844, parures of flowers composed of real or imitation gems.

Coral, branch or carved (*Figs.* 13a and b).   [1845]
Carbuncles and diamonds.
Mosaics (*Fig.* 8).
Inlaid work or Florentine mosaics (Plate I).

Collet-set gems (*Fig.* 11b).   [1850]
In 1857, coral and onyx cameos, by Isler of Rome. 'A parure of these cameos
  is altogether aristocratic, and wholly unlike the cameos with which all the
  world is acquainted [perhaps the writer is here referring to shell cameos].
  They are pure works of art, modelled and cut by artist-gravers, and mounted
  and ornamented by artists in *bijouterie*.'
Parure Louis XV, of stones of all colours, to be worn with a maize-coloured
  ball-dress, together with field flowers which repeat the colours of the stones.
Rubies and diamonds, to be worn with a white ball-dress, together with
  purple rhododendrons.
Turquoise ornaments, to be worn with a blue *robe de bal*.

[1] Roman pearls were artificial pearls produced by introducing an iridescent paste made from
the scales of a fish called the bleak (*albinus lucidus*) into spheres of very thin glass.

DEMI-PARURES

[1840]   Necklace and earrings. *Fig.* 10a shows one in blue enamel and diamonds.
Necklace and brooch. *Fig.* 14a shows one in gold and peridots.
Brooch and bracelet. *Fig.* 10c shows one in gold.
Brooch and earrings. *Fig.* 11a shows one in gold and paste.

[1850]   Carved coral. Brooch and earrings in *Figs.* 10b and 12a.
Carved ivory. Pendant and earrings in *Fig.* 12b.
Lava (as the bracelets in *Fig.* 38).

Note: Sets in inexpensive materials abounded in the fifties. Some of the most popular kinds are mentioned in the advertisement in *Fig.* 15.

2. Head Ornaments

Ornaments preferred:

Ornaments preferred:

1837–1844, Ferronnières and Pins most fashionable.
1844–1850, Combs.
1850–1860, Wreaths, which droop at the ears.

(A) ORNAMENTS THAT ENCIRCLE THE HEAD

1. Ferronnières, fashionable (*see Fig. 2*).   [*c.*1837–1844]

   Thin chains or cords from which fell an ornament of
   gold and jewels (*as the central ornament of the necklace in Fig.* 19c),
   pearl,
   silver, or
   jet.
   Entirely made of pearls.
   Entirely of gold, silver or other beads.

2. Bandeaux, worn straight across forehead.   [*c.*1837–1844]

   Burnished gold in flat bands. Usually one was worn alone; but sometimes two
   or three together, caught by a brooch over each ear.
   Pearl beads.
   Diamonds.
   Gold serpent with head and tail forming knot on the forehead. Worn with
   coiffure *à la reine Blanche* in 1837. (*Fig.* 3).
   Spray of jewelled flowers, going straight across forehead.

3. Tiaras, Diadems and Wreaths   [1837–1844]

   Couronnes moyen âge and *couronnes renaissance*, which were bands of gold with
   small triangles or semi-circles rising in the front, set with coloured gems
   (*Fig.* 16c).
   Diadems of gold and stones (Plate II).
   1838. *Coiffure à la Ninon*, decorated with vine leaves in gold, with small
   diamond grapes.
   1839. Couronnes of diamond *épis* and roses.
   Wreaths of silver wheat-ears.
   Gothic diadems (*Fig.* 16a).
   Diamond tiaras of floral design with 'rains' of diamonds falling over the ears   [1840–1860]
   (*as the ornament in Fig.* 27).
   Artificial flowers with dewdrops of diamonds or pearls.
   1843. At a fashionable wedding, the bride's silver filigree diadem, with
   flowers which trembled on their stalks, was acclaimed by all.

[1850–1860] Diamond tiaras (*Fig.* 16b).
Wreaths of branch coral (*Fig.* 13a).
Circlet of stars in invisible setting (*Fig.* 5).
Flowers powdered with silver.
Gilded leaves, on a coiffure powdered in gold dust.
1853. Mrs Ruskin describes a party at Stafford House in June where 'the ladies were all astonished and so were the gentlemen at the appearance of Frances, Ctess Waldegrave and Lady Desart with their heads powdered with gold . . .'
1851. At the Great Exhibition, Hunt & Roskell's branch coral tiara, ornamented by leaves of enamel and gold, enriched with diamonds.
A tiara of sapphires and diamonds, made for the Queen of Spain, the points being composed of diamond leaves, and having bands of diamonds falling in loops at the sides.
1855. A tiara of lilies, by Phillips of London, at the Paris Exhibition.

4. BEADS

[1837–1860] Beads of silver, gold or pearl entwined in, or encircling the hair (*Fig.* 4).
[1837–1844] Beads worn straight across forehead as bandeaux.
[1843–1860] Pearls or diamonds, falling irregularly in a 'rain', set on fine wires.

(B) COMBS

[*c.*1842] Combs become fashionable, as chignon descends to the back of the head (*Figs.* 4b and f).

[1842–1850] High combs, rather narrow.
Gold-topped combs studded with pearls or diamonds, or with cameos.
Gold headings carved to resemble wood.
Peigne d' Alger, with a large top covered with Moorish designs.

[1840–1860] *Peigne Joséphine*, studded with a row of gold or pearl beads. (*A variation of this can be seen in Fig.* 7a.)

[1850–1860] Metal headings carved into twists, or a series of knots.
Metal headings with scallops.
Metal headings of pierced work.
Metal headings in two tiers.
Tortoiseshell combs become fashionable.

(C) PINS

[1837–1844] Gold arrows, eight to ten inches long, decorated with pearls or diamonds.
Gold daggers, eight to ten inches long, decorated with pearls or diamonds on the hilts.
In 1838, 'In most full-dress toilettes, a poniard of gold adorned with jewels is passed through the knot in which the hind hair is arranged'.

Butterflies in coloured gems.

Pins with heads of cameos or of diamonds, pearls, etc, in the shape of berries, flowers, grapes, stars, or balls.

Pins with heads of twisted gold (*Fig.* 17, *No.* 1).

Glauvina pins: hexagonal in shape, set with gems.

In 1838, 'Stars of either brilliants or burnished gold have a superb effect on a coiffure *à la Grecque*'.

Venetian pins of gold, the heads enriched with precious stones. [1837–1855]

Silver and gold filigree bonnet-pins for day wear. [1840–1850]

Pins with large heads, from which pendants fell (*Fig.* 17, *No.* 2). [1850–1860]

(D) AIGRETTES

Aigrettes of pearls or gold frequently used. [1837–1850]

Clusters of pearls as holders for plumes or sprays of flowers.

3. Earrings

1837–1840, LONG EARRINGS were worn with evening dress.

1840–1850, almost no earrings were worn, as the hair completely covered the ears. The few which were worn were usually long.

1850–1860, EARRINGS gradually regained popularity, as the ear-lobes began to appear once more. Earrings of the fifties are usually small.

Queen Victoria's Coronation Earrings were horizontal bars from which hung three drops.

[1837–1840] Long elaborate jewelled earrings (*Figs.* 9 and 10a).

Long elaborate jet earrings for mourning (*Fig.* 1).

Long gold earrings (*Fig.* 18d).

Girandoles.

Round drops, single, double or triple (*Fig.* 7a), of

    Roman pearl.

    Gold.

    Silver.

    Glass.

    Jewels.

Small flowers of seed-pearls or stones.

1837. 'The most novel form of setting diamond earrings is a grape between two vine leaves, the grape is in brilliants, the leaves and the stalk in small diamonds.'

1839. Earrings become noticeably less fashionable.

[1840–1850] Rare.

[1850–1860] Small earrings the rule.

[1850–1860] Creole earrings—small hoops of gold or hair, thicker at the bottom than at the top (*Fig.* 18a).

Hoops of coral (*Fig.* 18e).

Ball drops, double or single—pearls, gold, or other materials.

Chased gold, simulating leaves and tendrils with a jewel as a bud (*Fig.* 18c).

Small hoops, flattened (*Fig.* 19d).

Elongated bead shape   trimmed with smaller beads, or with gold appliqué (*Fig.* 19b).

Gothic (*Fig.* 20).

Flowers of diamonds, or other gems.

    Roses of carved coral (*Fig.* 12a).

Hands in carved coral (*Fig.* 10b).

Ammonites (*Fig.* 18b).

Flat discs, decorated with
    Mosaic (*Fig.* 8).
    Enamelled eyes, hands, etc. (*Fig.* 19a).

Lava.

Pebble—Celtic shields or St Andrew's crosses.

1851. Earrings by Hunt & Roskell at the Great Exhibition, in emeralds, diamonds, carbuncles, etc., after the sculptures from Nineveh.

4. *Necklaces and Pendants*

Jewelled and bead necklaces, usually short ones, were worn during the late thirties and from 1850 to 1860.

Long fine chains were worn all through this period.

Ribbons crossed at the throat, and held together with a button or slide were characteristic of this period.

(A) NECKLACES

1. OF BEADS, sometimes with pendants. Usually short necklets.

[1837–1840]
and
[1850–1860]

Single or double rows of pearls (*see Fig.* 3).
Coral.
Gold.
Silver.
Glass (*see Fig.* 7a).

2. DECORATIVE NECKLACES of gold and jewels

[1837–1842]
and
[1850–1860]

Clusters of jewels connected by pearls or chains (*Figs.* 2 *and* 5).
Cameos connected by pearls or chains or gold links (*Fig.* 22).
Jewels hanging as a series of pendants from a chain (*Fig.* 21).
Coral drops hanging from coral beads.
Chains joined by a jewel, with two short ends hanging (*Fig.* 19c).
1838. 'A single row of gold chain, in the centre of which is a knot of gold with two short ends, to which gold acorns are suspended.'
Gold serpents with heads of enamel and jewels (*Fig.* 14b).
Serpents with turquoise-studded scales (*as the chain in Fig.* 9).
Seed-pearls (*Figs.* 6 *and* 7b).
Gems in collet settings (*Fig.* 11b).

3. GOLD NECKLACES

[1837]
[1837–1840]

Thick gold chokers.
Gold beads with decorative links (*Fig.* 23, *No.* 1).
Colliers *à la chatelaine*, with massive gold flat links.

4. OTHER MATERIALS

[1837–1860]

Jet necklaces for mourning (*Fig.* 1).
Mosaics (*Fig.* 8).
Lava (*as bracelets in Fig.* 38).

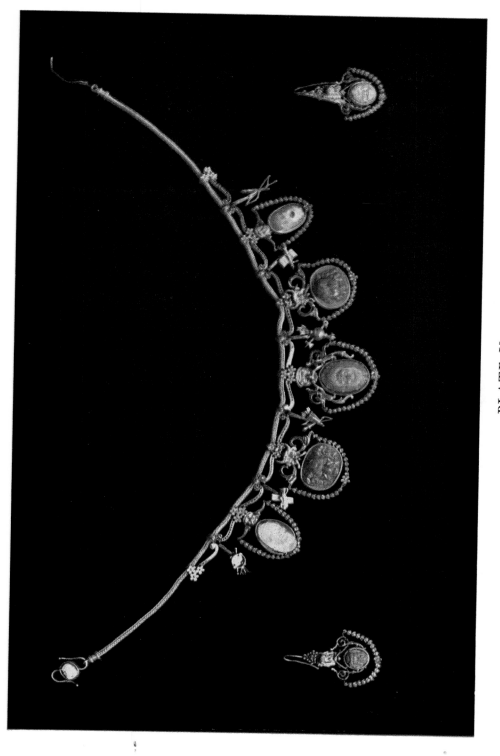

PLATE V

Necklace and pair of Earrings

Enamelled gold hung with cameos in chalcedony and onyx. Made by John Brogden, and shown at the Paris Exhibition of 1867.

(*Victoria and Albert Museum*)

Ribbon necklaces with jewelled slides.

(These necklaces may be seen in the portraits of Florence Nightingale by Sir George Scharf (1857) (*see Fig.* 26a), and of Charlotte Brontë by George Richmond (1850) in the National Portrait Gallery.)

1838. 'A very pretty ornament for the throat is composed of a band of velvet about an inch broad; it is fastened at the throat by a button of gold or precious stones; the ends of the velvet are crossed, and descend a little on the neck.'

(B) CHAINS

Used all through the period, to support a watch at the waist, or bearing a pendant, or alone.

1837. 'A minute gold or hair chain, to which the eye-glass is suspended, is more frequently seen than a necklace.'

Fine gold.

Serpent links of gold.

Gold and enamel (*Figs.* 20, 23, *No.* 3, *and* 24).

Hair.

Horsehair (*Fig.* 25a).

1853. In *The Heir of Redclyffe*, Mary Ross has a long chain put round her neck, as the finishing touch to her ball toilette.

(C) PENDANTS

Cross, hanging from a heart, the favourite style. (Plate III, b *and Fig.* 3, *centre*.) [1837–1842] This ornament, called by the French a *Croix à la Jeannette*, was a survival from the distant past. It was one of these which, Balzac tells us, Charles Grandet gave as a present to *la grande Nanon* when he left for the Indies. The name, according to Henri Vever, came from the practice of giving or buying them on St John's Day; and servant-girls in France from time immemorial had worn them hanging from a black ribbon. (There was also a bracelet *à la Jeannette*, which was a simple silk ribbon passing through a gold buckle.)

These *Croix à la Jeannette* were of gold, pearl, turquoise, garnet, rubies, diamonds or other gems.

Small gold crosses worn hanging from strings of pearls.

Flowers in seed-pearls or jewels or gold.

Birds or butterflies in seed-pearls or jewels or gold.

Maltese cross in blue enamel and diamonds (*Fig.* 10a).

Small round lockets, usually containing an inscription and a lock of hair (*Fig.* 25c).

Larger jewelled pendants. [1842–1860]

Serpents and leaves (*Fig.* 29a).

In carbuncles and diamonds.

In turquoise, enamel and diamonds.

Crosses in gold and jewels (*Fig.* 20).
  Amethyst (*Fig.* 11b).
  Carved ivory (*Fig.* 12b).
  Carved or polished coral.
Oval lockets of chased gold.
Enamel lockets with diamond flowers or insects.

5. Brooches

Usually large, and of an oblong, oval or lozenge shape. One, two or three pendants very often hung from them—pendeloque pearls, tassels, a jewel on a chain, or a small band of gems. The axis tended to be horizontal, whereas in the seventies and eighties it was usually vertical. As the sixties approached, brooches became smaller.

Many brooches were fitted with a hook or ring so that they could be worn as pendants. Large brooches were sometimes *en suite* with belt buckles.

(A) IN GOLD AND JEWELS

1. CORSAGE ORNAMENTS, or STOMACHERS, and SHOULDER ORNAMENTS   [1837–1860]

   In carbuncles and diamonds (*Fig.* 25d).

   Queen of Spain's bouquet and shoulder knot by Lemonnière of Paris in diamonds, pearls, rubies and emeralds. The aiguillette is of diamonds, pearls, and a large emerald (*see Fig.* 27).

   Strapwork ornament with pendant, in gold, enamel and jewels (*Fig.* 24, *centre*).

   Twigs and leaves of gold, enamel and jewels (*Fig.* 24).

   Branch coral (*Fig.* 13b).

   In 1851, the best of the English jewels at the Exhibition was Morel's diamond and ruby stomacher. 'It was originally intended and designed as a bouquet . . . moreover, it was so constructed as to separate into several distinct pieces of jewellery, according to requirement. The setting was contrived with springs, resulting in a waving or slightly oscillating motion when in use, which displayed to the fullest extent the brilliant colours of the stones.'

   A brooch by Messrs C. Rowlands & Son of London: A carbuncle set in gold, surmounted by a bust of a winged female, and flanked by two cupids, holding trumpets; a pendent gold mask, and drops of brilliant.

   A corsage ornament of rubies and diamonds by Rowlands.

   A bouquet of diamonds with bands of diamonds falling as pendants by Rowlands.

   A brooch by Froment-Meurice: a step-cut jewel in a frame resembling a Gothic window, flanked by angels playing harps.

2. BROOCHES

   Central gem, surrounded by foliate, twisted or strapwork border (*Figs.* 14a *and* 28a).   [1837–1855]

   The same, with a pendant (*Fig.* 29c).

   Girandoles, having three drops.

[59]

Ovals with four balls at the points of the compass shape from 1837 to about 1847. (*A variant of the bracelet clasp in Fig. 36c.*) were the favourite *this shape is seen in*

Medieval themes
Gauntlet (*Fig. 23, No. 4*).
Ecclesiastical (*Fig. 20*).
Knights, pages, angels.

Bows or knots of ribbon in diamonds (*Fig. 30b*).

Bows of ribbon in gold and turquoise (*Fig. 28c*).

Floral ornaments combined with bows of ribbon or with strapwork.

Knots
Gold serpents twisted (*Fig. 10c*).
With tassel (*Fig. 11a*).
Algerian knots.

Naturalistic (*Fig. 2*).
Flowers (*Fig. 24*).
Serpents and leaves (*Fig. 29a*).
Vine leaves and seed-pearl grapes (*Fig. 28d*).

In 1837, the new brooches for evening were 'composed of pearls and turquoises; the pattern is a hazel nut placed on a branch of foliage. The fruit which is of a tolerable size, is formed of a single pearl, the leaves tastefully grouped, are of small turquoises placed very close together.'

[1850-1860] Leaves and flowers in gold, pearls and light-blue enamel.

Cinquefoil in white enamel with pearl centre surrounded with enamelled green leaves from ends of which hang three small pearls.

Leaves and an insect in blue enamel, pearls and diamonds.

Star in black enamel and diamonds, with pendent pearls.

Diamond bird pecking at ruby cherries.

At the Great Exhibition of 1851.
Cameos set in diamonds on blue enamel by Phillips (*Fig. 30b*).
A diamond flower with a rain of pink pearls designed by Lemonnière for the Queen of Spain.
Copies of ancient Irish penannular brooches. By Messrs West of Dublin (*Fig. 30a*).
A brooch by Rudolphi, with two knights tilting on horseback against a background of leaves and strapwork. Another of ivy leaves and a third of acanthus leaves.
A round brooch designed by Messrs West of Dublin, to be presented by the people of Dublin to Miss Helen Faucit. It has a laurel-wreath border, and the centre is composed of a kneeling female figure, flanked by two masks. All three of which are framed in the coils of a large serpent in relief (*Fig. 30a*).

(B) IN LESS EXPENSIVE MATERIALS

In 1839. 'The prettiest undress brooches are of a round shape, and of a deep
blue enamel ground, on which is a bouquet of small flowers of the natural
colours.'

Coral (*Fig.* 12a).

Ivory.

Mosaic.

Fossils.

Oxidized silver: Rudolphi's angel, etc (*Fig.* 29d).

Aventurine quartz in gold frame.

Horsehair (*see Figs.* 26b *and* c).

Gold and aquamarine (*Fig.* 32a).

From 1847. Parian (*Fig.* 29b). Belleek (*see Fig.* 33c).

Enamelled eyes or hands on gold.   [1850]

Silver brooch with green ivy leaves and grapes of facetted coral.

White cornelian, ornamented with filigree flowers (*Fig.* 32b).

Miniatures set in gold or pearls (*Fig.* 28b). This may represent St. Rosalie,
patron of Palermo, who is always depicted in a cave, with a cross and a
skull.

In 1849, safety-chain brooches, in two parts, of scrollwork patterns, Devonshire pebbles inlaid in the scrolls.

Scottish pebble jewellery.

    Shields.

    Garters (*Fig.* 31a).

    Crosses.

Carved bog oak from Ireland, set with Irish pearls.

SENTIMENTAL BROOCHES

    Of gold and hair. Bow-knot shown in *Fig.* 31b.

    Flowers entirely of hair.

    Hair landscapes (*Fig.* 31d).

    Hair feathers in gold frames (*Fig.* 31c).

    Black enamel background with small ivory flowers.

6. Bracelets

Most popular ornaments of the Romantic Period, bracelets were consistently worn, even in the forties, when other jewellery went out of fashion. Two or three bracelets were usually worn on each arm; in the evening they were worn on the short white evening gloves, and also between the glove and the elbow. Pairs of bracelets, one on each wrist, were popular in the thirties and fifties.

The following quotation from the *World of Fashion*, Sept. 1844, makes clear what bracelets the well-dressed woman was then expected to wear:

'Bracelets are now considered indispensable; they are worn in the following manner: on one arm is placed the *sentimental* bracelet, composed of hair, and fastened with some precious relic; the second is a silver enamelled one, having a cross, cassolette, or anchor and heart, as a sort of talisman; the other arm decorated with a bracelet of gold net work, fastened with a simple *noeud*, similar to one of narrow ribbon; the other composed of medallions of blue enamel, upon which are placed small bouquets of brilliants, the fastening being composed of a single one; lastly, a very broad gold chain, each link separated with a ruby and opal alternate.'

(A) BANGLES

[1837]   Serpent bracelets in gold, enamel and diamonds.
> Queen Victoria wore one of these at her First Council (*Fig.* 34a).

Serpents pierced by arrows.

Serpents about to swallow birds.

Serpents coiled and holding a heart pendant (*Fig.* 32d).

Serpents entwined in knots (*Fig.* 10c).

A bracelet by Froment-Meurice, with the arms of Marseilles in the centre, and on each side three enamel portraits of city worthies of former days.

Foliage patterns in enamel, set with pearls and diamonds (Plate III, *Fig.* a).

Gold twisted into a knot, with a central star in pearls and enamel (*Fig.* 32c).

Simulated ribbon, in enamel and gold, set with gems. The ends of the ribbon terminate in *ferrets*, or tags, of diamonds (*Fig.* 33a).

In 1844, A bracelet containing a watch is a new article of jewellery.
> 'The dial plate is covered in the evening by a cameo or an enamelled case, with a cypher in diamonds. By touching a spring, a lady can always know the hour, and she can do that behind her fan, without being observed.'

In 1849. A carved tortoiseshell bangle in the style of natural wood, with gold leaves (*Fig.* 39b).

A bracelet of leafage design, with a crowned eagle as a centre.

In 1850. A strap and buckle bangle, in gold enamelled light-blue with the buckle of rose diamonds.

In 1851. A bangle with diamonds set in gold and green enamel by Phillips (*Fig.* 30b).

Gold bangles set with cabochon garnets.   [1850]

Bangles pavé-set in facetted garnets, with central garnet cluster.

Turquoise clusters on gold bands.

Gold bangles with scalloped tops.

Manchette bracelets, like wide cuffs, following the shape of the arm, enriched with a motif in diamonds, such as a large flower with pendants, or tiny diamond ribbons apparently lacing it shut.

Manchette bracelets, of narrow gold bands, set with gems (*Fig.* 36b).

Plain gold bangles.

Twisted gold, like rope.

'Creole' bracelets of gold rings and hair.

(B) LINK BRACELETS

Ornamental links in chased gold, decorated with enamel, very wide (*Fig.* 37).   [1837]

Flexible serpents of gold links with enamelled and jewelled heads.

Enamel miniatures, set in engraved frames (*Fig.* 39c).

Chased gold links with pendants (*Fig.* 36a).

Curb chain bracelets with pendants.

Narrow bracelets of collet-set gems (*Fig.* 11b).

Facetted cylinders of malachite or granite with pendants (*Fig.* 35b).

Moyen-âge bracelets, with ogive-shaped links, containing knights in armour standing sentinel.

In 1837. 'A bracelet of fine gold chain, with a clasp either of rubies or any other coloured gem, from which a large pearl depends.'
'A serpent which encircles the arm three times.'

In 1839. 'A bracelet of narrow gold chains, clasped by a rose encircled by a foliage of rubies.'

In 1842. A bracelet in massive silver by Froment-Meurice, showing scenes from the life of St Louis. Shown in London in 1851 (*see Fig.* 40a).

In 1845. Gold foliage links, each set with an emerald, with a central ornament of emeralds and diamonds, and an emerald pendant (*Fig.* 41a).

Square links, outlined in pearls, with a quatrefoil central ornament, enriched   [1845]
with gems throughout (*Fig.* 20).

Quatrefoils in enamel and gems, linked ornaments of twisted gold wire (*Fig.* 41b).

Semi-circular links, set with carbuncles and diamonds, with a niello miniature in the centre (*Fig.* 35a).

Jewelled oval links round an ornamental centre flanked by winged figures.

Silver with bosses of burnished gold, and medallions of medieval figures (*Figs. 40d and* 42c).

Cabochon stones outlined with pearls or diamonds, and linked together.

In 1849. Heavy gold link chain, from which depends a carbuncle, carved as three grapes enriched with diamond leaves.

[1850] Enamelled links, with an all-over decorative pattern.

Lava medallions, linked together (*Fig.* 38).

In 1851. Diamonds and amethysts on green enamel; a central motif and small motifs, connected by gold links (*Fig.* 40b).

Blue and white enamel links, on which notes of music are represented (*Fig.* 40c).

Diamonds and enamels with a carbuncle centre.

Carbuncles set with diamonds, the precious stones **connected** by gold cross-bands enamelled in turquoise-blue scrollwork.

In 1855. A pair of gold bracelets, chased and enamelled in the oriental style.

(C) FLEXIBLE BRACELETS

In 1837. Woven gold bracelets. Queen Victoria wore one of these bearing the words *Honi soit qui mal y pense* at her Coronation (*see Fig.* 34b).

[1837] Enamel serpents, encircling the arm several times.

Flexible gold bands with central jewelled ornament (*see Fig.* 39a).

In 1839. 'A bracelet of rubies and diamonds, with a clasp formed of a brilliant set in rubies. The bracelet is twisted in such a manner as to resemble a striped ribbon unrolling in serpentine folds.'

'Another of *or-lisse*, narrow and flexible, with gems incrusted, clasped by a serpent enamelled in colours.'

[1840] Hair plaited into flat bands, or coiled into ropes, clasped with a miniature, or a fastening of chased gold (*Figs.* 43c *and* 44a, b *and* c). (In 1837, hair bracelets had been considered in the worst taste).

Hair or ribbon, passing through a gold buckle (*Fig.* 42b).

Serpent chains of gold, with pendants (*Figs.* 42a *and* 43a).

In 1843. Elastic bracelets are a novelty.

[1848] Carved ivory, strung on elastic (*Fig.* 33b).

Flexible gold bands, with Assyrian rosettes, or lotus flowers, in jewels (*Fig.* 24).

In 1851. Cable of massive gold, with a pendant of vine-leaves set with brilliants,
   by Attenborough.
   A bracelet of rubies and gold.
In 1857. 'A broad ribbon of gold, fastened with a large buckle of black enamel
   and gold, through which the pointed lappet of the ribbon passes.'
   'Another, more costly, has a buckle set with diamonds, and the lappet is
   finished with five diamond tags.'

(D) BEAD BRACELETS

Pearls, several rows, held by a clasp.
Beads of coral, garnets, or other materials, often with short strings of beads
   falling as pendants.
Seed-pearls sewn into patterns (*Fig.* 6).
Facetted coral beads, with a carved coral clasp (*Fig.* 36c).

(E) BRACELET CLASPS

Bracelets of velvet, silk ribbon, embroidery or bead work, were usually adorned
   with ornamental clasps.
Large stones, or coloured pastes, on ornamental borders of foliage, strapwork   [1837–1845]
   or scrollwork (*Fig.* 43b).
Flat oblong catches of chased gold (*Fig.* 44a).
Barrel-shaped catches of chased gold (*Fig.* 44c).
Square buckles.
Miniatures set in gold, pearl or diamond frames (*Fig.* 44b).   [1837–1860]
Cameos in gold or jewelled frames.
Ovals set with mosaics or lava (*Fig.* 8).   [1845–1860]
Parian clasps (*Fig.* 43d).
In 1854. Three large pearls are the clasp for a green velvet bracelet.
   Emerald buckles fasten black velvet bracelets.
   Clusters of gems fasten black velvet bracelets.
   Clasps of brilliants on bracelets of ruched pink ribbon.

(F) CHAINS ON BRACELETS

A fine chain was often attached to a bracelet, the other end joined to a jewelled
   vinaigrette which was held in the hand, or to a small finger-ring.

7. Rings

Queen Victoria's coronation ring: the bezel was a sapphire, on which five rubies were set in the manner of a Cross of St George, surrounded by a circle of diamonds.

(A) DECORATIVE RINGS

Prince Albert's gift to Princess Victoria on his first visit to England was a narrow enamel ring set with a tiny diamond.

[1837]
Clusters of gems on narrow bands (*Figs.* 45b *and* d).
Daisies of pearls, diamonds and garnets (*Fig.* 45g).
Concentric circles of diamonds and turquoise (*Fig.* 45f).
Forget-me-nots or pansies in enamel and gems.
Serpents with jewelled eyes.

[1844]
Figures chiselled in relief (*Fig.* 46b).
Groups of angels.
Two children clasping hands over the bezel of a ring.
Heraldic patterns.
Ecclesiastical patterns (*Fig.* 20).
Ivy leaves and trefoils in naturalistic rings (*Fig.* 24).
Large gem set in gold resembling flowers (*Fig.* 24).
Rings with coral hands or coral flowers as bezels.
Single-stone gem rings (*Fig.* 45a).
Half-hoop rings (*Fig.* 45c).
Rings with floral designs in enamel on bezel and shanks.
Rings in the shape of a belt and buckle.
In 1856, a young girl's ring, of small rubies and diamonds (*Fig.* 46c).
Favourite stones: Diamonds, pearls, rubies, emeralds, turquoise, garnet and coral.

(B) RINGS WITH VINAIGRETTES ATTACHED

[1837]
Ring, chain and vinaigrette decorated in enamel (*Fig.* 23, *No.* 3).
1843. Queen Victoria's pearl, gold and pale-blue enamel ring, attached to a vinaigrette by a fine gold chain (*Fig.* 46a).

(C) ENGAGEMENT RINGS

Queen Victoria's betrothal ring was a gold serpent studded with emeralds. Pearl half-hoops were favourite engagement rings in the fifties.

(D) SOUVENIR RINGS

Fluorspar rings from the Blue John mine.
Lava.
Mosaics.
Shell cameos.

(E) MOURNING RINGS

Gold bands encircled by a plait of hair, sometimes set with a piece of facetted
   jet (*Fig.* 46e).
Gold bands ornamented with black enamel.
Gold and black enamel, with a heart-shaped bezel (*Fig.* 46d).

8. *Miscellaneous*

(A) BELTS

[1837–1840] Wide ribbon belts with jewelled buckles.
  On these were sometimes placed *watch-hooks*, as the hand in *Fig. 23, No. 2*.
Jewelled girdles, inspired by those of the Middle Ages.
Cordelières, or girdles knotted in front with the two ends hanging down.
In 1837, with full evening dress, a fashionable girdle was a *cordelière* of silver beads, fastened at the waist with bead cluster and having two more clusters holding the descending ends together until they terminated in a single bead tassel. This was *en suite* with a necklace and earrings of silver beads.
In 1839, *cordielières* were composed of silk, roses and pearls.
In the early forties, pointed waists superseded round ones, and belts and girdles were no longer fashionable.

(B) BUCKLES AND AGRAFES

[1837–1844] Large jewelled oval or oblong buckles *en suite* with brooches.
Gold lizards studded with diamond spots as agrafes.
Pearl and gold clusters, as agrafes.
Blue and gold butterflies, as agrafes.
Silk bows pierced by gold arrows.
In 1849. Narrow vertical buckles of leaves and scrollwork.

[1850–1860] Ovals of pearls used as agrafes.

(C) CHATELAINES

[1837–1840] Chatelaines worn with '*grandes costumes*'.
In 1839, the *World of Fashion* describes chatelaines as 'those large, heavy, chased gold hooks, with which our great-great-grandmothers used to fasten their massive watch chains to their waists. These are now revived, not only in their antique form, but even in their antique rust, if we may so express it, for the more they bear the stamp of antiquity, the more fashionable they are. The watch, the smelling-bottle, and eye-glass, suspended from the chatelaine, are all of modern and elegant workmanship, which forms a contrast ridiculous enough; *mais la mode le veut*, and we all know that she is an absolute Queen.'

[1840–1850] Chains at the waist suspending a small evening bag, or gold smelling-bottle.

[1849–1855] Steel chatelaines fashionable.
  A steel chatelaine was shown at the Great Exhibition of 1851 with scissors, watch, notebook, knife and vinaigrette, highly ornamented in floral patterns.

[1852–1860] Chatelaines in pierced and engraved gold, often with Moorish patterns.

(D) LORGNETTES

In 1857. Lorgnettes were decorated with gems and pearls, or set in jet. Others were made of sculptured rosewood, with 'medallions set round with pearls, and of *mosaïque Louis XVI*—beautiful as works of art, and wholly distinct from the ebony or ivory type of Lorgnette we have been so long accustomed to'.

(E) DRESS CLIPS

In 1846, clips called *Pages*, in the form of negroes' heads, were attached to the waist by a chain, and used to hold up the skirt while walking.

(F) STUDS

In 1852, fashionable with the *gilet*, or waistcoat.
  Made of gold, pearl, jet, turquoise or similar materials. 'Some ladies have had old-fashioned, obsolete articles of jewellery reset for studs, with very good effect, emeralds, rubies or amethysts being shown to great advantage on the white watered-silk *gilets*.'

(G) BUTTONS

Buttons worn very large.   [1843–1847]
  Enamel, circled with marcasite.
  Garnet, surrounded with pearls.
  Amethyst ⎫
  Turquoise ⎪
  Marcasite ⎬ Many of these shaped as flowers.
  Cut steel ⎭

Fancy buttons, of gilt, pearl, pebbles, mosaic.   [1850–1860]

(H) CHILDREN'S JEWELLERY

Coral beads were a customary christening present for a girl baby, and she wore these during her childhood. A rattle of silver bells on a coral stem was the corresponding present for a boy.
Tiny crosses and lockets on a chain.
Wide black velvet, or ribbon bracelets.

Summary

1837 – 60

I. MATERIALS CHIEFLY USED

FOR PRIMARY JEWELLERY

Amethysts (often cut *en cabochon*)
Cameos (gem).
Carbuncles.
Chrysolite.
Coral.
Diamonds (rose and brilliant cut)
Emeralds.
Enamel.
Gold (Of 18 and 22 carats. Also of different colours—red, green and yellow—used together. The preferred setting for all precious stones).
Gold filigree.
Niello.
Opals (rarely).
Pearls.
Peridots.
Rubies.
Sapphires.
Seed-pearls.
Silver.
Silver filigree.
Topaz.
Turquoise.

FOR SECONDARY JEWELLERY

Bog-oak.
Cameos (of shell or glass).
Coral.
Enamel.
Fluorite.
Fossils.
Garnets (small and facetted, often pavé-set).
Gilt (mercury-gilding was usual but electro-gilt articles were shown as early as the Paris Exhibition of 1844).
Gold (Of 9, 12 and 15 carats).
Hair.
Horsehair.
Ivory.
Jet.
Lava.
Malachite.
Marcasite.
Mosaics.
Parian.
Paste.
Pearls, Roman or other imitations.
Pebbles (of limestone or marble).
Pinchbeck.
Quartz in various forms, as
Amethyst	Cornelian
Aventurine	Onyx
Cairngorm	Topaz
Steel (late forties and early fifties).
Silver (plain and oxidized).
Tortoiseshell.

II. MOTIFS MOST TYPICAL OF THIS PERIOD

Algerian knots.
Angels.
Arabesques.
Arches, pointed.
Arrows.
Assyrian.
Belt and Buckle.
Bows of ribbon.
Celtic.
Clusters.
Crosses.
Daggers.
Daisies.
Doves.
Eyes.
Flowers.
Garters.
Gauntlets.

Girandoles.
Gothic.
Grapes.
Hands.
Hazel-nuts.
Hearts (as pendants or slides).
Heraldic.
Ivy-leaves.
Knights.
Knots.
Moorish.
Scrollwork.
Serpents.
Stars.
Strapwork.
Tendrils.
Thistles.
Vine-leaves.

III. OTHER FEATURES CHARACTERISTIC OF THIS PERIOD

Bracelets with pendants, usually heart-shaped.
Brooches with pendants hanging from coiled or knotted chains.
Carved coral, ivory or tortoiseshell, imitating twigs, leaves and branches.
Chains attaching vinaigrettes to rings or bracelets or belts.
Collet-set single stones forming bracelets or necklets.
Diamonds set in parallel falling bands.
Ferronnières (1837–43).
Figures carved in relief.
Hoop, or Creole earrings (1850–55).
Manchette bracelets (1850–60).
Scrollwork patterns engraved or enamelled on gold.
Slides or buttons, often heart-shaped, for ribbons or neck chains.
Strapwork frames in chased gold.
Trembling ornaments.

Fig. 1. 'Morning, Walking and Evening Dresses to be worn as the
Mourning for the Lamented King, William IV'

From the *World of Fashion*, July, 1837

(*Mrs Doris Langley Moore*)

Fig. 2. A Presentation to Queen Victoria
By H. Robinson after A. E. Chalon R.A., 1837–8
(From a print belonging to Mrs Doris Langley Moore)

Fig. 3. Morning, Dinner and Evening Dresses
From the *World of Fashion*, April, 1837
(*Mrs Doris Langley Moore*)

Fig. 4.

From the *Ladies' Cabinet,* 1844.

Evening dresses and coiffures

A. Shaded velvet robe, a low corsage trimmed *en Berthe* with four rows of lace. Short tight sleeve, lace cuff. Blonde lace *bonnet paysanne* ornamented with a wreath of roses in different shades of red, and a knot of ribbon at the back.

B. Green satin robe, the corsage trimmed with a lace pelerine. Short tight sleeve finished with three rows of lace. The hair is decorated with silver bands and a tuft of exotics.

C. White satin robe, the corsage, low and square, is decorated with lace disposed *à la vielle.* Demi-long sleeve. Fancy turban of white spotted gauze decorated with three dahlias brought very low on one side.

D. Shaded satin robe, the corsage partially covered by a *tulle* pelerine of a novel form. . . . The hair is decorated with a double row of pearls terminated by pearl tassels.

E. Violet velvet róbe, *berthe* of *point d'Alençon. Tulle* cap, a round shape profusely trimmed with the blossoms of the cotton-tree.

F. Shaded satin robe, the corsage trimmed with a double fall of lace. The hair is decorated with lace brought round the back of the head, an ornamented comb, and a bouquet of flowers.

(*Mrs Doris Langley Moore*)

Fig. 5. Sortie de Bal and Ball Dress
From the *Journal des Demoiselles*, March, 1854
(*Mrs Doris Langley Moore*)

[78]

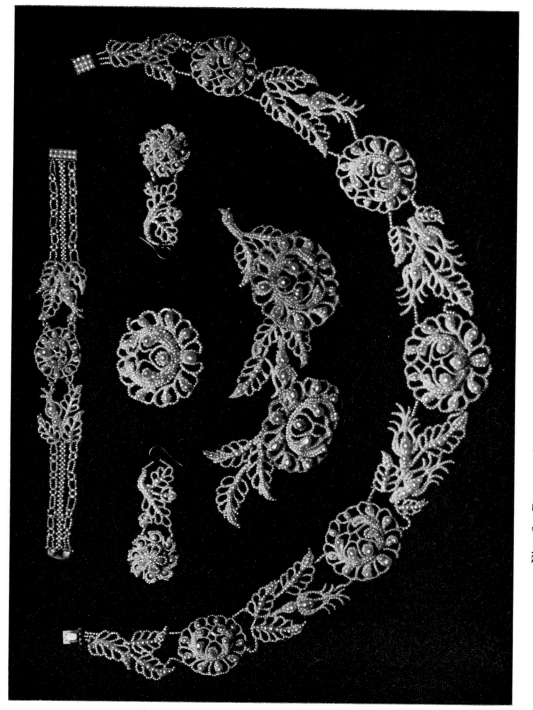

Fig. 6. Parure of seed pearls in a pattern of flowers and leaves
consisting of a necklace, a brooch, a corsage ornament with the two oval flowers set on springs,
and a pair of bracelets (one shown). *c.* 1840.

(*Mrs James Walker*)

A

B

Fig. 7a. Parure in light-blue blown glass and gold
consisting of a modified Joséphine chignon comb, a necklet of
graduated beads and a pair of earrings. 1837
(*Mrs James Walker*)

Fig 7b. A seed pearl necklet
By Franklin and Hare. *c.* 1837.
(*Mrs Patrick Hancock*)

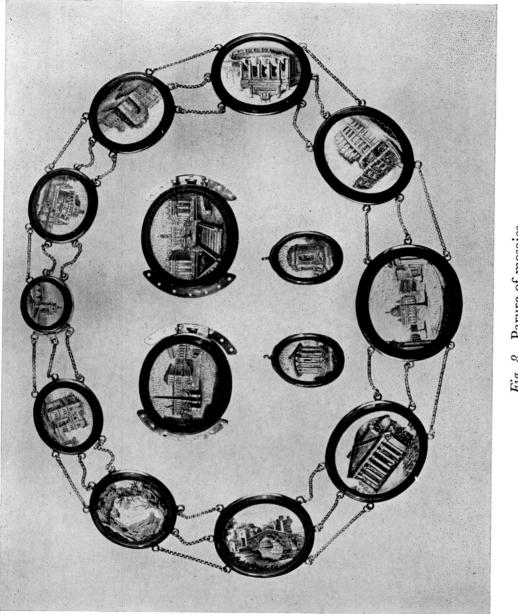

Fig. 8. Parure of mosaics

showing views of Rome, set in blue frames mounted in gold. The set consists of a necklace *en esclavage*, a pair of bracelet clasps and a pair of earrings. *c.* 1840.

(*Messrs Harvey and Gore*)

[81]

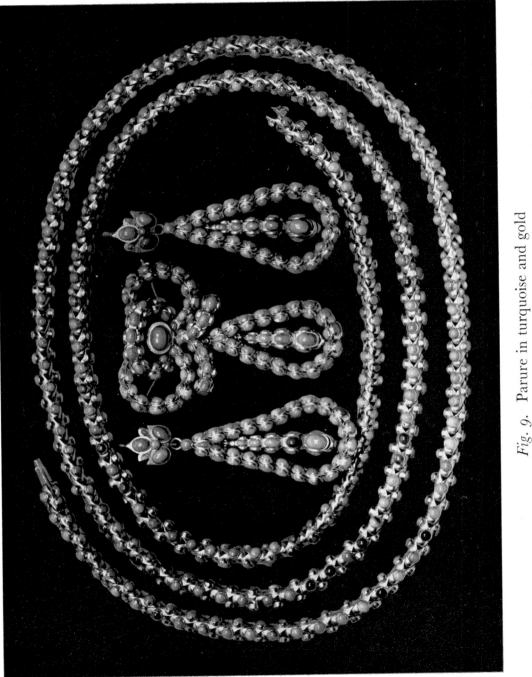

Fig. 9. Parure in turquoise and gold
comprising a long flexible chain, a pair of earrings and a brooch in the form of a knot of riband.
By Storr and Mortimer. *c.* 1840.

(*Cameo Corner*)

[82]

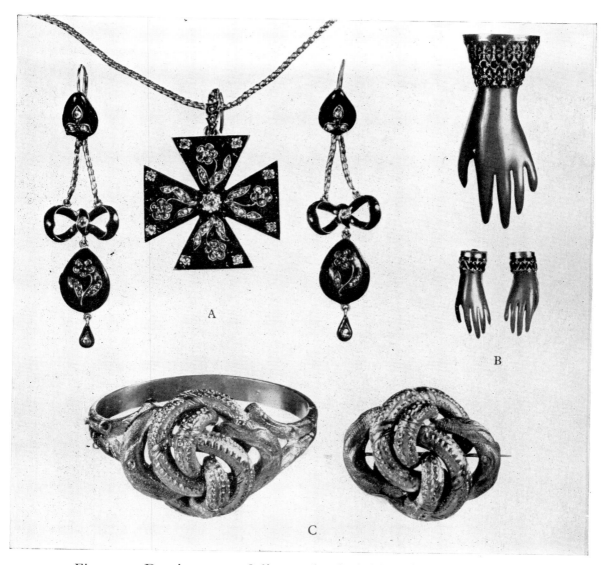

Fig. 10a. Demi-parure of diamonds, dark-blue enamel and gold
The Maltese cross pendant can be worn as a brooch if desired. *c.* 1840.
(*Messrs Harvey and Gore*)

Fig. 10b. Demi-parure of gold and coral
the coral carved into the shape of hands with gold lace cuffs. *c.* 1845.
(*Mrs Barbara Neill*)

Fig. 10c. Gold brooch and bangle *en suite*
each decorated with a knot formed of two coiled serpents. These knots are twisted hollow tubes of gold, chased to resemble snakeskin. *c.* 1845.

(*Mrs Wilfrid Nicholson*)

Fig. 11a. Gold and paste demi-parure. *c.* 1845
(The Author)

Fig. 11b. Suite of Siberian amethysts set in gold collets. *c.* 1850
(Mr Collins)

A

B

Fig. 12a. Carved pink coral pendant and earrings with
gold and pink coral brooch. *c.* 1855

(*Mrs James Walker*)

Fig. 12b. Cross and earring in carved ivory. *c.* 1850

(*The Author*)

Figs. 13a and *b.* Tiara and corsage ornament of branch coral
to be worn *en suite. c.* 1850.

(*London Museum*)

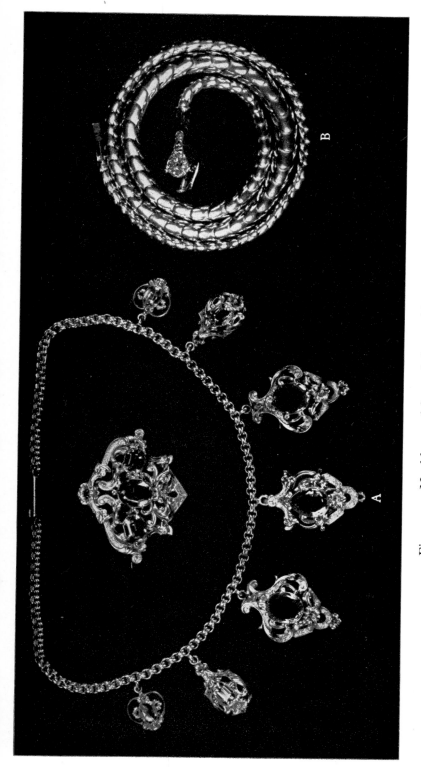

Fig. 14a. Necklet and brooch in peridots and gold

Seven graduated peridots in gold mounts hang from a chain. The gold mounts are ornamented in chased strapwork, and in shells, flowers and foliage. (The gold work is open and is built up on several different levels.) The brooch *en suite* is set with three peridots. A small gold ring on the reverse permits it to be worn as a pendant on a fine chain. *c.* 1840.

(*Mrs James Walker*)

Fig. 14b. Gold serpent necklet

The blue enamel head of the serpent is set with diamonds. Two garnets form the eyes. *c.* 1840.

(*Mrs Gilbert Debenham*)

[87]

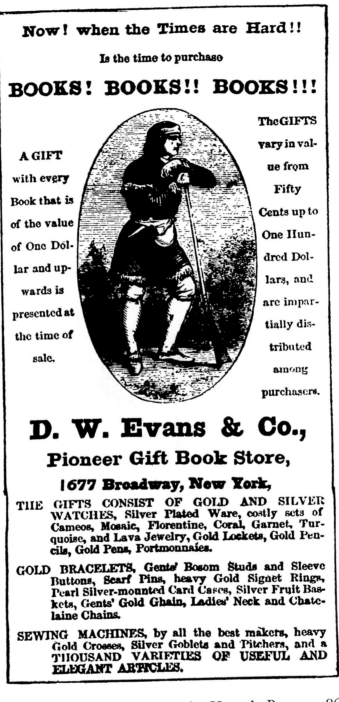

Fig. 15. An advertisement in *Harper's Bazaar,* 1861

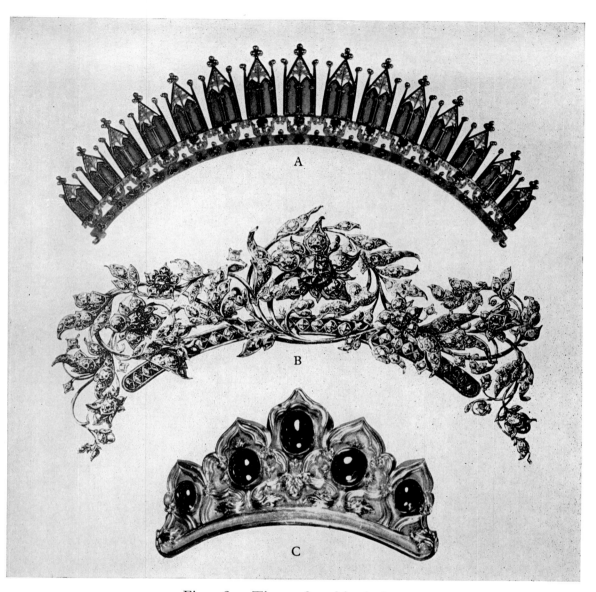

Fig. 16a. Tiara of gothic design

Gold, set with rubies and enriched with black, green and blue
enamel. *c.* 1848. (*H. Steiner*)

Fig. 16b. Tiara in gold and jewels

designed by James Brown, and executed by Watherston and
Brogden. From the *Art Journal*, 1852.

Fig. 16c. Diadem in gold and carbuncles. *c.* 1840
(*Mr Albert A. Julius*)

Fig. 17.

1. Hair ornament with twisted gold heading. *c.* 1838.

2. Hair pin with ornamental head with pendants. Gold and
    pale-blue glass. *c.* 1850.

3. Lace-pin or tie-pin with a head in the form of a horseshoe.
    Gold, set with pearls. *c.* 1890.

4 & 5. Silver filigree hair pins with flower heads which tremble.
    c. 1868.

(*The Author*)

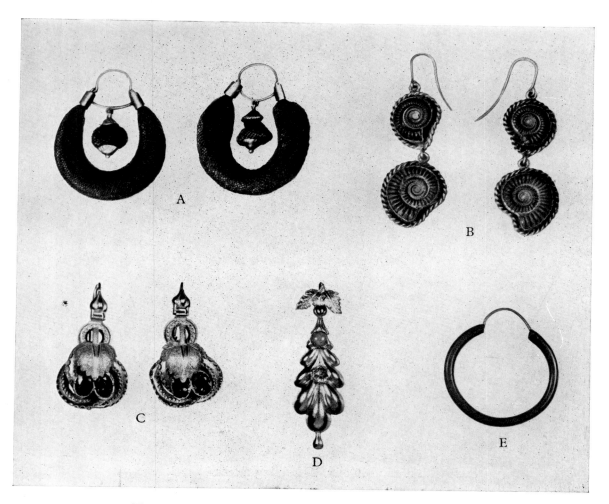

Fig. *18a*. Creole earrings in gold and hair. *c.* 1850

(*Mrs James Walker*)

Fig. *18b*. Earrings of fossils mounted in silver. *c.* 1850

(*Mrs James Walker*)

Fig. *18c*. Earrings of gold and garnets. *c.* 1855

(*Mrs James Walker*)

Fig. *18d*. Gold earring set with a turquoise and an
imitation diamond. *c.* 1838

(*The Author*)

Fig. *18e*. Hoop earring of polished coral. *c.* 1850

(*The Author*)

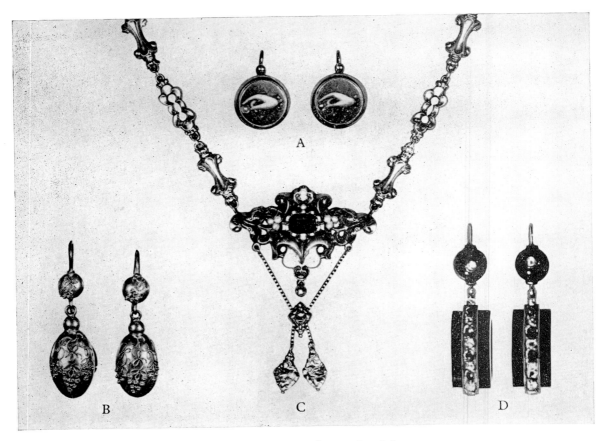

Fig. 19a. Earrings of gold

each with a hand in enamel holding a small pearl. *c.* 1855.

(*Mrs James Walker*)

Fig. 19b. Small gold earrings

ornamented with a grape and tendril pattern in fine gold grains
and wire. *c.* 1855.

(*Cameo Corner*)

Fig. 19c. Necklace of fancy gold links

with central ornament in leaf and scroll design, from which hang two fine
chains joined by a small gold motif and terminating in two small gold
pendants. The central ornament has a table-cut garnet or spinel in the
centre and eight small pearls. It is decorated with dark-blue and white
champlevé enamel. *c.* 1838.

(*Mrs Eric Ambler*)

Fig. 19d. Hoop earrings of jet

ornamented with a gold band set with imitation diamonds and
garnets. Formerly belonged to Lady Nias. *c.* 1855.

(*London Museum*)

[92]

Fig. 20. Jewellery designed by Pugin and executed by
Hardman of Birmingham

Pugin designed the pieces at some time between 1844 and 1850.
They were shown at the 1851 Exhibition.

Fig. 21. Necklet in gold, garnets and diamonds
The gold is chased to resemble ribbon. *c.* 1843.   (*Mrs Evelyn Verschoyle*)

[94]

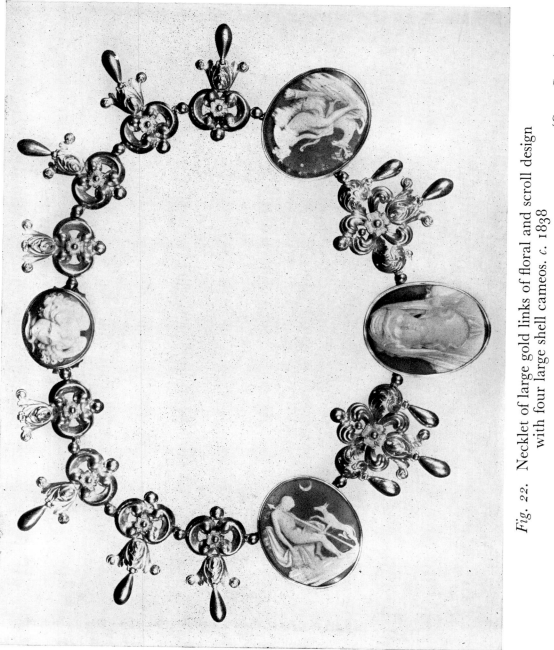

Fig. 22. Necklet of large gold links of floral and scroll design
with four large shell cameos. *c.* 1838

(Cameo Corner)

[95]

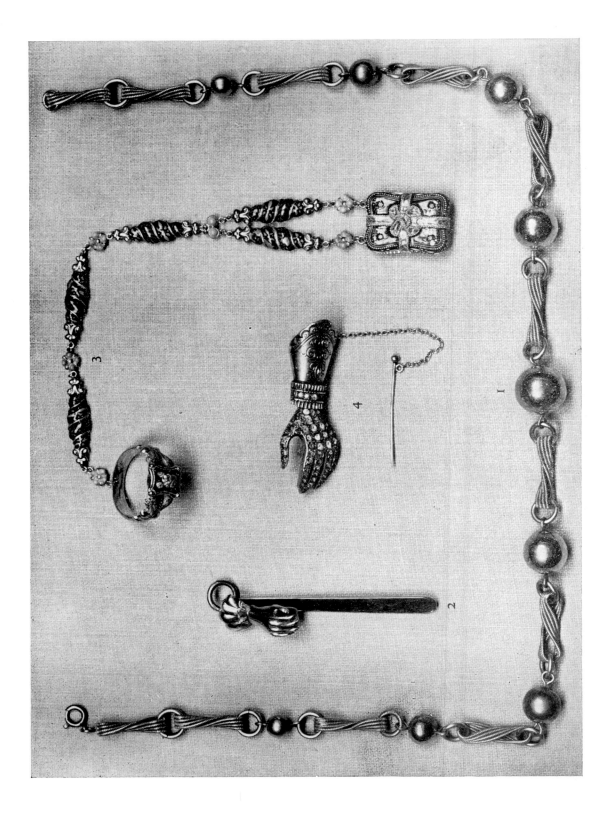

Fig. 23.

1. Pinchbeck necklet

c. 1838. Balls of gold-coloured metal in graduated sizes are connected by twists of very fine chain and by round gold links.

(Mrs James Walker)

2. A gold watch-hook

c. 1835. A hook for the watch is directly under the hand, which thus appears to be holding the watch. The long piece of gilt metal is to be thrust inside a wide belt. A guard chain may be inserted into the round link above the hand.

(The Countess of Crawford)

3. Enamel and gold vinaigrette pendent from a finger-ring

c. 1838. The vinaigrette is in the form of a box in dark-blue enamel orna-mented with white flowers, green leaves and small grains of gold, tied up with a bow of rose-coloured ribbon. The gold ring has bezel and shanks enamelled in floral patterns. The connecting gold chain has long links in a flat spiral pattern, in dark-blue enamel decorated with flowers and leaves. Between the long links are pale-blue enamel flowers.

(The Countess of Crawford)

4. Brooch in silver and paste

in the shape of a gauntleted hand. *c.* 1842. The cuff is trimmed with chased ornaments and raised border. The back of the glove is covered in pavé-set paste. A small safety chain and pin are seen at the bottom.

(Mrs James Walker)

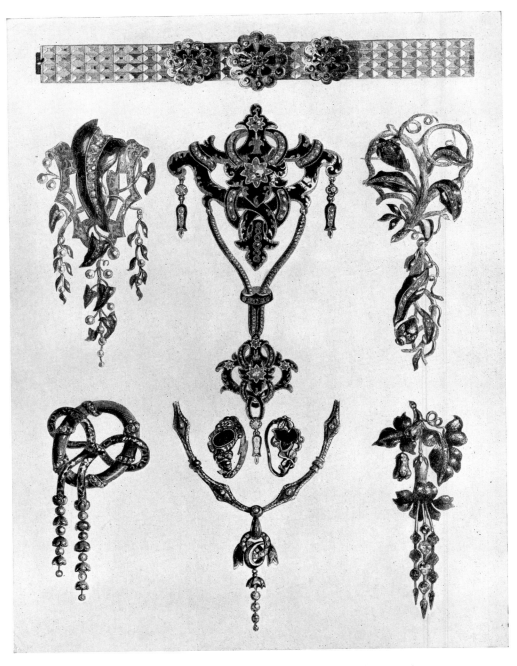

Fig. 24. Jewels shown by Watherston and Brogden at
the 1851 Exhibition

The design of the bracelet was suggested by jewellery discovered
at Nineveh. From the *Art Journal*, 1851.

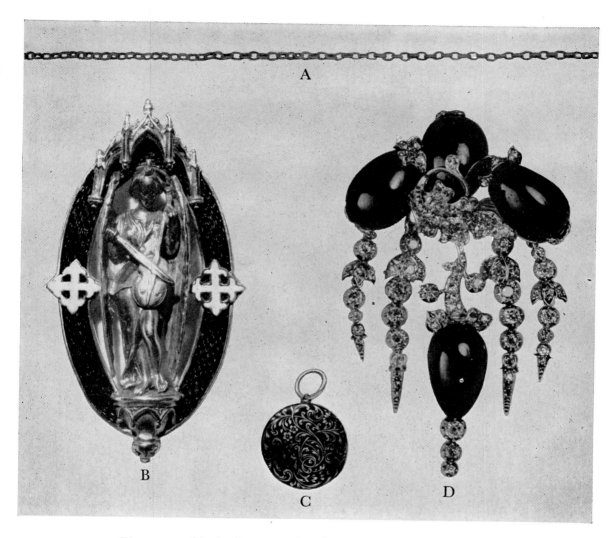

Fig. 25a.   Chain in natural coloured horsehair. *c.* 1845
(Mrs James Walker)

Fig. 25b.   Brooch in enamelled silver
showing an angel playing a violin.
Made by Froment Meurice. *c.* 1850
(Victoria and Albert Museum)

Fig. 25c.   Locket in black enamel and gold
Actual size, both sides the same. Inscribed 'Bolton King obt.
Nov 7th 1840, at 12 Years'.
(Miss Hilford)

Fig. 25d.   Corsage ornament in carbuncles and diamonds. *c.* 1850
(Miss M. J. Biggs)

Fig. 26a. Florence Nightingale, by Sir George Scharf
Pencil drawing of 28 December, 1857
(*National Portrait Gallery*)

Fig. 26b. Brooch in natural coloured horsehair
composed of three nosegays and ten separate flowers with three
long drops. *c.* 1845.

(*Mrs James Walker*)

Fig. 26c. Brooch in dyed red horsehair
built up of motifs of flat discs. Three trefoil pendants. *c.* 1845.

(*Mr Michael Dowling*)

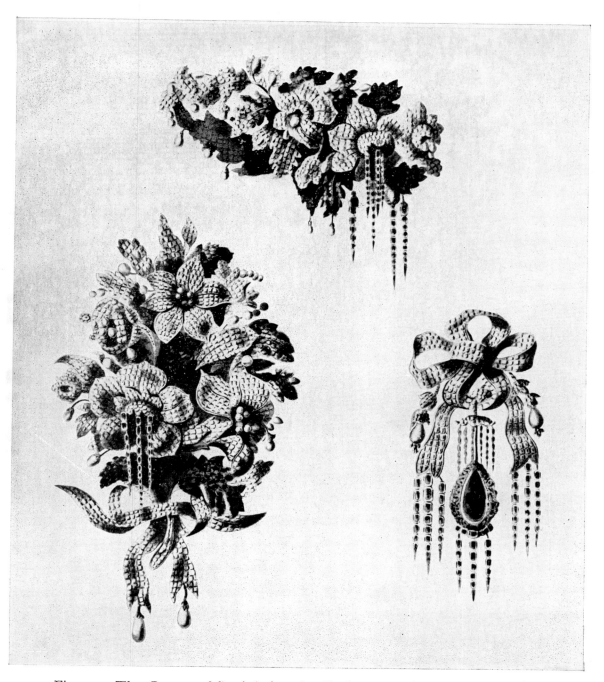

Fig. 27. The Queen of Spain's jewels, displayed at the 1851 Exhibition
Head-dress and shoulder-knot in diamonds, pearls, rubies and emeralds.
Bouquet in diamonds, pearls and rubies. Made by Lemonnière.
From Tallis's *History and Description of the Crystal Palace.*

(*Mrs James Walker*)

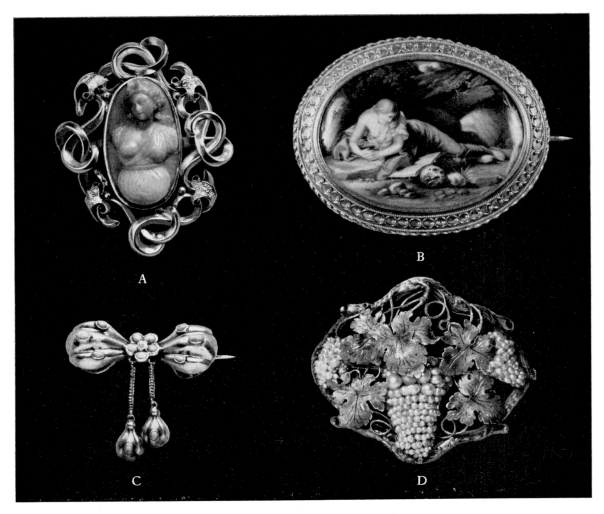

Fig. 28a. Brooch of coral

carved *en cameo* in gold strapwork frame. *c.* 1840.

(*Mrs. Pindar*)

Fig. 28b. Miniature painting on ivory

mounted as a brooch in a gold frame decorated with twists and grains. *c.* 1858.

(*Miss Joan Maude*)

Fig. 28c. Brooch in gold, set with small turquoises. *c.* 1840

(*Miss Hilford*)

Fig. 28d. Brooch of gold and seed pearls

The gold is worked into the form of a vine, with tendrils and finely-chased leaves. The seed pearls represent bunches of grapes. *c.* 1840.

(*Miss Joyce Abbott*)

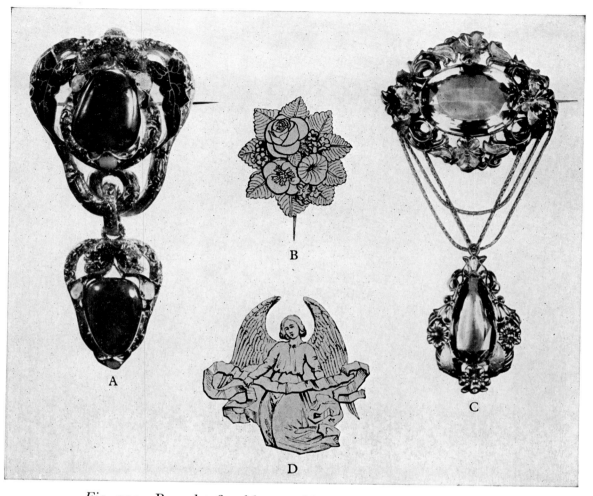

Fig. 29a. Brooch of gold, set with two large carbuncles and
five small opals, ornamented with dark-green enamel
c. 1846

(Messrs. H. J. Tuson & Sons Ltd)

Fig. 29b. Engraving of a brooch in Parian, by Messrs Minton
From the *Journal of Design*, vol. III, 1850.

(Mrs James Walker)

Fig. 29c. Brooch with pendant hanging from a looped gold chain
each part being composed of a Brazilian topaz set in a border of
gold flowers and leaves. Size slightly reduced. *c.* 1840.

(Mrs B. H. Liddell Hart)

Fig. 29d. Engraving of a brooch in silver by Rudolphi
From the *Journal of Design*, vol. I, 1849.

(Mrs James Walker)

Fig. 30a. Brooches by West of Dublin, shown at the 1851 Exhibition
The three smallest are inspired by ancient Irish jewellery. The
large upper one, a new design, was presented by the people of
Dublin to the actress, Helen Faucit.

Fig. 30b. Brooches by Phillips Brothers, shown at the 1851 Exhibition
1. Diamonds set in gold and green enamel.
2. A cameo surrounded with diamonds on blue enamel, with a diamond
   eagle at the top.
3. A knot of riband in diamonds.

Fig. 31a. Brooch in the shape of a garter, in silver and
Scotch pebbles. *c.* 1850

(*The Author*)

Fig. 31b. Brooch in hair and gold. *c.* 1845

(*Mrs James Walker*)

Fig. 31c. Mourning brooch

with curls of hair, seed pearls and gold thread, set in frame of
black enamel and gold. Dated 1850.

Fig. 31d. Brooch in gold, ivory and hair

Flowers in hair on front and romantic scene in hair on the back. *c.* 1856.

(*Both from H. Steiner*)

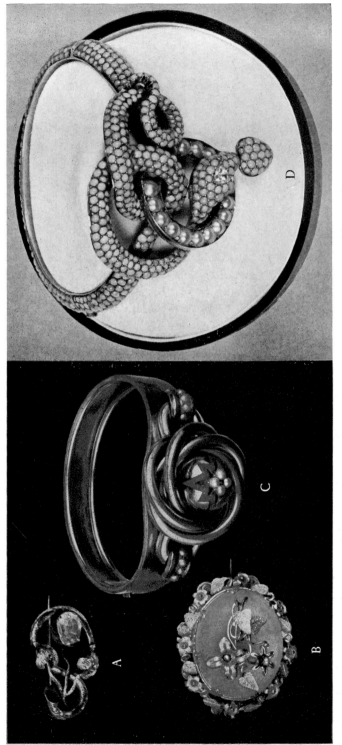

Fig. 32a. Brooch of an aquamarine and chased gold. *c.* 1850   (*The Author*)

Fig. 32b. Coloured gold wire ornamentation on white
cornelian brooch. *c.* 1855   (*Mrs Edward L. Barnes*)

Fig. 32c. Gold bangle with light-blue enamel and pearls. *c.* 1855
(*Miss Hilford*)

Fig. 32d. Serpent bracelet of gold, turquoise, pearls and diamonds

The serpent, composed of pavé-set turquoises with a large diamond in his head and tiny
diamond eyes, is coiled round and through a circle set with pearls, and holds in his mouth a
heart-shaped turquoise locket. *c.* 1840.

(*Messrs Harvey and Gore*)

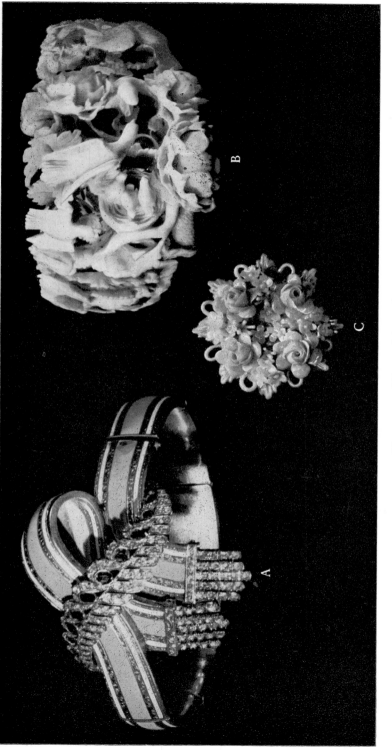

Fig. 33a. Hinged bangle

in the form of a twisted ribbon, with fringed ends, of gold, pale-blue enamel, white enamel, and small diamonds and garnets. *c.* 1855.

(London Museum)

Fig. 33b. Bracelet of carved and polished ivory

showing a dove defending its young against a serpent. *c.* 1855.

(The Countess of Huntingdon)

Fig. 33c. Brooch of Belleek porcelain

a nosegay of roses and forget-me-nots. *c.* 1848.

(Mrs James Walker)

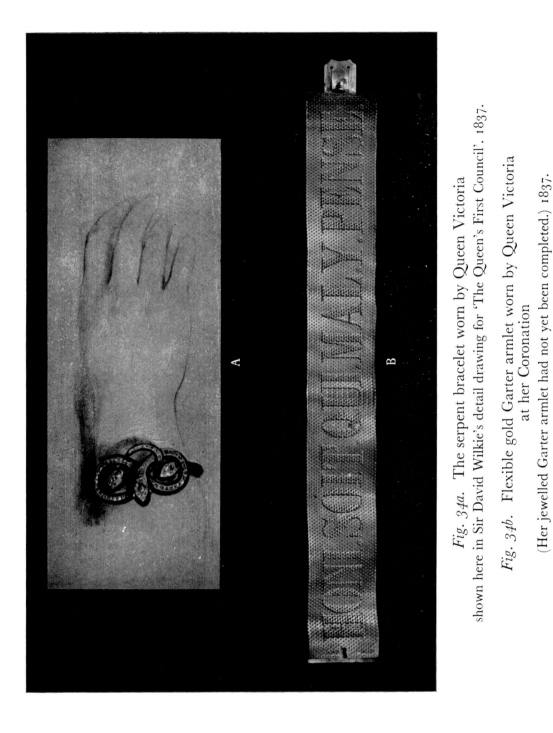

A

B

Fig. 34a.   The serpent bracelet worn by Queen Victoria
shown here in Sir David Wilkie's detail drawing for 'The Queen's First Council'. 1837.

Fig. 34b.   Flexible gold Garter armlet worn by Queen Victoria
at her Coronation

(Her jewelled Garter armlet had not yet been completed.) 1837.

(*Both by gracious permission of H.M. THE QUEEN*)

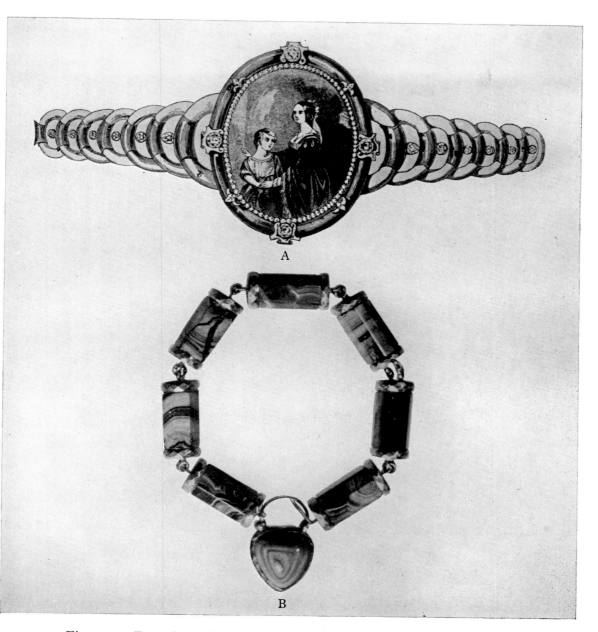

A

B

Fig. 35a.   Bracelet exhibited by Messrs S. H. & D. Gass of London
'Set with diamonds and carbuncles, with portraits of the Queen and the
Prince of Wales, after Thorburn A.R.A., and executed in niello, engraved
by J. J. Crew.' From the *Art Journal*, 1851.

Fig. 35b.   Bracelet of malachite and silver
Formerly belonged to Lady Nias. *c.* 1850.

(*London Museum*)

Fig. 36a. Bracelet of chased gold fancy links with a
clasp formed of an engraved gold heart
One side of the heart has a garnet set in it, the other a glass box
for hair. *c.* 1842.

(*Mrs Eric Ambler*)

Fig. 36b. Manchette bracelet
of narrow gold bands, set with small diamonds, emeralds,
rubies and sapphires. *c.* 1858.

(*Cameo Corner*)

Fig. 36c. Bracelet of facetted beads in light-red coral
The clasp is of gold with a coral medallion carved *en cameo. c.* 1843.

(*Mrs Pindar*)

Fig. 37. A pair of bracelets in pinchbeck and enamel

The pinchbeck is of two colours which resemble green and yellow gold. The *champlevé* enamel is light-blue, dark-blue, red, yellow, pale-green, pink, black and white. *c.* 1838. (*Mrs Eric Ambler*)

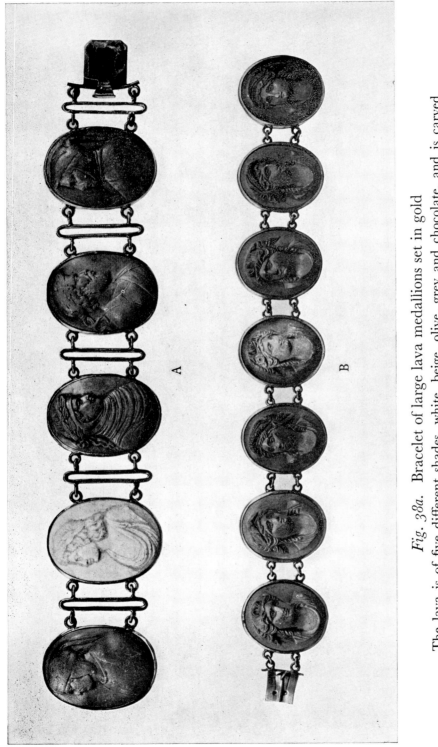

Fig. 38a. Bracelet of large lava medallions set in gold

The lava is of five different shades, white, beige, olive, grey and chocolate, and is carved *en cameo* with medieval and classical heads. *c.* 1850.

Fig. 38b. Bracelet of small lava medallions set in silver

The lava is cream, grey and terra cotta in colour, and carved *en cameo* with classical heads of females. *c.* 1850.

(*Both from Cameo Corner*)

Fig. 39a.   Bracelet of flexible gold with a centre of rubies and diamonds. *c.* 1850

(*Mr Collins*)

Fig. 39b.   Bracelet of carved tortoiseshell
mounted with gold and enamelled leaves. By Phillip of Paris. From the *Journal of Design,*
vol. III, 1850.

(*Mrs James Walker*)

Fig. 39c.   Bracelet of enamel miniatures set in engraved pinchbeck. *c.* 1845

(*London Museum*)

Fig. 40a. Bracelet of the early medieval style, by Froment Meurice
'In a rich gothic framework are three compartments, containing, we presume, representations of scenes in the life of St Louis; the centre, or chief one, seems to represent his death.' *c.* 1842.
From the *Art Journal of the 1851 Exhibition*.

Fig. 40b. Bracelet of diamonds and amethysts set in green enamel with golden links
Shown by Phillips Brothers at the 1851 Exhibition

Fig. 40c. Bracelet of blue and white enamel, on which musical notes are represented
Shown by Phillips Brothers at the 1851 Exhibition

Fig. 40d. Bracelet in silver with burnished gold bosses, by Phillips
Shown at the Dublin Art Exhibition of 1853

Fig. 41a. Bracelet in emeralds, diamonds and gold

Inscribed on the back as follows: 'Lascelles Cup
by subscription of gentlemen hunting with the Harewood races November 5th, 1845 Earl of
Harewood's hounds. Won by Colonel Thompson's B. H. Hamlet, ridden by the owner. In
celebration of the coming of age and marriage of Viscount Lascelles.'   (*Messrs S. J. Phillips*)

Fig. 41b. Bracelet of gold and enamel

Inscribed on back of clasp, 'May 20 1859 from #.' In the centre of each quatrefoil is a small
carbuncle; pearls or turquoises form the ornaments at the points of the compass.

(*Mrs Barbara Neill*)

[115]

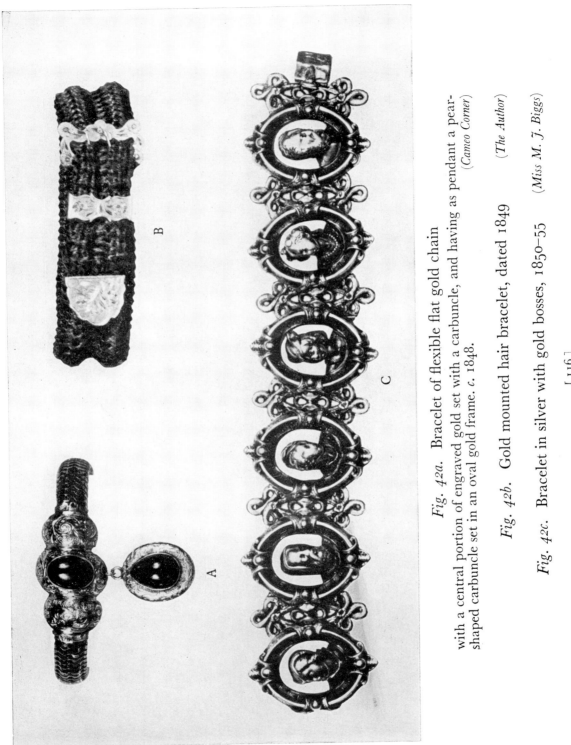

Fig. 42a. Bracelet of flexible flat gold chain

with a central portion of engraved gold set with a carbuncle, and having as pendant a pear-shaped carbuncle set in an oval gold frame. *c.* 1848.

(Cameo Corner)

Fig. 42b. Gold mounted hair bracelet, dated 1849   *(The Author)*

Fig. 42c. Bracelet in silver with gold bosses, 1850–55   *(Miss M. J. Biggs)*

Fig. 43a. Bracelet of flexible gold chain
having six gold pendent balls. *c.* 1850.　(*Cameo Corner*)

Fig. 43b. Bracelet clasp in amethyst and pinchbeck
(now made into a brooch). *c.* 1838. (*Mrs Evelyn Verschoyle*)

Fig. 43c. Bracelet of three twisted ropes of light-brown hair
with gold-engraved clasp and safety chain. *c.* 1840.　(*The Author*)

Fig. 43d. Bracelet clasp in Parian, by Mrs Brougham
From the *Journal of Design*, vol. IV. *c.* 1850.

(*Mrs James Walker*)

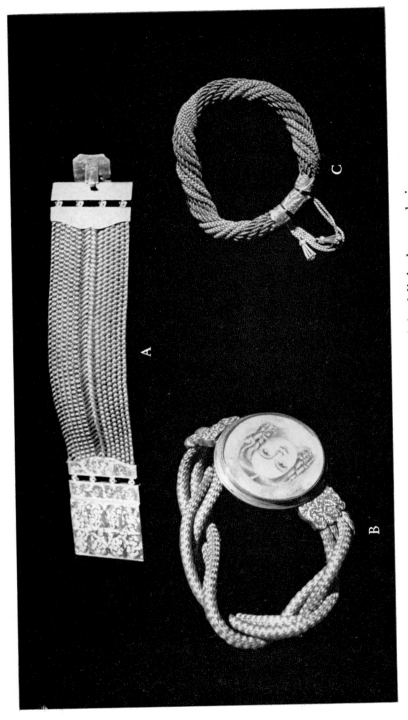

Fig. 44a.   Wide bracelet of plaited light-brown hair
Engraved gold clasp which opens to disclose a miniature painting of the head of a little girl.
c. 1845.

Fig. 44b.   Bracelet of four ropes of pale-brown hair
Large miniature of child's head set in clasp. A lock of hair enclosed in the compartment at the back of the clasp. *c.* 1840.

Fig. 44c.   Bracelet of twisted chains of hair in two colours, light and dark brown
Engraved gold clasp. Safety chain in gold with two pendent tassels. *c.* 1845.

(All from H. Steiner)

[118]

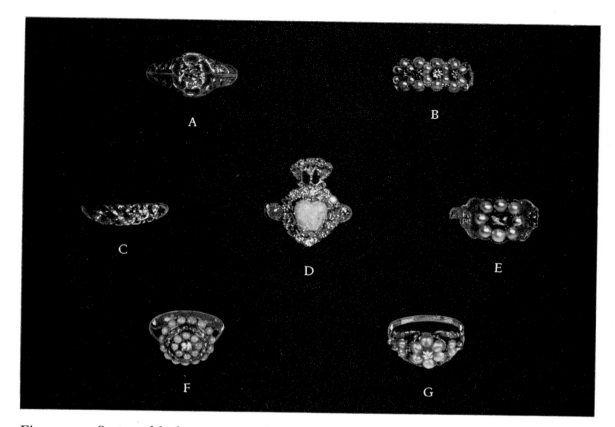

Fig. 45a. 18-ct. gold ring, engraved shoulders set with an old Brazilian diamond.
c. 1845–50

Fig. 45b. Ring composed of four clusters of pearls with
diamond centres, engraved and pierced shoulders. *c.* 1840

Fig. 45c. 18-ct. five-stone diamond half-hoop ring, carved gallery setting. 1855–65

Fig. 45d. Diamond cluster heart surmounted by a coronet, with opal heart centre
Two diamonds on carved shoulders. Silver mounting, gold shank. *c.* 1890.

Fig. 45e. Gold ring with pearl cluster surrounding hair box
Gold shank with carved and pierced decoration. Dated 1831.
(*All from Mr Fred Hurst*)

Fig. 45f. Ring of concentric circles of diamonds and
turquoises with gold open shoulders. *c.* 1855

Fig. 45g. Ring of a pearl flower with diamond centre,
and small garnets at the side, set in engraved gold. *c.* 1840
(*Both belonging to Mrs James Walker*)

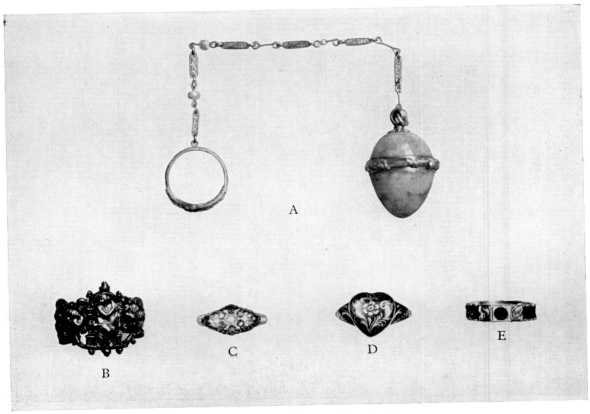

Fig. 46a. Queen Victoria's vinaigrette

which she carried clasped in her left hand in case she might feel faint. The vinaigrette was brought to the Queen as a present from France in 1843. It is attached by a chain to a gold, pearl and light-blue enamel finger-ring.

(By gracious permission of H.M. THE QUEEN)

Fig. 46b. Ring in chiselled steel and gold

Made by Froment Meurice. *c.* 1850.

(Victoria and Albert Museum)

Fig. 46c. Ring for a young girl of small rubies and diamonds set in gold. 1856

(Mrs Rita Smith)

Fig. 46d. Ring of black enamel and gold

with a heart-shaped bezel and a box at the back for hair. *c.* 1840.

Fig. 46e. Mourning ring in gold, jet and hair. *c.* 1840

(Both belonging to the Author)

VI
MID-VICTORIAN
JEWELLERY
1860-1885

PLATE VI

Pendant and chain by Carlo Giuliano

A large central straw-coloured topaz, surrounded by diamonds,
each set in a petal of gold, is placed upon an enamel background
of scrolls and leaves, embellished with six pearls. There are
three pendants, each of a small diamond and large cairngorm.
The chain is of pearls, enamel and gold. The enamel is of white,
dark red, green, black and vermilion. c. 1870.

(Mrs Gilbert Debenham)

1. Parures

[1860]

Gold, set with onyx and diamonds.

Gold, set with emeralds and diamonds, by West of Dublin (*Fig.* 52).

Gold and pearls, by Castellani (*Fig.* 60b).

Gold butterflies suspended from twisted gold chains.

Pendent gold oyster-shells, each disclosing a pearl.

In 1866. 'A dress of pale pink satin with white tulle draperies fastened in front and on the shoulders with artistic cameos. A band of pink satin ribbon, with a cameo for a clasp. The necklace, bracelets, and ornaments for the hair were in the same style.'

'Pink coral necklace, earrings and bracelets, and strings of pink coral beads in the hair. Worn by a young lady in a white ball dress.'

In 1867, a set of earrings, necklace and bandelettes for the hair, 'each earring composed of two ovals of cut crystal, encircled with gold, and fastened together with tiny gold chains; a beautiful insect of emerald green and gold is placed in the centre of each oval. The necklace is formed of a supple gold cord, to which are suspended seven ovals of cut crystal with emerald and gold insects. Similar ovals are placed upon the bandelettes of gold cord to wear in the hair.'

A suite of cinquecento design in enamel, gold and precious stones: £26–36 from Mr. Green, of the Strand.

At the Paris Exposition: Messrs Hancock's suites—one of rubies, bought by the Earl of Dudley, one of opals and diamonds, and one of emeralds and brilliants.

[1868]

Amethysts or carbuncles inlaid with jewelled motifs.

Tiger claws set in gold (*Fig.* 53).

Turquoises pavé-set.

Turquoises laid on white enamel.

In 1869, 'a very coquettish suite, of dogs' heads cut in coloured coral and set in polished jet.' This was considered particularly suitable for wear in a country house.

Chiselled gold set with jet, in imitation of ancient Norman jewels which had been set with black diamonds.

Louis XVI enamelled sets with small stones of all colours.

Byzantine jewellery in old silver.

White filigree silver.

Gold filigree (*Fig.* 56).

[1870]

Cameos set in gold.

Pink coral, with diamonds and emeralds.

Chased or raised gold, with fringes or without.

In 1872, Messrs Hancock's gold 'sporting' suite (*see P. 34, above*).

In 1875, Mr Godwin's Etruscan set, with amphorae and balls, and his Egyptian set, with sphinxes, rams' heads and lotuses, both copied from originals in the Louvre.

[1875]   Sapphires and rubies in modified lotus-flower pattern (*Fig.* 54).

Diamonds alone, or diamonds and pearls, in such patterns as the swan and harp (*Fig.* 57).

Golden bees (*Fig.* 58).

DEMI-PARURES

BROOCH and EARRINGS or LOCKET and EARRINGS

[1860]   Turquoise, diamonds and gold (*Fig.* 60a).

Coral set in gold circles.

Ivory flowers on a jet ground.

Mosaic pictures set in jet.

Jet cameos.

[1867]   Small diamond motifs on gems set in gold (*Fig.* 59a).

The 'Patti' jets: polished jet balls popularized by Adelina Patti.

Jet clusters, as worn by Adelina Patti (*Fig.* 55a).

In 1868, Assyrian patterns in gold.

Coloured gold set with pearls or other stones often in Etruscan patterns (*Figs.* 59b *and* c).

Silver buttercups, rosebuds or daisies, at 5s. the set.

Scissors, keys, fans, etc., in silver, steel, gilt, or enamel, at 1s. 6d. the piece.

[1878]   Valentine sets, expressing nationality, as follows:

Ireland—bog-oak,

Scotland—cairngorms in silver,

England—roses in various metals.

In 1880, birds, flowers or insects in chased metal.

[1881–1885]   Ivory elephants' heads.

Ivory and jet railway engines.

Gold heraldic lions.

Silver circular shields with round bosses (*Fig.* 55b).

2. Head Ornaments

(A) COMBS

Most popular head ornaments of the period, worn either on the forehead as diadems, or above the chignon. Combs of the sixties usually have tortoiseshell teeth and a hinge. The direction of the hinge indicates where the comb was worn on the head.

Peigne Joséphine  with gold or pearl or tortoiseshell balls. [1860–1880]

A variation with two rows of balls.

1862. Tortoiseshell studded with steel.

1867. The 'Empire' coiffure, with a gold and pearl diadem comb (*Englishwoman's Domestic Magazine*, January 1867)

Combs with gilt headings. [1860–1872]

    Set with gems (*Fig.* 70a).

    Ornamented with enamel patterns, usually Greek.

    Set with cameos.

    Bearing a buckle motif.

    Worked into an open pattern.

Metal combs unfashionable. Replaced by tortoiseshell of which the 'blonde' variety was the most admired. [1868]

    Tortoiseshell combs (*Fig.* 62).

    With a twist or plait heading.

      In the shape of a ducal or baronet's coronet.

      With a row of round or square beads.

Bandeau combs worn just over the fringe, stretching all the way across the forehead. (*Fig.* 63a). [1870]

    Pearl, coral, gold or jet for evening.

    Tortoiseshell for day.

Vogue for high Spanish combs in tortoiseshell, worn over a high chignon with a mantilla. [1872–1875]

(B) BANDELETTES, WORN TWINED IN THE HAIR OR ENCIRCLING IT

1867. Velvet ribbon trimmed with jet ornaments at regular distances. Finished with lappets fringed with jet. Necklace to match. Called the 'Dubarry coiffure'.

1867. Gold braid, trimmed with diamond-shaped pieces of velvet, which were edged with pearls. With matching necklace. Called the 'Psyche coiffure'. Suitable for young ladies.

Black velvet with amber grelots.

Gold braid with balls of coral.

(C) STRINGS OF BEADS ENTWINED IN THE HAIR

Pearls most popular.

Gold beads, in 1861 worn coming to a point on the forehead.

Gold chains.

(D) DIADEMS

1860s. *A la Grècque.* Style probably set by Empress Eugénie. See her portrait by Winterhalter, 1862.

1866. In gold and pearls, *à la* Mary Stuart.

1867. Castellani's diadem of 'decussated and reticulated gold' at the Paris Exhibition.

1870s. Tiaras with small spikes began to be worn.

(E) PINS. WORN IN THE CHIGNON

[1860–1870] Flat pieces of gold, decorated with pendent chains or beads (*see Fig.* 47).

With large round heads of:

Gold, jet, filigree, piqué.

With heads of fancy patterns, as in brooches, e.g.

Guitars, boats, helmets, suns, moons, stars,

Butterflies, humming-birds, peacocks,

Gold bulrushes, flowers.

1861. 'Mme. de Walewski wore gold wheat-ears in her hair.'

[1865–1880] Stars, in diamonds, jet or steel (*Fig.* 63b).

Filigree flowers (*Fig.* 17, *Nos.* 4 *and* 5), or butterflies.

Gilt cornflowers.

*c.*1875. Gilt arrows and daggers have a short revival.

(F) ARTIFICIAL FLOWERS

Used purely for ornaments or to hide the tops of plain combs (*Figs.* 48 *and* 49).

1867. Norma bandeaux: 'Bronzed and emerald-green foliage, enriched in front with a bunch of golden acorns, and at the back with trailing sprays of leaves, and here and there a golden acorn.'

Water-flowers and foliage fastened by a chain of coral.

Flowers sprinkled with crystal dewdrops.

Anemones with trembling diamond stamens on silver stems.

(G) PLUME-HOLDERS

In 1861. Pearl cluster on forehead.

Round gold brooches.

Flower-shapes.

In 1870. Aigrettes of cut jet were fashionable.

3. Earrings

Earrings were worn consistently throughout this period, by day and during the evening. The sizes of earrings fluctuated as follows:

They were generally small before 1865. From 1865 to 1870 they grew longer and longer, until, when they began to tangle with bonnet-strings, bonnets had to be made without strings.[1] Evening earrings about 1868–70 were so long that sometimes they rested on the shoulders. About 1876, small earrings reappeared, and by the eighties they had almost entirely replaced the large ones.

(A) SMALL EARRINGS, 1½ INCHES LONG OR LESS

[1860–1870]　Gold by day, and precious stones or pearls by night, were the most usual material. Small pearl drops were the most common evening earrings of the sixties.

Ball drops—one or two balls. In gold, pearl, piqué, jet, glass (*Fig. 68*).

Pear- or tear-shaped drops in the same materials.

Two or three short strings of beads, as drops.

Small pieces of natural or carved coral.

Hoops of gold or beads, either round or oval in shape (*Fig. 68*).

Gold hoops with gold or coral balls suspended in the centre (*Figs. 67 and 68*).

Spheres with pendent gold fringe or gold tassels (*Fig. 64c*).

Crescents with fringe.

Fringe alone, hanging from a bar (*Fig. 64b*).

Gold tassels.

Amphorae (*Figs. 64e, 66 and 67*).

Crosses, Latin or Maltese. Made of beads, gold, pearl, piqué, or black glass (*Fig. 66*).

Discs of mosaic, or gold circles with central boss.
Fig. 65b, shows some of these made with granulations in the Etruscan manner.

[c.1867]　Tiger claws, set in gold (*Fig. 53*).

Cabochon stones, such as carbuncles or amethysts, having small motifs—diamond or pearl stars or flowers—set in the stone (*Fig. 59a and 64f*).

[c.1868]　Ivory flowers on a jet ground.

Mosaics or cameos on a jet ground (*Fig. 61*).

Gold star set on a jet ground.

---

[1] Benoîton chains (p.33) were introduced to replace bonnet-strings.

Fancy shapes.
Beetles.
Bells (*Fig.* 64d).
Birds (*Fig.* 64h).
Bridles.
Butterflies (*Fig.* 66)
Croquet mallets

Fish.
Flies.
Flowers.
Horseshoes,
(to be worn with riding dress).

Ladders.
Saddles.
Tyrolese hats.
Sabots.

Crosses,
Hearts,
Stars,
} with or without fringe.

{ Gold filigree (*Fig.* 56).   [1870–1880]
Gold.
Pearls.

Facetted jet balls (*Fig.* 61).

Ball drops of gold or onyx.

Etruscan hoops, with gold grain ornaments (*Fig.* 67).

Sphinxes.

Rams' heads.

Lotus flowers.

1875. From the *Watchmaker, Jeweller & Silversmith* for July 5:
'Parisian ladies are wearing earrings, representing monkeys, guinea-pigs, lizards, chandeliers with candles in them, birdcages with birds within, tortoises, spades, spurs, officers' epaulettes, etc.'

1876.   In England, ladies are wearing:
Monkeys, acorns, saucepans, birdcages, candelabra, cockroaches, tortoises, tongs, and shovels.

1878. Bells, in honour of the successful play *Les Cloches de Corneville*.
Ivy leaves.
Silver dove holding a crystal drop.
Gridirons.
Pierced hearts.
Grapes.
Butterflies.
Cockleshells.
Sea shells.

Monograms.
Buttercups.
Turkish earrings in gold or silver.
Gold sailor-hat and oar.
Scissors.
Keys.
Fans.

Disc shape preferred (*as in Fig.* 51), often with Etruscan ornamentation.   [1880]

Discs set with pearls or diamonds (*Fig.* 59c).

Tiny gold earrings:
daisy, clover leaf, pine-cone, bees.

Coins.

Ball drops of onyx, pearls, or other stones.

Balls of gold, which clasp round solitaire diamonds during the day.

(B) LARGE EARRINGS, OVER 1½ INCHES IN LENGTH
(*See Figs.* 47–50).

1. Drops.

[1860–1870] Pear-shaped gems, hanging from a small diamond. Cf. Queen Alexandra's corbeille, Fig. 69.

Three balls, one under the other.

[1865] Triple drop earrings—a lengthened variation of the girandole (*Figs.* 60b, 65a *and* 66).

Beads strung together forming one, two or three drops.

Bunches of grapes in gold, pearl or gems.

Flowers hanging upside down, the stem attached to the ear.

Long golden flies.

In 1868. Two diamond stars, connected by a gold wire so thin as to be nearly invisible.

18-carat gold earrings advertised: long drops with delicate chain work round them; others of Italian, Grecian, Egyptian or Assyrian designs (*Fig.* 65c).

[1870–1876] Most characteristic earring is the gold, pear-shaped drop, decorated with stones and/or Etruscan patterns (*Fig.* 68).

Sphinxes.

Ivory anchors or crosses.

1872. Earrings described as 'Forms within other forms . . . Violence of contrast, and, in the majority, eccentricity rather than beauty, together with . . . angularity of finish . . . appear to have been the chief point aimed at' (Cf. *Fig.* 64g *and* 67).

[1870–1880] Large gold or bead or ivory hoops (*Fig.* 50).

Long Crosses.

Peapods in gold or tortoiseshell with pearls or gold balls for peas.

Large hearts.

Two small hearts suspended from a bead on the ear.

Drops showing Etruscan influence (*Fig.* 67).

1878. Pierced silver in classical, Moorish or Arabesque patterns.

2. Medallions.

From 1865. Large oval discs with *repoussé* or chased patterns with pendent beads or fringe.

In 1867. Vogue for Algerian earrings.

From 1865. Enamel medallions with jewelled motifs and gold fringe (*Fig.* 68).

4. Necklaces and Pendants

During this period necklaces almost invariably had something hanging from them, small motifs such as masks, amphorae and the like, from the Greek and Etruscan originals, festoons, large oval medallions, or a single rich pendant. For less wealthy people—a locket suspended on a velvet ribbon (*Fig.* 48).

(A) NECKLACES

Simple necklaces of a single or double row of pearls.

'Empire' necklaces, formed of loops of beads and pendent ornaments either of pearl, amber, garnet or cut jet.

Heavy gold chokers.

Thin gold chains.

'Most fashionable are heavy gold chains from which hang medallions enriched with diamonds and precious stones' (*Fig.* 48). These medallions might be:
Onyx with diamond stars,
Carbuncles or amethysts with diamond stars (Plate IV),
Blue enamel with a jewelled star (*Fig.* 70b), cross, flower or fly,
Flies or butterflies under, or on crystal (*Fig.* 72),
Plain gold enriched with classical patterns.

In 1868. Gold ivy-leaves hanging from a gold chain, life-size and modelled from leaves brought by the future wearer.

Pearl necklaces with vari-coloured jewels (*Figs.* 69 *and* 73).

Greek and Etruscan reproductions. Giuliano's beads covered with gold grains alternating with carved onyx beads or gold chain.

Brogden's cameo necklace (Plate V).

Gold necklaces with pendent urns, acorns, or masks.

Jewelled and enamelled necklaces with small drops (*Fig.* 50).
By Castellani (*Fig.* 74). By Giuliano (*Fig.* 75).
In carbuncles and diamonds (*Fig.* 71).

Long pearl strings, terminating in tassels (*Fig.* 51), or in pearl crosses (*Fig.* 49).

Jet necklaces with pendent stars, or amphorae, or cameos.

Polished jet necklaces (*Fig.* 61).

'Résilla' necklaces of a network of jet or amber beads (*Fig.* 61, *low right*).

Pearls alone replaced by diamonds alone in popularity.
Wide diamond necklaces in fine lace-like patterns.

Flat silver links (*Fig.* 76).

Wide silver chains, with chased links for day wear, usually with a silver locket (*Figs.* 55b *and* 77b).

[1860–1867]

[1867]

[1870]

[1879]

[1880]

(B) PENDANTS

[1860]   Richly jewelled pendants hung from strings of pearls.
    Many of these had attachments which enabled them to be worn as brooches, and further information will be found in the section on brooches (*Figs.* 78 *and* 79a).

Emeralds, rubies, or other precious stones surrounded by pearls, with a pearl drop (*Figs.* 69 *and* 82).

Jewelled and enamelled pendants with matching chains.
    (*See Giuliano's*, Plate VI *and Figs.* 77a *and* 78b).

Jewels showing Renaissance influence.
    (*See Giuliano, Castellani and Novissimo pendants*, (Plate VII, *Figs.* a, b *and* c).

Jewels of classical inspiration.

Cut jet (*Fig.* 84).

[1878]   Diamonds, or pearls and diamonds together, in more delicate patterns with smaller pendants, began to replace the rich jewels of the previous decade.

(C) CROSSES

Latin, Greek, Irish or Maltese, of:
    Gold and jewels (*Figs.* 79b *and* c),
    Precious stones, set clear, as amethysts, emeralds, rubies, diamonds,
    Opaque stones: pearl, turquoise, coral,
    Gold, silver, enamel, piqué, jet or glass (*Fig.* 84).

(D) LOCKETS

Most popular neckwear of the Seventies. [1]

Jewelled lockets.
    Onyx and pearl, from Queen Victoria to her grandchildren (*see Fig.* 80c).

[*c.*1868]   Standard shape, oval. Standard material, gold (*Fig.* 68).

Next most frequent material, jet, with carved ornaments in relief (*Fig.* 80a).

Ornamented with jewels, and enamel, or simply chased, with one of the following motifs:

Monograms,	Butterflies,	Names,[2]
Stars,	Cameos,	Lizards.
Crosses,	Hearts (*Fig.* 68),	
Garters (*Fig.* 80b),	Flowers (*Fig.* 68),	
Cable chain,	Urns,	
Cupids,	Torches,	

[1] 'A cross or locket is becoming quite *de rigueur* with bodices open *en châle*, and seems an indispensable finish to the toilet.' *Englishwoman's Domestic Magazine.* 1870.

[2] 'Lockets formed of different letters spelling the Christian name of the wearer. The letters are of gold, or of enamel inlaid with pearls and precious stones.' *Young Ladies' Journal.* 1870.

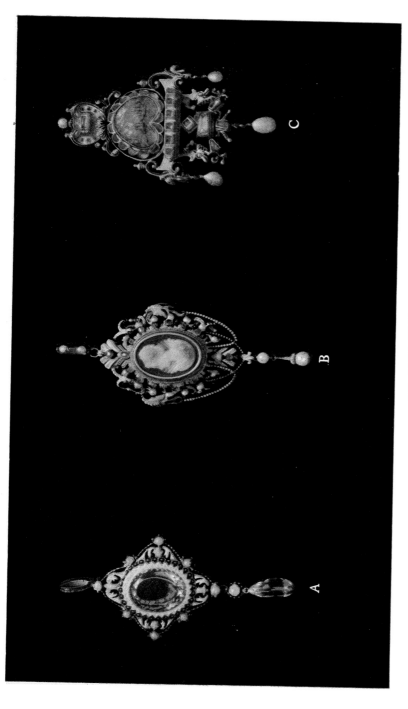

PLATE VII

Fig. a. Pendant

of enamelled gold, set and hung with amethysts and pearls. Made about 1880 by Pasquale Novissimo (*d.* 1914).

Fig. b. Pendant

of enamelled gold enriched with rubies, sapphires and pearls; enclosing an onyx cameo portrait of Maria de Medici, Queen of France (*d.* 1642). Signed G. Bissinger. Made by Carlo Giuliano. *c.* 1875.

Fig. c. Pendant

of enamelled gold, enriched with rubies, pearls, a diamond, and a sapphire intaglio of a battle-scene. Made by Castellani. *c.* 1868.

(All from Victoria and Albert Museum)

Classical figures or 'Watteau' patterns in Etruscan enamelled porcelain.

In 1869. Mr Green of the Strand, had lockets fitted with slides which could be moved at will; '*par exemple*, a plain gold locket with raised monogram is worn all day. At night the monogram slide is removed, and a slide on which a diamond star is set is inserted in its place. One day's locket is of pearls and coral, another turquoise and diamonds, or emeralds and opals. In mourning, too, a black enamelled monogram or cross can be introduced.'

Silver lockets with intricate chased patterns became more fashionable than the gold and jewelled ones worn before (*Figs.* 55b *and* 77b). [*c.*1878]

5. Brooches

These were usually interchangeable with pendants.
(For further information, see Pendants).

[1860] Flowers or birds in jewels (*see Princess of Wales's flower-spray Fig.* 85).

Jewelled medallions with pendants (*see Giuliano brooch Fig.* 81d).

Round gold brooches with centres of stones or enamel most generally worn. (*See illustration at right*).

This brooch has a brown and white onyx centre, mounted in gold, decorated with blue and white enamel and small twists and grains in the Etruscan style. (*From Miss Hilford*).

Moorish influence (*Fig.* 81a).

Etruscan influence (*Fig.* 59b).

Round shields with central boss of coral or pearl.

Round or oval gold frames with cameo centres (*Fig.* 83).

Round or oval gold frames with miniatures (*Fig.* 86a).

Gold of several colours inlaid with tiny pearls.

Piqué brooches (*Fig.* 66).

Celtic influence—Scottish brooches in topaz, pebbles and silver.

Anglo-Saxon designs on bonnet brooches.

In 1867. Brooches admired at the Paris Exhibition:

Diamond branch of lilac with trembling blossoms,

Butterfly with gold and turquoise body, and wings of diamonds and emeralds,

Humming-bird in diamonds and emeralds, made for Empress Eugénie,

Peacock feather in diamonds with its eye in emeralds and sapphires,

Fly with opal body, and wings and head set with rubies, brilliants, emeralds and sapphires.

[1867] Cabochon stones set with small diamond motif, and encircled in gold (*Fig.* 59a).

Egyptian brooches with sphinxes and Klaft-covered heads,

Etruscan brooches with diamond centres and small pointed pendants.

Blue enamel, set with a pearl star.

Cog-wheel, with a lapis lazuli centre.

Gold buckle with strap and band of turquoise.

For mourning: gold and black enamel, set with an onyx bearing a diamond star.

In 1868, Mr Green advertised these brooches:

Gold with three intersecting triangles raised on it,

Carbuncle, with a diamond star let into the stone,
A gold butterfly with a tube underneath, through which a flower is passed,
so that the butterfly appears to have settled on the flower.

Jet brooches set with: [1868]
Enamelled miniatures,
Mosaics,
Ivory flowers.

In 1868. Curiosities in gold, pearl and jewels
Barrel, Pipe,
Champagne bottle, Postage stamp,
Death's head, Tooth.
Lantern,

Brooches begin to be inscribed with mottoes.

In 1869. *Bijoux Normands* in reddish gold with black stones.

The triple locket brooch, round and 'surrounded by a cable twist, very finely executed; a raised centre holds two lockets concealed, and a third is placed at the back, as usual in brooches'.

In 1872. A contemporary critic's[1] view of brooches: 'Happily, the style of brooch which prevailed so largely a few years ago, with its twisted scrolls and Louis Quinze details, has given way to a more rational and severe form of article in which the use of the object as a species, at least, of *fibula*, is recognized, if not always intelligently followed out, and thus the decorations are subordinated to the general outline and contour'. However, he objects that some of the brooches have 'too much the appearance of the highly finished details of mechanical engineering; smooth and angular, with uncomfortable-looking points as details'.

Twisted borders round central jewel. [c.1873]

Cameos *habillés*.

Painted enamel miniatures in filigree frames.

Monograms (*Fig.* 81c), and mottoes.

Presentation brooch in onyx and pearls with diamond crown and 'V' (*Fig.* 86c). This is dated 1889 but belongs to mid-Victorian design.

Horseshoe brooches in pearls, diamonds and gold.

Hunting brooches, with saddle and stirrup.

Diamonds and pearls in light, open design. [c.1878]
(*Fig.* 81b *shows such a brooch, which is influenced by Indian jewellery*).

Silver becomes more fashionable than gold.

Novelties such as the 'Don't be cross' brooch—a silver cross, bearing the word DONT and a bee. (This sold for 3/6.)

Fans in gold and diamonds (*Fig.* 86b).

In 1880, Elaine de Marsay, writing in the *Queen*, says: 'Brooches were given this season in preference to lockets, and took curious forms; enamelled flowers, especially violets; a large gold walnut, studded with pearls; a spray of eglantine, with silver and gold foliage; a pea pod half opened disclosing

[1] *Art Journal Exhibition Catalogue*, p. 35.

pearls for peas; an enamelled fan; a delft plate with a gold spoon in it . . . Some represent a graceful spray of flowers, with the foliage of encrusted diamonds, or a ruby in the centre of a wild rose, or else rosebuds of pearls of different colours, such as the pink pearl, the yellow pearl, or the pear-shaped white pearl. A favourite design is a gold bar, with a diamond sunk in the centre. What is called the gipsy setting—where the diamond is embedded in the gold—is more fashionable than the knife-edge setting that merely caught the stones'.

[c.1882]   Brooches for day wear begin to be replaced by small pins.

6. Bracelets

Two or three were usually worn on each arm (*Figs.* 49 *and* 51).

(A) BANGLES

Hoops, or half-hoops of diamonds, or other precious stones (*Fig.* 91b).

Gold, set with gems and/or decorated with enamel (*Figs.* 82, 86d, 87d *and* 89b).

Wide bands of plain gold, bearing a central jewelled ornament (*Figs.* 83, 85 *and* 87a).
>   The centre might be a cameo, a Greek, Assyrian, Egyptian or Celtic design, or a single stone.

Gold bands studded all round with cabochon or facetted stones.

Wide bangles decorated with serpents (*Fig.* 87c).

Strap and buckle bracelets (*Fig.* 85).

Wide gold bangles engraved in scrollwork or other patterns (*Figs.* 87e, 88c *and* 90a).

Gold bangles with motifs:
>   From Greek art (*Figs.* 88a *and* b).
>   From Assyria (*Figs.* 87b *and* 91a).

Wide or narrow twists.

Gauntlet cuffs in gold, to be worn with riding costume.

'Life and death bracelet' advertised in 1868, with the lotus and scarab (emblems of life and death) placed on medallions going round it.

Plain gold bangles (*Fig.* 50). Most popular bracelet of the seventies. Eugène Fontenay traces the vogue of this bracelet to the circles of buffalo's horn, narrow, square-edged and as thick as they were wide, introduced by Algerian merchants as a '*porte-bonheur*'. The circles were soon copied in redgold. Everyone wore them. Contrary to the usual course of fashion, this one began at the bottom, and then, as a circle of diamonds, took the highest society by storm.

Silver bangles, as above.   [1870]
>   Indian motifs.
>   Scandinavian motifs.

Thinner bands of gold with ornamental medallions or horseshoes in diamonds.   [1880]

(B) LINK BRACELETS

Round or rectangular links, united to make a flexible bracelet (*Fig.* 90b).

Links decorated with gold and jewels, or gold alone or enamel alone (*Hancock's bracelet Fig.* 91c, *Castellani's Fig.* 92c, *Giuliano's Fig.* 90c, *Brogden's Fig.* 92b).

Scottish patterns in pebbles and enamel (*Fig.* 92a).

Medallions set with round stones.

Miniatures set with jewels (*Fig.* 85).

Curb chains in gold, sometimes with pendent charms.

(C) FLEXIBLE BRACELETS

Diamond bracelets, in small sections, joined by links (*Fig.* 89a).

Jewelled patterns set on flexible gold bands instead of stiff ones.

Diamonds set in wide flexible bands, in open patterns resembling lace or embroidery.

Ribbon of gold passing through a jewelled buckle or slide, the free end set with jewels. Called '*Bracelet Jarretière*'. (Early sixties.)

Ovals of polished jet, strung on elastic.

Hair bracelets with ornamental clasps (*Fig.* 92d).

Bead bracelets.

Pearls most popular. Two or three strings often twisted round the wrist (*Figs.* 49 *and* 51).

Coral, jet, ivory.

Wooden bead bracelets.

Serpent bracelets; larger and longer than before.

In 1878, 'Ladies who wear long gloves wear, in addition to the gloves, a bracelet of plain gold, twisted round and round the arm, in serpent fashion, up to the elbow. I have counted as many as nine of these serpent coils round an arm. The serpent's head is generally on the wrist.'

Serpent bracelets were made also in jet and ivory (*Fig.* 93a).

(D) BRACELET PENDANTS[1]

Chains, acorns and medallions hung from Moroccan and Algerian-inspired bracelets.

Chains of gold beads very common.

Hearts.

Drops of pearl or other jewels.

A final curiosity. Souvenir of the Paris Exhibition of 1878. 'Exhibition bracelet, a gold circlet, ornamented by a representation of the Trocadéro, in bas-relief, and pierced with innumerable holes, through which can be seen minute pictures of the gardens and the animals illustrating the four quarters of the globe.' The *Ladies' Treasury*.

---

[1] In 1877, Victor Hugo was so moved by Bernhardt's acting in *Hernani*, that he wept. In admiration he sent Bernhardt a gold chain bracelet from which hung a diamond tear.

7. Rings

Except for the finest rings set with large stones as in Fig. 93d, and enamelled or engraved by a master, rings were inexpensive during this period. Bright gold rings were about half the price of coloured gold. Those shown in *Fig.* 94, ranged at wholesale from No. 1 at 7/6 to No. 27 at £35.

(A) DECORATIVE RINGS

In 1869. Gold rings set with pearls and turquoise or pearls and coral.
    Diamonds with rubies or emeralds are set clear in gold.
    Opals and diamonds are much favoured for brides' guard rings.
Gold rings studded all round with gems.
Gold rings with stones set in clusters (*Nos.* 13, 25, *Fig.* 94).
Gold rings with stones set in half-hoops (*Nos.* 16, 27, 28, *Fig.* 94).
Gold rings with stones in star settings (*Nos.* 17, 18, *Fig.* 94).
Gold rings with stones in coronet settings (*No.* 27, *Fig.* 94).
Gold rings with stones in boat settings (*No.* 28, *Fig.* 94).
Gold rings with stones in claw settings (*Nos.* 22, 23, *Fig.* 94, *Fig.* 93c).
Gold rings with stones in carved gallery settings.
    Favourite stones: Diamond, ruby, sapphire, emerald, turquoise, garnet, opal, pearl, coral.
A new style, the Gipsy Ring, in which the stone is set deep in the metal, so   [*c.*1875] that the surface of the stone is flush with the surface of the metal (*see No.* 24, *Fig.* 94).
In 1880, a gipsy ring set with diamond, sapphire or ruby is thought very fashionable.
In 1875, the *Young Ladies' Journal* informs us:
    'Any pretty fancy ring may be worn as an engagement-ring. Pearls or diamonds are considered the proper gems. The engagement-ring is not considered after marriage to answer the purpose of a keeper. A keeper should be a chased gold ring without stones in it. It is worn on the same finger as the wedding-ring.' And 'opals, on account of their signification being "sorrow" are not fashionable for engagement rings'.

(B) PLAIN GOLD RINGS

Wedding rings.
Serpent rings (*Nos.* 19–21, *Fig.* 94).

(C) SIGNET RINGS

Plain gold or with cartouche or square or oval in such stones as bloodstone, onyx and cornelian (*Nos.* 9–12, *Fig.* 94).

(D) MEMORIAL RINGS

Gold rings with a braid of hair round them (*see Nos.* 1–8, *Fig.* 94).
The same with enamel and pearl decoration (*Nos.* 6–8, *Fig.* 94).

(E) HANDKERCHIEF RING

In 1870 this was fashionable. To the gold finger-ring, a larger ring was attached by a chain; and through the larger ring the handkerchief was passed (*Fig.* 93b).

8. Miscellaneous

(A) BELTS

Filigree silver ceintures encompassing the round waists. [1860–1870]
Velvet ribbon, more usual, with a large buckle at the front.
In 1866. The Emerald belt, of chains of gold, with green crystal beads.
   The Oriental, of pearls and gold.
   The Indian, of amber.
   The Peruvian, of garnet.
   The Naïad, of white crystal, in imitation of drops of magic water.
   The Joan of Arc, of cut jet; 'it is a wide strip formed of a tissue of beads, as strong and supple as a coat of mail'.
   The Egyptian girdle is of coloured enamel, with hieroglyphics in black and gold.
Belts of oxidized silver, sometimes with chatelaine-holders. [1870–1880]

(B) BUCKLES AND CLASPS

Ornamental buckles *en suite* with brooches or diadems, in gold and imitation [1860–1870]
   stones.
Large oval, hexagonal or oblong buckles (*as in Fig.* 47), in gilt, silver filigree;
   or in beads.
Agrafes made of clusters of pearls.
Buckles of jet beads. Clasps of carved and polished jet. [1870–1878]

(C) CHATELAINES

Worn rarely in the sixties; with moderate frequency from 1870–85.
Cloisonné enamel. [1860–1870]
Open-worked gold.
Oxidized silver, steel, or electro-plate, sometimes hanging from metal belts. [1870–1875]
   Contained: purse, memo book, scent-bottle, pins, thimble, pen-knife, etc.
Jet combined with steel. [1875–1885]
Silver with silver watch and silver-bound prayerbook.

(D) FAN-HOLDERS

1875. Height of popularity.

(E) FAN-CHAINS

1879. 'Great luxury is being displayed in the chains which are destined to
hold the fan at the side. Some are of pure gold and are composed of
several chains joined together by a clasp, forming a jewelled flower.
The newest chains of this description are so made that they can be
transformed into a necklet, bracelet, watch-chain or chatelaine.'
(The *Ladies' Treasury*.)

(F) BOUQUET-HOLDERS

Of crystal and jewels (*see Fig.* 85), gold and jewels, filigree silver or gold, and
gilt. Usually suspended from a small ring, so that the bouquet could dangle
while its wearer was dancing.

(G) PORTE-JUPE

Introduced in 1867 by the celebrated French jeweller, Rouvenat, this article
was described as follows:
'A gold clasp which is fastened to the waist-band, from which depends a
brooch or medallion, held on by three gold chains, and which serves to loop
up the dress by inserting the long pin of the brooch through very small gold
rings sewn on to the widths of the skirt. Thus the dress is elegantly draped
in front and at the sides but the train remains sweeping behind. Clasp and
brooch are frequently of gold and enamel, studded with very small pearls, in
the Byzantine style, or else of plain gold, set with jewels, or again of beautifully carved oxidized silver. But it is also made much plainer in jet, or steel,
to wear out walking in the streets. In that case, it is called a Macadam
porte-jupe.' (*Englishwoman's Domestic Magazine*.)

(H) LINKS

[*c.*1865]   Fanciful sleeve-links, such as:
Pearl buttons set in gold, with gold threads crossing the centre,
Playing cards in enamel,
Bees, flies, flowers,
Enamel masks.

(I) CHILDREN'S JEWELLERY

Necklets of coral beads.
Necklets of silver daisies.
Tiny crosses worn on ribbon.
Small earrings in silver or gold.
Bracelets of pearl, silver, coral, or wooden beads.
Brooches of filigree silver, in the form of insects or flowers.

Summary

(1860-85)

I. MATERIALS CHIEFLY USED

FOR PRIMARY JEWELLERY.

Amethyst.
Cameos (gem).
Carbuncles.
Coral.
Crystal.
Enamel.
Diamonds (rose and brilliant cut).
Emeralds.
Gold;
    Plain and coloured, (*see* P.30),
    Red gold—dark red in late sixties,
    Green gold,
    Orange gold,
    Yellow gold.
Malachite.
Onyx.
Opal.
Pearls.
Rubies.
Silver.
Tiger-claws, set in gold.
Turquoise.
Sapphires.

FOR SECONDARY JEWELLERY.

Amber.
Bog-oak.
Cairngorms.
Garnets.
Glass;
    black glass or French jet.
Gold;
    low carat,
    Imitation gold.
Ivory.
Jet;
    from Whitby,
    French jet and black glass.
Paste.
Pearls.
Pebbles.
Shells;
    natural or carved *en cameo*.
Silver;
    plain or oxidized,
    Imitation silver.
Steel;
    for buttons and chatelaines.
Tortoiseshell;
    dark and blonde,
    Plain or piqué.
Wood.

II. MOTIFS MOST TYPICAL OF THIS PERIOD

Acorns.
Amphorae.
Anchors.
Animals.

Bees.
Bells.
Birds.
Birdcages.

Buckles.
Butterflies.
Byzantine.
Celtic.
Crosses.
Daisies.
Dragonflies.
Etruscan.
Fans.
Flies.
Flowers.
Geometrical.
Greek, e.g. Walls of Troy.
Initials.

Insects.
Locomotives.
Lotus flowers.
Masks.
Monograms.
Mottoes.
Norman.
Roses.
Scandinavian.
Serpents.
Shells.
Sphinxes.
Stars.
Swans.

III. OTHER FEATURES CHARACTERISTIC OF THIS PERIOD

Cable twists.
Curb chains.
Enamel work of high quality.
Etruscan decoration, i.e. gold grains and fine gold wire.
Inlaying of small stones into larger ones.
Medallions with small motifs under crystal.

Network patterns, set with diamonds, resembling lace, or networks of beads.
Open settings for crosses and necklaces.
Pendent fringes.
Pendent medallions.
Round shield shape with central boss.

Fig. 47. Fashions for day wear. From the *World of Fashion,*
September, 1865

(*Mrs Doris Langley Moore*)

Fig. 48. Fashions for evening. From *Le Follet*, July, 1867

(*Mrs Doris Langley Moore*)

Fig. 49. From *La Mode Artistique*, 1870

(*Mrs Doris Langley Moore*)

Fig. 50. Fashions for day and evening wear.
From *Le Follet*, October, 1875

(Mrs Doris Langley Moore)

Fig. 51. Latest Paris Fashions. From the *Queen*,
February, 1883

(*Mrs Doris Langley Moore*)

Fig. 52. Parure in gold, emeralds and diamonds
by West of Dublin

comprising a gold flexible snake-chain with fringed pendant, a
bangle and a pair of earrings. *c.* 1865.   (*Cameo Corner*)

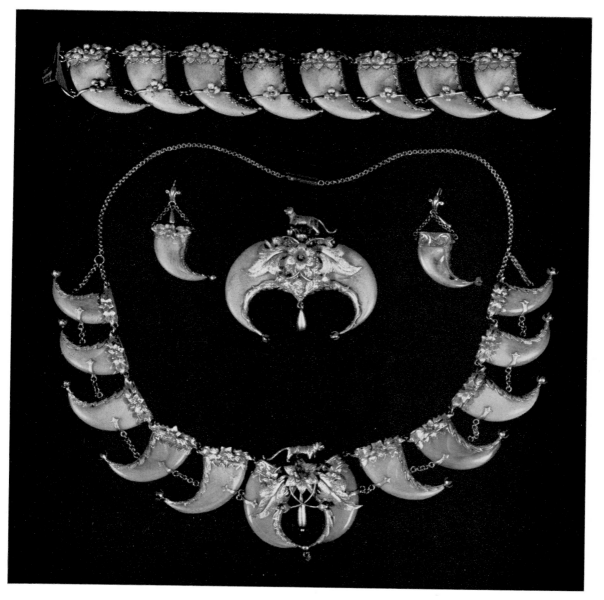

Fig. 53. Parure of tiger's claws set in gold floral and
leafage mounts. *c.* 1872
(By courtesy of Messrs Christie, Manson and Woods)

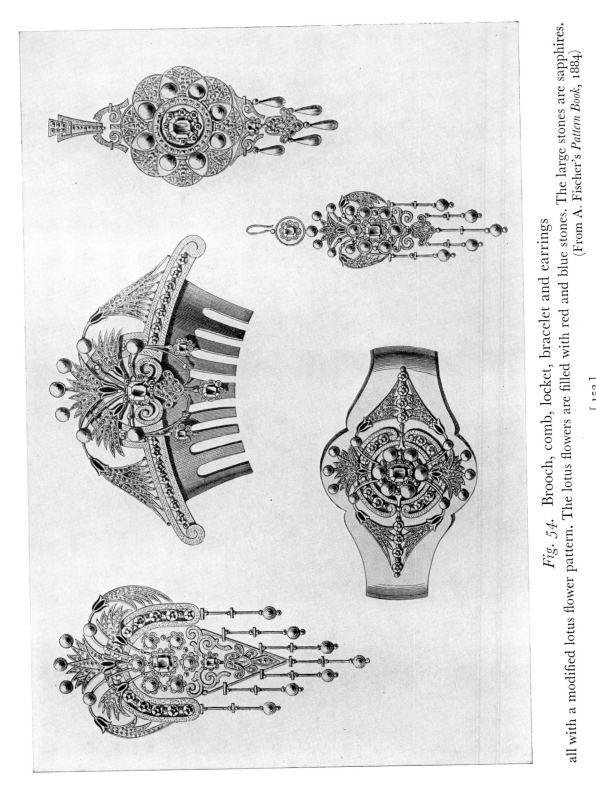

Fig. 54. Brooch, comb, locket, bracelet and earrings all with a modified lotus flower pattern. The lotus flowers are filled with red and blue stones. The large stones are sapphires. (From A. Fischer's *Pattern Book*, 1884)

A

Fig. 55a.   Adelina Patti wearing her jet jewellery. c. 1867

Fig. 55b.   Demi-parure. Locket and chain in silver. c. 1882

B

(From a photograph belonging to Mrs Doris Langley Moore)

[153]

Fig. 56. Gold filigree parure
the pattern made up of bows of ribbon and Maltese crosses. *c.* 1875.
(The Author)

Fig. 57. Silver parure with brilliants and white oriental pearls. *c.* 1878
(From A. Fischer's *Pattern Book*, 1884)

Fig. 58. A brooch, a pair of earrings and a pair of studs
in the shape of bees

in gold-coloured metal, in a box formed as a beehive. By
Harvey and Gore. *c.* 1880. *(The Author)*

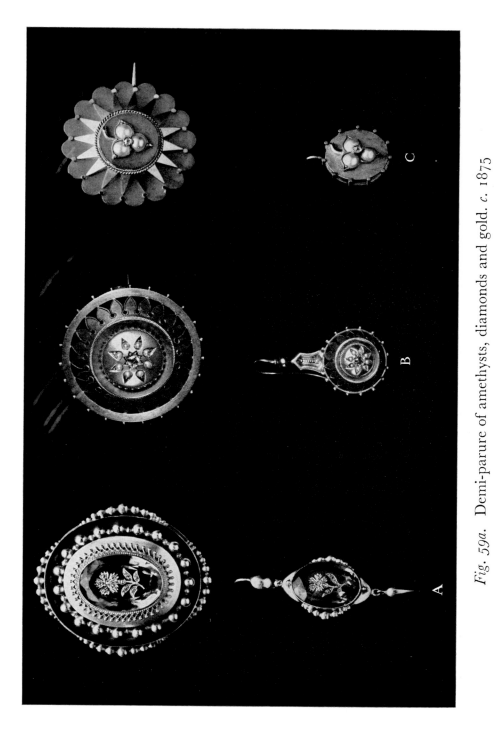

Fig. 59a. Demi-parure of amethysts, diamonds and gold. *c.* 1875
(*Mrs James Walker*)

Fig. 59b. Demi-parure of coloured gold, pearls and garnets. *c.* 1875
(*The Author*)

Fig. 59c. Demi-parure of coloured gold, pearls and diamonds. *c.* 1883
(*Mrs James Walker*)

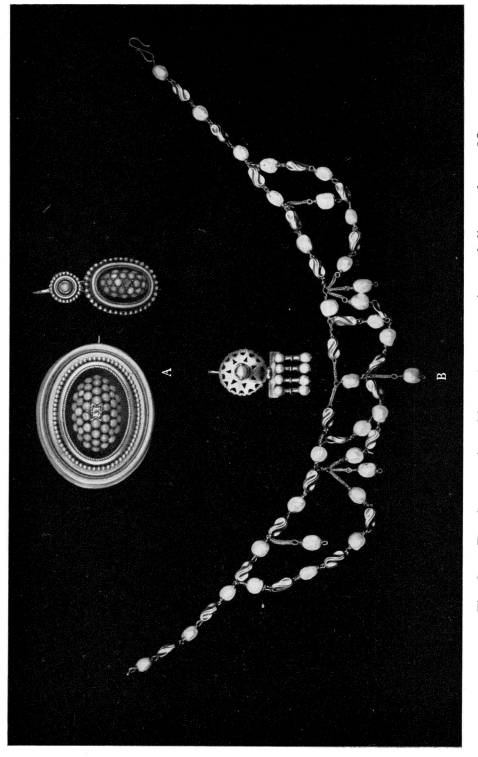

Fig. 60a. Demi-parure in gold, pavé-set turquoises and diamonds. *c.* 1860
(*Mrs James Walker*)

Fig. 60b. Necklace and earrings

(belonging to a parure of necklace, tiara and earrings). Gold, set with pearls. Made by Castellani
of Rome, with suggestions for the design from Michangelo, Duke of Sermoneta. *c.* 1875.
(*Victoria and Albert Museum*)

[158]

Fig. 61. Jet necklaces, brooch and earrings. *c.* 1875

(*Mrs James Walker*)

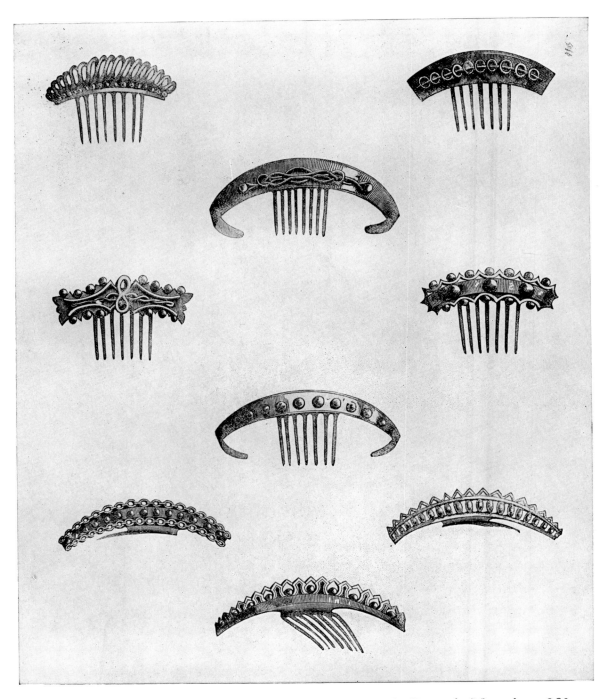

Fig. 62. Tortoiseshell combs, from the *Englishwoman's Domestic Magazine*, 1868
The curved combs form bandeaux. The straight ones are worn within
the chignon.   (*Mrs James Walker*)

[160]

Fig. 63a. Combs, from the *Englishwoman's Domestic Magazine,* 1868

    1. Coiffure with straight comb
    2. Coiffure with straight comb
    3. Coiffure with comb forming a bandeau
    4. Coiffure with diadem comb
    5. Coiffure with large comb

(Mrs James Walker)

Fig. 63b. Hair pin with head formed of a star in cut jet (black glass). *c.* 1870

(The Author)

Figs. 64a to e. Some typical gold earrings of the sixties

(*Mrs James Walker*)

Fig. 64f. Earrings of carbuncles and gold
with a pearl star set on each carbuncle, and pendent gold fringe. *c.* 1868.

(*Mrs James Walker*)

Fig. 64g. Earrings with three pendants hanging within
hollows cut to receive them

A coral bead is on the end of each pendant. *c.* 1873.   (*The Author*)

Fig. 64h. Gilt earring in the form of a bird on a nest. *c.* 1878

(*The Author*)

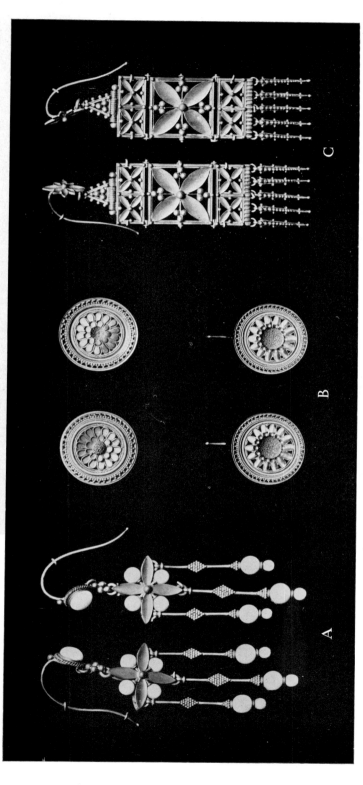

Fig. 65a. Earrings of gold, set and hung with sweet-water pearls
By Giuliano. *c.* 1870.

Fig. 65b. Earrings of gold
with central bosses granulated after the ancient Etruscan manner. By Carlo Giuliano. *c.* 1870.

Fig. 65c. Earrings of gold
Made by Giuliano. *c.* 1870.

Fig. 66. Earrings, brooches and buttons in piqué (tortoiseshell with gold and silver inlaid). *c.* 1865

(*Mrs James Walker and the Author*)

[164]

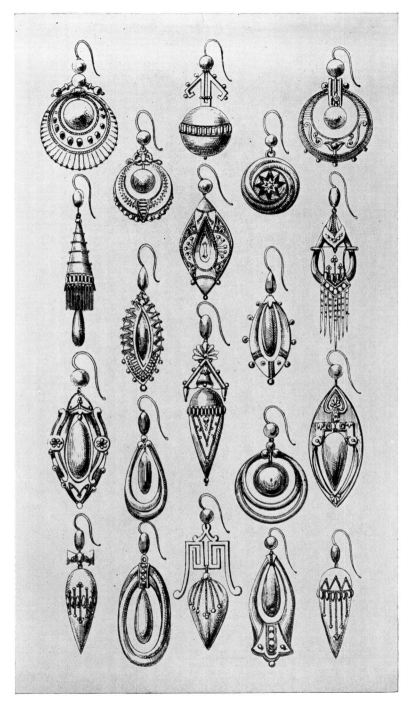

Fig. 67. Coloured gold earrings
From R. Pringle's *Illustrated Catalogue and Price List of Jewellery*, April, 1876.

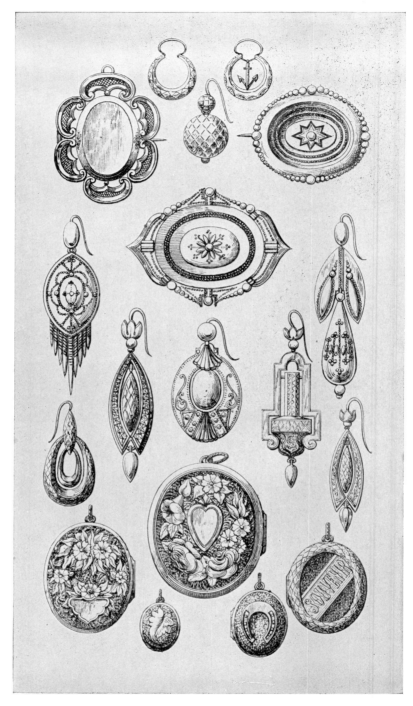

Fig. 68. Brooches, earrings and lockets
From R. Pringle's *Illustrated Catalogue and Price List of Jewellery*, April, 1876.

Fig. 69. Presents given to Princess Alexandra of Denmark
on her marriage with the Prince of Wales in 1863

The centre necklace was on display at the Exhibition of 1872. Presented
to the Princess by her father, the King of Denmark. 'It is composed of
very large pearls and diamonds, and has suspended a facsimile of the
Cross of Dagmar in *cloisonné* enamel, ornamented with diamonds and
pearls. The style is Byzantine: the manufacturer is JULES DIDRICH-
SEN, the crown-jeweller of Copenhagen.'

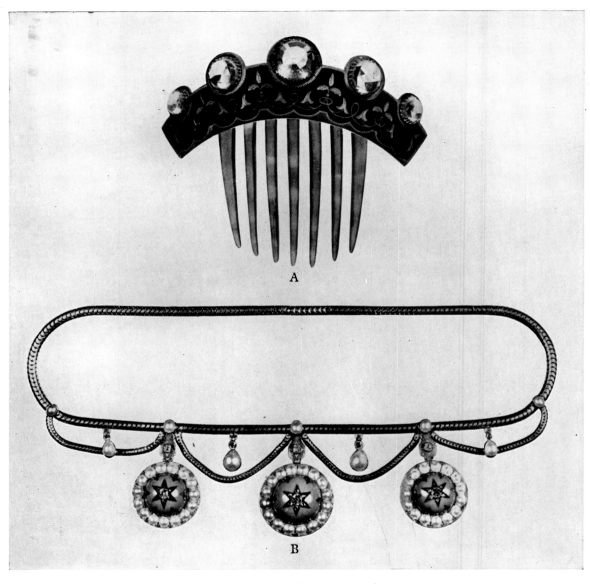

Fig. 70a. Chignon comb

with a metal heading ornamented in black enamel and set with
five graduated pieces of facetted crystal. *c.* 1865.

(Mrs James Walker)

Fig. 70b. Necklet

of flexible gold chain, with three pendent medallions, each of light-blue
enamel set with a diamond star and surrounded with pearls. Four
festoons of narrower gold chain fall from five small pearls, and within each
festoon hangs a pearl from a small diamond. By Parkes of Vigo Street,
London. *c.* 1868.

(Cameo Corner)

[168]

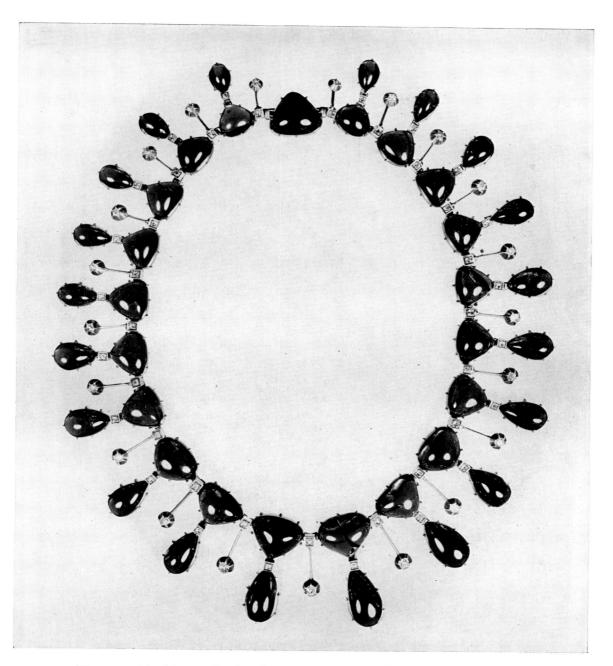

Fig. 71. Necklace of cabochon garnets and diamonds set in gold

The graduated cabochon garnets in open claw settings have each a pear-shaped carbuncle as a pendant. A diamond in a square setting appears between each garnet and its pendant, also between each stone and its neighbour in the main row. Between the carbuncles depend brilliant-cut diamonds, mounted on knife-edge stems of gold. *c.* 1868.

(Cameo Corner)

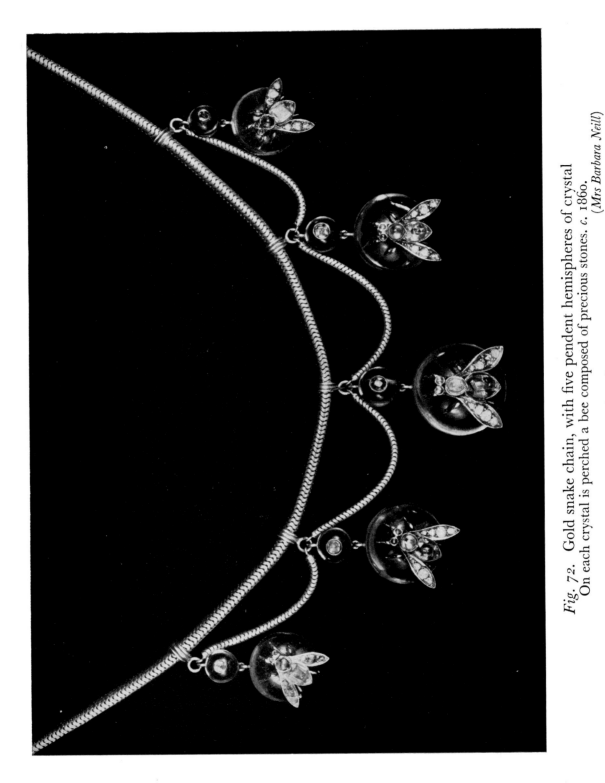

Fig. 72. Gold snake chain, with five pendent hemispheres of crystal
On each crystal is perched a bee composed of precious stones. *c.* 1860.

(*Mrs Barbara Neill*)

[170]

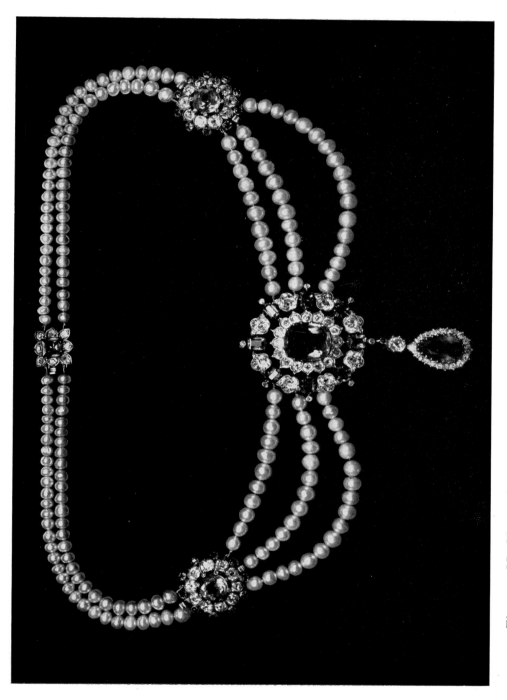

Fig. 73. Necklace of emeralds, amethysts and diamonds, joined by strings of pearls. The three larger jewelled pieces can be dismounted and worn as brooch and earrings. *c.* 1865.

(Miss Joan Maude)

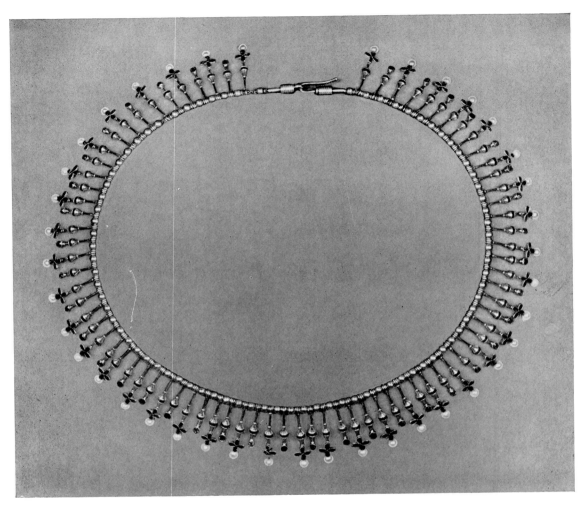

Fig. 74. Necklace by Castellani in rubies, pearls, enamel and gold
Each drop is crossed by a band of dark-blue enamel; the smaller drops
end in rubies set in collets, the larger ones in a blue enamel quatrefoil and
spherical pearl. Each drop swings freely on a gold chain. In the space
between every two drops is a gold bead and two gold rings. *c.* 1868.

(*Mrs James Walker*)

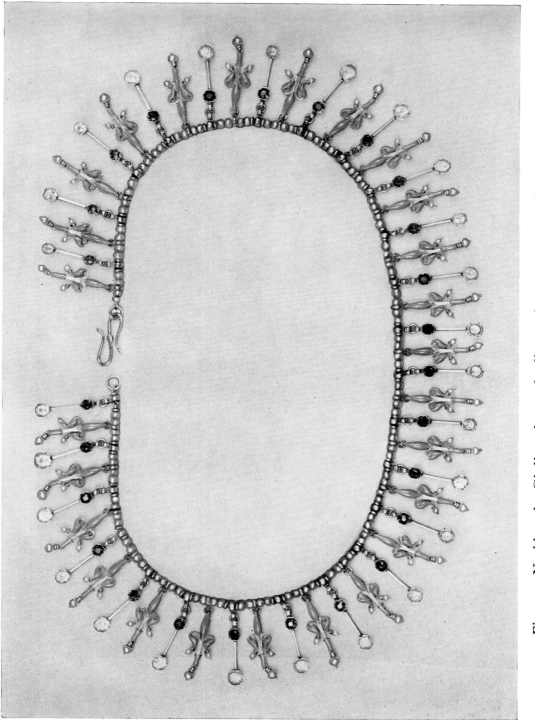

Fig. 75. Necklace by Giuliano in pearls, diamonds, garnets, enamel and gold. *c.* 1867

(*Mrs Gilbert Debenham*)

[173]

Fig. 76. Necklace of flat silver pieces, given to Jenny Lind by Queen Victoria. *c.* 1880

(*Miss Joan Maude*)

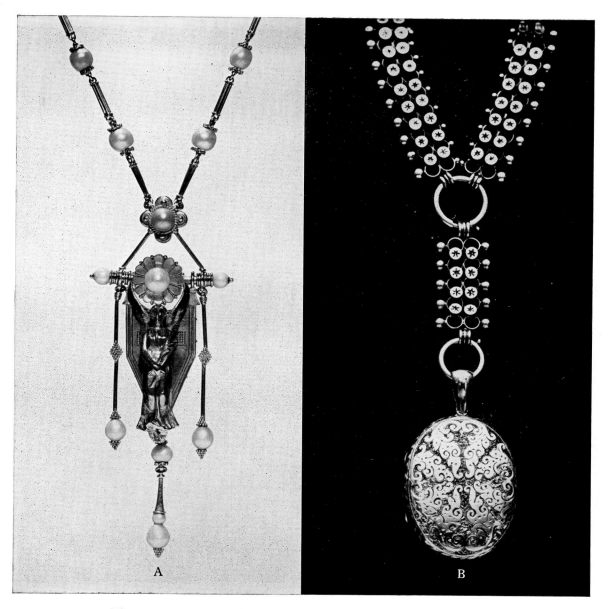

Fig. 77a. Pendant and chain, signed by Carlo Giuliano,
in gold and fresh-water pearls

The lotus flower and the angel on the pendant lift up to disclose a cross
composed of grains of gold. The decorations are of gold grains and twists
of fine gold wire. Very similar to the gold and pearl earrings by Giuliano
in the Victoria and Albert Museum. *c.* 1870.   (*Messrs Harvey and Gore*)

Fig. 77b. Silver locket and chain. *c.* 1882

(*Mrs Norman Reid*)

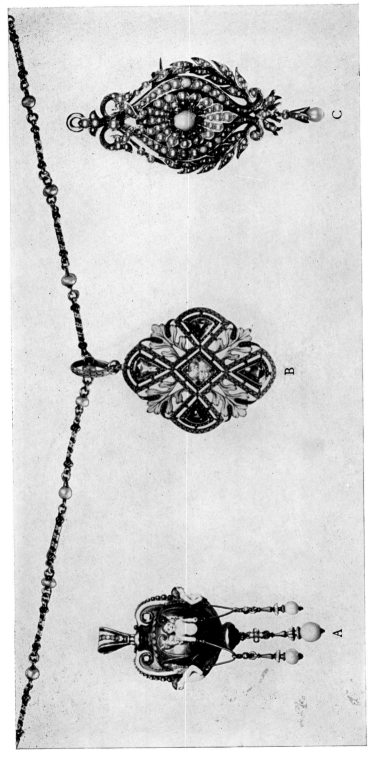

Fig. 78a.   Pendant of enamelled gold, enriched with rubies, diamonds and fresh-water pearls
Made by Carlo Giuliano, c. 1867. (*Victoria and Albert Museum*)

Fig. 78b.   A gold pendant and chain set with topaz and enamelled
By Carlo Giuliano. *c.* 1875.

(*Messrs Bracher and Sydenham*)

Fig. 78c.   Pendant or brooch in gold, turquoise, pearls and diamonds
the central pearl flower framed in a scroll and two branches of laurel. *c.* 1885.

(*Mrs James Walker*)

Fig. 79a. Pearl and diamond pendant. *c.* 1880
(The Goldsmiths & Silversmiths Company Ltd)

Fig. 79b. Cross of black enamel and gold
decorated with pearls and with rose diamonds set into stars and
flowers. *c.* 1870. *(Messrs Harvey and Gore)*

Fig. 79c. Cross by John Brogden
in coloured gold inlaid with pearls which are outlined in black
enamel. *c.* 1875. *(Messrs Harvey and Gore)*

A

B

C

Fig. 80a. Jet locket and chain. *c.* 1878

(*The Author*)

Fig. 80b. Coloured gold locket with garter in black enamel. *c.* 1870

(*Miss Joan Maude*)

Fig. 80c. Locket of gold, black and white onyx, pearls and enamel
Given by Queen Victoria to one of her grandchildren. The box at the
back of the locket contains a small photograph of Feodora, Princess of
Hohenlohe-Langenburg, Queen Victoria's half-sister. The gold frame
round the photograph at the back is inscribed: 'In recollection of dear
Gd. aunt Feodora b. Dec. 1807 d. Sep. 23, 1872 From Grandmama V.R.'

(*Mrs G. K. Lindsay*)

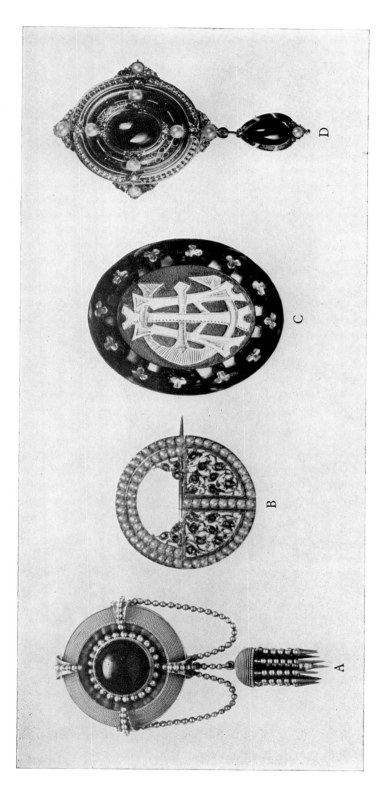

Fig. 81a. Carbuncle and gold brooch. *c.* 1865
(*Mrs James Walker*)

Fig. 81b. A gold brooch set with rubies and pearls
By Giuliano. *c.* 1883. (*Messrs Bracher and Sydenham*)

Fig. 81c. Brooch of carved bog-oak, decorated with gold shamrocks
and a gold monogram. *c.* 1870 (*The Author*)

Fig. 81d. Brooch in enamel, pearls, rose diamonds and carbuncles
By Giuliano. 1865–70. (*Miss M. J. Biggs*)

Fig. 82. Bracelets and brooches by Howell and James,
shown at the 1862 Exhibition
From the *Art Journal*, 1862.

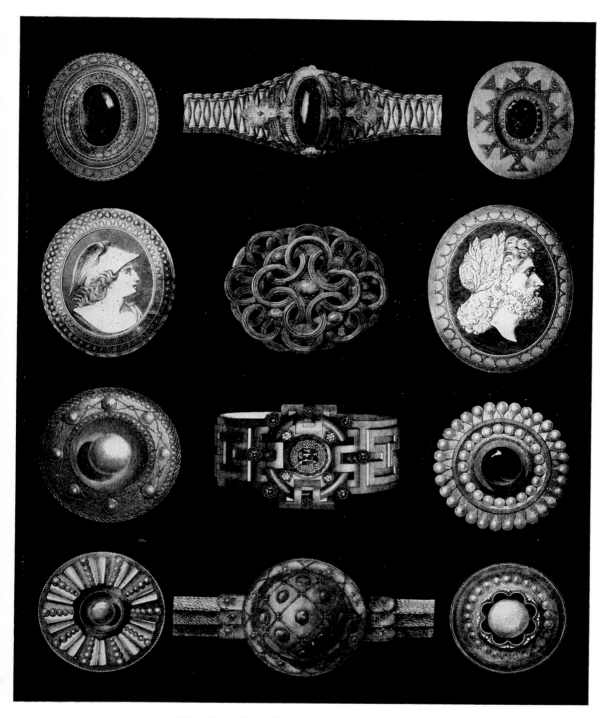

Fig. 83. Jewellery by Richard Green
shown at the 1862 Exhibition. From the *Art Journal,* 1862.

[181]

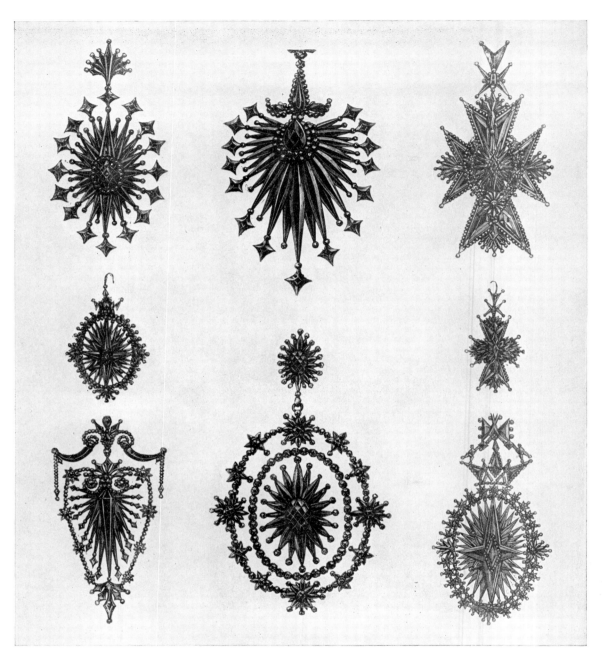

Fig. 84. Black glass jewellery by William Whiteley
From the *Art Journal*, 1872.

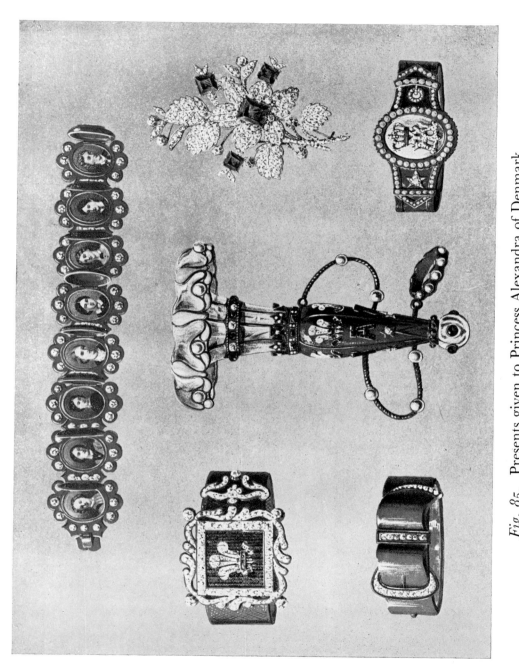

Fig. 85. Presents given to Princess Alexandra of Denmark
on her marriage to the Prince of Wales in 1863

The carved crystal bouquet holder attached to a pearl finger-ring was given by the Maharajah Duleep Sing.

[183]

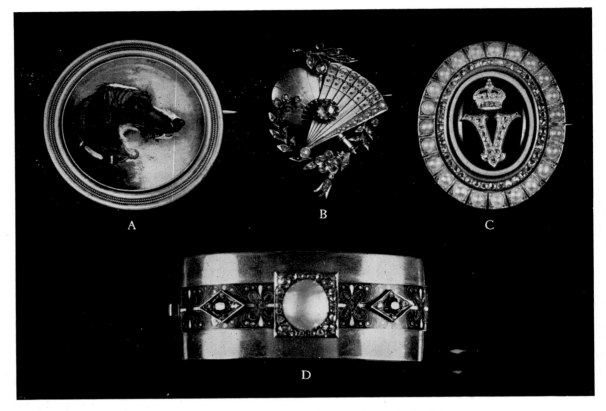

Fig. 86a.   A brooch of crystal set in gold

A dog's head is carved in intaglio on the bottom of the crystal
and then painted, so that from the front the dog's head appears
three-dimensional. *c.* 1865.   (*Messrs Bracher and Sydenham*)

Fig. 86b.   Brooch

Two fans and a laurel wreath spray in coloured gold, set with
diamonds and pearls. *c.* 1884.   (*Mrs James Walker*)

Fig. 86c.   Oval brooch

with brown and white onyx centre, set with a crown and a 'V' in gold and
diamonds, with a border of small diamonds and large pearls. Engraved
on the back 'Victoria Empress Frederick to M. E. Green 1881–1889'. The
brooch opens to disclose a photograph of the Empress (Queen Victoria's
eldest daughter).   (*Cameo Corner*)

Fig. 86d.   Wide gold bangle

decorated with a band of variously-coloured enamel, on which are set a
square containing a baroque pearl surrounded with diamonds, and two
lozenges containing rubies and diamonds. *c.* 1870.   (*Cameo Corner*)

Fig. 87a. Gold bangle

ornamented with twisted gold wire and set with a carved
amethyst having a pearl star in the centre. *c.* 1867.

Fig. 87b. Gold bangle

decorated with three lotus flowers in appliqué, between sheaves
formed of appliquéd gold wire. *c.* 1865.

Fig. 87c. Wide gold bangle

decorated with two coiled serpents, their heads set with pearls
and having diamond eyes. *c.* 1870.

(All three from Cameo Corner)

Fig. 87d. Gold bangle

with boss in pavé-set turquoises. *c.* 1860.

(Miss Hilford)

Fig. 87e. Silver-hinged bangle with bead border

bluebell heads in gold. *c.* 1876.

(Mrs B. H. Liddell Hart)

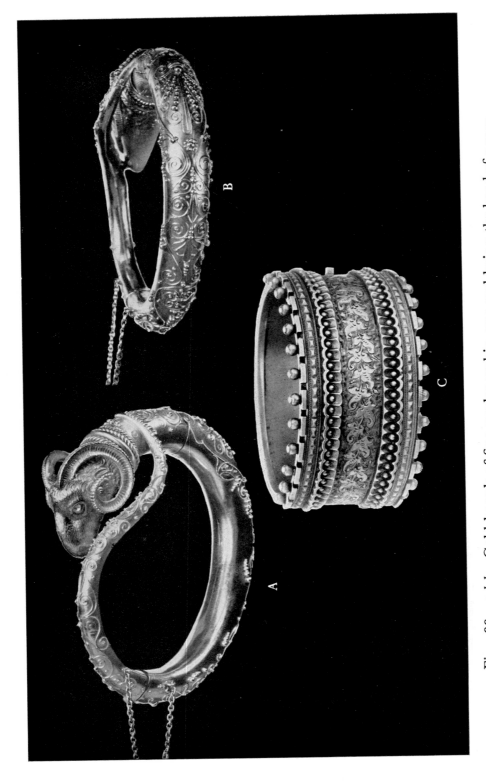

Figs. 88a and b. Gold bangle of fine workmanship, one end being the head of a ram The bangle as a whole is in the shape of a horn, tapering to a curved tip, and is decorated with gold grains and wire in various motifs from the ancient world, including the lotus and acanthus. *c.* 1862.

(*Cameo Corner*)

Fig. 88c. Gold-hinged bangle with bead border. *c.* 1875

(*Mrs B. H. Liddell Hart*)

[186]

Fig. 89a. Bracelet composed of brilliant-cut diamonds set in gold
The central piece can be dismounted and worn as a brooch or pendant. *c.* 1870. (*The Countess of Huntingdon*)

Fig. 89b. A 15-ct. gold bracelet with pink corals, pearls and diamonds
with inscription inside as follows: 'Given by H.R.H. Alexandra, Princess of Wales to F. I. C.
Vesey, Marchioness of Bath, Longleat 10th December, 1881'. (*Messrs Bracher and Sydenham*)

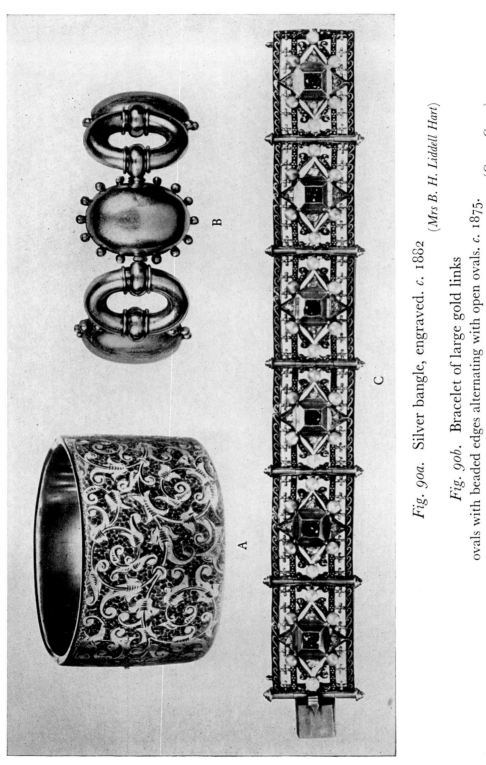

Fig. 90a. Silver bangle, engraved. *c.* 1882

(*Mrs B. H. Liddell Hart*)

Fig. 90b. Bracelet of large gold links
ovals with beaded edges alternating with open ovals. *c.* 1875.   (*Cameo Corner*)

Fig. 90c. A gold bracelet enamelled and set with sapphires and pearls
Signed C.G. (Carlo Giuliano). *c.* 1870.   (*Messrs Bracher and Sydenham*)

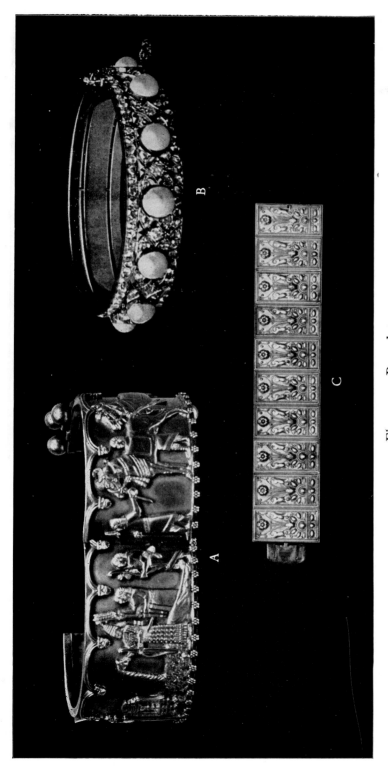

B

A

C

Fig. 91a. Bracelet

Gold with applied decoration representing Ashur-bani-pal, king of Assyria, sacrificing on his return from a lion hunt, after sculptures in the British Museum. On the clasp is a Babylonian cylinder in steatite. Made by John Brogden, London. *c.* 1865.   (*Victoria and Albert Museum*)

Fig. 91b. Pearl and diamond bracelet. *c.* 1875

(*Goldsmiths & Silversmiths Company Ltd*)

Fig. 91c. Bracelet

Gold with applied floral decoration. Made by Hancock, London. *c.* 1863.

(*Victoria and Albert Museum*)

[189]

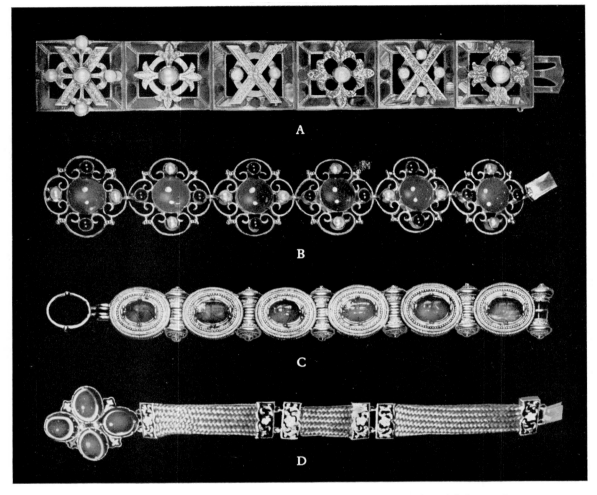

Fig. 92a. Scotch pebble, Scotch pearl and chased gold bracelet.
c. 1865

Fig. 92b. Bracelet in 18-ct. gold, lapis lazuli,
carbuncles and pearls
the quatrefoils in fine twisted gold wire. By John Brogden.
Between 1878 and 1884. *(Both from Mr Albert A. Julius)*

Fig. 92c. Bracelet
Gold, set with red agate scarabs. Made by Castellani. *c.* 1865.
(Victoria and Albert Museum)

Fig. 92d. Bracelet of plaited brown hair
The clasp is a quatrefoil of onyx. The sections of the bracelet are enclosed
in terminals of enamel on gold, white flowers and leaves on a black ground.
c. 1862. *(H. Steiner)*

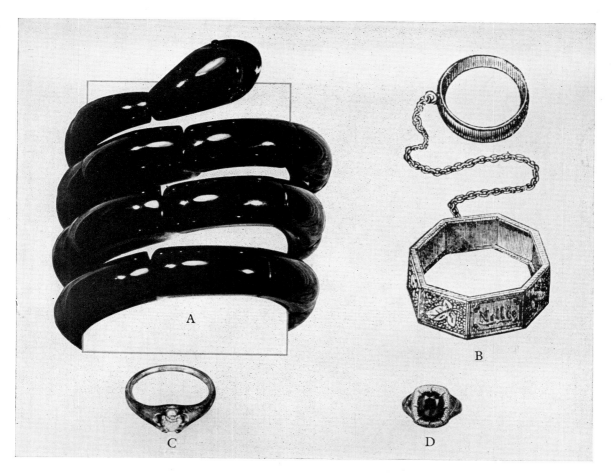

Fig. 93a. Serpent bracelet in polished jet. *c.* 1875

(Mrs James Walker)

Fig. 93b. Handkerchief ring

'This pretty invention consists of two gold rings, one round, for the little finger, connected by a small gold chain with an octagonal ring, bearing the name of the owner, through which the handkerchief is passed.' From the *Young Ladies' Journal*, 1870.

Fig. 93c. Brilliant-cut diamond, open set in six claws in gold ring

with shanks swelling to accommodate the diamond. *c.* 1865.

(Mrs Michael Robertson)

Fig. 93d. Ring

Enamelled gold, set with a sapphire. Made by Giuliano. *c.* 1875.

(Victoria and Albert Museum)

Fig. 94. Rings in gold, decorated with enamel and
semi-precious stones

From R. Pringle's *Illustrated Catalogue and Price List of Jewellery*, April, 1876.

VII
LATE VICTORIAN
JEWELLERY
1885-1901

PLATE VIII

Jubilee set

A bar brooch, with a rose, shamrock and thistle, a crown and the dates 1837 – 1897; a pendant and a necklace. In 15-ct. gold, diamonds, pearls, peridots and topazes, decorated with pink, green, blue and white enamel. (*Messrs Albert A. Julius*)

1. Parures

Large sets of matching jewellery were no longer in fashion.
Demi-parures were still made, and sometimes worn, as follows:

Brooches in round shield shape, with small circular discs as earrings (*as in Fig.*   [1885–1890]
55b).

Pearl cluster centre, on gold circular shield with bead edge.

A gold daisy in relief, on a circle with a bead edge.

In 1890. The Shamrock Parure Bracelet and Bar Brooch in gold and rubies. Three ruby shamrocks on bracelet of thin gold wire, and the same on a small bar brooch.

The Shamrock Parure Earring and Brooch in gold and rubies. The ruby shamrock is in the centre of an open circle, formed by its thin twisted stem. The earring is a spherical ruby, with a screw to hold it on the lobe of the ear.

Large brooches with pieces which could be dismantled and used as small brooches or hairpins. The *Queen*, in 1890, describes two of these, both in diamonds and rubies. One is made of five swallows, the other 'still more novel' is a spray of five orchids. The birds and flowers were graduated in size. 'The setting of the stones is platina, a new treatment which serves better than silver to enhance the brilliancy of the gems. So artistic is the workmanship, that the flowers tremble at the faintest touch, most delicately are they fastened on their stems.'

Earrings, bracelets, necklaces and belts were made in turquoise and silver with Egyptian motifs.

In 1897. The Jubilee set (Plate VIII).

2. Head Ornaments

(A) TIARAS

Necklaces were often made so that the jewelled front could be worn as a tiara.

> *c.*1887. Diamond tiara, in the form of a coronet (*Fig.* 95).
>
> *c.*1895. Diamond tiara, or necklace, with graduated spikes alternating with trefoils (*Fig.* 98a).

[1889] Tiaras of pearls and diamonds, with two rows of inverted festoons, rising from clusters, each festoon surmounted by a pearl.
Art Nouveau tiaras (*as in Fig. 98b*).

> In 1891. Tiara of pearls and diamonds, a single row of alternate clusters and flowers; no upright pieces.
>
> In 1893. Diamond tiara, the upright pieces very close together, resembling flower stems with leaves, each surmounted by a diamond.
>
> In 1896. Tiara of spikes, set close together, surmounted by alternate diamonds and pearls.
>
> In 1897. Tiara of five diamond stars.
> Diamond tiara of crescents, from each of which rises a small flower.
>
> In 1898. A diamond tiara composed of tiny fuchsias, each on its stem.

(B) PINS OR BROOCHES TO BE WORN IN THE HAIR

These were very popular for evening wear in the nineties, diamonds being the jewels almost invariably chosen. The pins were placed in the front hair or at the highest point of the topknot.

> In 1885. Golden crescent, set with ruby stars.
> Gold and pearl wings.
>
> In 1886. Stars, and constellations of stars were the most fashionable decoration for the hair. Among these, a favourite was the 'Southern Cross' brooch, a spray of diamonds representing the constellation which is the emblem of the Southern hemisphere.

[1888–1900] Diamond butterflies.
Diamond crescents.
Diamond feathers.
Diamond flower sprays.
Diamond stag-beetles.
Diamond stars.
Diamond swallows.
Diamond swords.

Diamond trefoils.

In 1889, diamond flowers and foliage were the most favoured hair ornaments.

Pearl double hearts with true lovers' knot in diamonds. [1891–1900]

Diamond bats.

Diamond bees.

Diamond crescent and star.

Diamond double circles, interlaced.

Diamond doves.

Diamond horseshoes.

Diamond knots.

Diamond moons, i.e. flat crescents.

Diamond owls.

Diamond violins.

Dragonflies in enamel and jewels (Plate IX *Fig.* a, and *Fig.* 112, *No.* 5).

(C) COMBS

A vertical tendency is noticeable in these. The hair is arranged in a top-knot, and the heading of a comb stuck into the topknot rises even higher. Most combs have a foundation of tortoiseshell with a gold or jewelled heading. (*Fig.* 96).

In 1885. High Spanish combs fashionable, worn with mantillas over powdered hair. The high combs were of tortoiseshell, sometimes plain, sometimes decorated with gold or silver.

Peigne Joséphine worn in front, on pompadour.

Peigne Joséphine with alternate large and small balls.

In 1887. Combs of solid tortoiseshell, no pattern or decoration whatever.

Galatea comb, with three or five vertical stalks, each surmounted by a jewel, [1890] becomes favourite style.

Combs with three loops as heading.

Side combs set with turquoise, coral or rose diamonds (*see comb at back of head in Fig.* 96).

Small combs with a band of gold, set with five or seven stones.

Semi-coronet shapes with pearls.

Combs with high scrollwork tops, surrounding a central diamond.

Trefoil of sapphires and diamonds as comb-top.

Flowers, bees, etc, in semi-precious stones and enamel, being Art Nouveau [1895] comb-tops.

In 1895. Diamond scrollwork tops on tortoiseshell combs.

*c.*1900. Comb-tops of silver and turquoise, with scarabs and other Egyptian motifs (*Fig.* 99, *No.* 4).

(D) HAIRPINS AND ORNAMENTS
IN TORTOISESHELL OR METAL

In 1890, 'two-pronged tortoiseshell pins, with a gold coil or band round the upper part, are the favourites. One has a gold cable twisted into a knot at the top.' Others were trimmed with gold open-work.

Also, 'a small dagger of pale amber tortoiseshell, the hilt and point encrusted with diamonds. A fairy-like chain of interlinked pearls and diamonds was fastened at either end; the setting in this case was literally invisible.'

In 1897. Silver hair pin with engraved open-work heading (*Fig.* 100b).

*c.*1900. Two-pronged ornaments, like that in Fig. 100c, of carved and tinted horn.

(E) PLUMES, FEATHERS AND AIGRETTES

In 1885. Diamond aigrettes in powdered hair.

[1889]   Diamond crescent and star forming base of aigrette.

In 1890. Feathers in diamond holders (*Fig.* 100a).

Plumes supported by *peigne Joséphine*.

[1898–1901]   Circles of pearls with aigrette in the centre.

Aigrettes rising from a small two-row pearl comb (*Fig.* 96).

In 1898. Black aigrettes with diamond star.

Feathers rising from a holder in gauze and diamonds (*Fig.* 99, *No.* 3).

(F) MISCELLANEOUS

*c.*1900. For young women, Venetian hair nets, of pearls or of gold thread and mother-of-pearl shells (*Fig.* 99, *No.* 7).

Gauze bows (*Fig.* 99, *No.* 5).

Wreaths of tinselled leaves (*Fig.* 99, *No.* 8).

(G) BONNET PINS

Inserted into the coils of hair at the back to keep the hat or bonnet in its place, they usually had three prongs and a flat top in chased metal.

3. Earrings

Very small earrings, or none.

Small discs of silver or gold, edged with beads, or having a small decoration of pearls or diamonds in the centre. [1885–1890]

In 1887. Earrings almost never worn.

Stud earrings with a hook fixture. [1888–1901]

Pearl and diamond clusters.

Turquoise and diamond clusters.

All-diamond clusters.

Single-stone diamonds (*as in Fig.* 95). The Goldsmiths and Silversmiths Company advertised these in a variety of sizes, ranging from £15 to £650 the pair, in 1888.

In 1890. Studs with a screw fixture were a novelty. The *Queen* noted in that year that 'Earrings with drops are beginning to be seen again, but the drops are quite in miniature so far. A dainty little pair are formed of thistles in diamonds, just the flower falling downwards. Pear-shaped pearls, pendent from a diamond in the ear' were also fashionable again. Queen Victoria was accustomed to wear spherical pearl drops in the nineties.

'Gray pearls for ear-drops are in better taste than diamonds.' *Young Ladies' Journal* for 1890.

In 1897, through the example of the Duchess of York, now Queen Mary, who wore earrings constantly, they began to return to favour.

4. Necklaces and Pendants

(A) DOG-COLLARS

The neckwear most characteristic of this period, worn consistently from 1885–1901 *Fig.* 96.

> In 1885, The *Ladies' Treasury* says: 'For the neck, nothing but dog-collars are seen. These may be of plain or beaded velvet for ordinary mortals, whilst possessors of pearls, diamonds and other gems, cover them with real stones. Sometimes necklets are worn as well as dog-collars'.
>
> Red velvet collars, bordered with rows of pearls.
>
> Jet or bead fringes on dog-collars.
>
> In 1886. Rows of pearls replaced the ribbon collars. The pearls were held in place with jewelled upright bands and an upright catch at the nape of the neck.
>
> In 1893. Dog-collars of pearls were worn with matching girdles.
>
> In 1894. The Princess of Wales wearing a pearl dog-collar (*Fig.* 102).
>
> By 1900. Dog-collars were very high, consisting of as many as eleven rows of pearls (*Fig.* 103a).
>
> Collars were also made of coral beads and of jet (*Fig.* 103b).
>
> *c*.1901. Edema collarettes, or jewelled bars through which lace, ribbon or velvet might be threaded to form a soft dog-collar for day wear (*Fig.* 99, *No.* 2).

(B) JEWELLED NECKLACES

Sometimes worn below pearl dog-collars. Colourless stones, as diamonds, pearls and moonstones had replaced the bright colours of the former periods. One of these, showing Indian influence, is in *Fig.* 104b. A fine moonstone and amethyst necklace by Giuliano is shown in Plate X.

[1885]
> Diamond rivières.
> Diamond necklets with drops of alternate single stones and trefoils.
> Pearl necklace of daisies (*Fig.* 104a).
> Necklets with fronts which can be detached and worn as tiaras.
> Single row necklet with pearl daisies at intervals.
> Pearl daisies and taper drops.
> Pearl daisies joined by festoons.
> Three pearl crescents and stars separated by a series of drops.
> Double festoon pearl and diamond necklet.
> Pearl fuchsia drops from single-row necklet.
> Row of pearls with small diamond drops.

Asymmetrical necklaces with a spray of flowers in diamonds and pearls en- [1890]
twined round one side only.

c.1896. Moonstone necklace, decorated with black and white enamel. By
C. R. Ashbee & Hugh Seebohm (*see Fig.* 105a).

(C) BEAD NECKLACES

Pearls were worn consistently through these years. Single, double and
triple row necklaces, often with pearl or diamond pendants.
Small gold bead necklets.

In 1890. Chokers of large pearls with small heart pendants.

'Cleopatra' necklace. A row of turquoises from which hung a fringe of coral, [1890–1892]
agate and other beads.

'Gipsy' necklace. A double row of turquoise and coral beads, interblended
with gold devices. Three pendent amulets fringed with beads hung from the
necklace.

'African' necklet. Amber beads, set off with tassels and small bugles in red silk.

(D) CHAINS

Fine chains, rather short, were used with jewelled pendants.
Narrow chain necklets of gold, in the following patterns:
    Fancy links,
    Link and disc,
    Single link,
    Small curb,
    Twist woven.

c.1896. Silver chain set with moonstones (*Fig.* 105b).

In 1897. The *Young Ladies' Journal* describes 'a pretty necklet of gold studded
with turquoise or other precious stones, with a gold link in front under which
is fastened a tiny hook, to which is fastened a watch-chain long enough for
the watch to be slipped into the belt'.

(E) SAUTOIRS

Long chains of gold links with a pearl or diamond, or a cornelian or agate bead [1890]
set at intervals of one or two inches, along the whole length.

In 1890. 'The great novelty, in the way of jewellery, this winter, is the long,
narrow gold chain, with pearls inserted every two inches; it is passed round
the neck, and falls a good deal below the waist.' *Young Ladies' Journal.*

These sautoirs frequently had jewelled slides. They sometimes terminated in
tassels. They were tucked in at the waist or caught up by a brooch (*see Fig.*
97).

The Princess of Wales frequently wore a pearl sautoir (*Fig.* 102).

(F) WATCH COCK NECKLACES

[*c*.1885–1890]   See p. 45 and Fig. 106b.

(G) PENDANTS

1. LOCKETS

[1885–1890]   Small oval lockets in plain gold, with monogram, or with a pearl star, or diamond star.

Small lockets decorated with enamel (*Fig.* 108b).

A novelty in 1885. A new *porte-bonheur* jewel called the *oudja*. 'It was in fashion in Egypt some three thousand years ago. It consists of a large eye, with eyebrow, and also with a tear glistening in it. It is encased in silver, and is worn like a locket.'

In 1886, another *porte-bonheur*. A crystal locket containing a four-leaved shamrock.

2. JEWELLED PENDANTS

Interchangeable with brooches. The Heart is the favourite shape.
The Princess of Wales wore a pear-shaped pearl pendant on a pearl necklace with a pearl dog-collar.

[1885–1901]   Diamond crosses, on diamond necklets (*Fig.* 95).

Pearl hearts, stars and daisies, worn on strings of pearls (*Fig.* 104a).

Open-work pendant in jewels and enamel, by Giuliano (Plate IX, *Fig.* b).

In 1890, H. M. Stanley, on his marriage, gave as presents to the bridesmaids, rock crystal double-hearts, surmounted by true lovers' knots in turquoises and pearls.

[1890]   Ornamental crosses, in a new and freer style (*Fig.* 107b).

Moonstone hearts bordered with diamonds.

Cluster composed of a large pearl framed in a double row of diamonds.

Pearl crescent and star.

Pavé-set pearl and diamond hearts.

Diamond cluster with spear points radiating from it.

[1894]   Pendants by Ashbee and his school.
      Topazes on fine gold wire.
      Silver, enamel and pearl blisters (*Fig.* 108a).
      Carbuncle surrounded by amethysts, set in silver (*Fig.* 106a).

c.1901. Art Nouveau pendants.
      Barley motif in green gold, by Miault (*Fig.* 107a).

PLATE IX

Fig. a. Dragonfly hair ornament by Lacloche of Paris

The body is of diamonds, the head of bright green enamel set with a large diamond. The wings, of pale green and blue *plique-à-jour* enamel, are set with tiny diamonds. *c.* 1890.

Fig. b. Pendant by Giuliano

composed of seven emeralds, two diamonds and a pendent pearl set in gold, decorated with black and white enamel. *c.* 1885.

Fig. c. Ring by Giuliano

A topaz and two diamonds set in gold. The ornamental open-work frame round the topaz is decorated with blue, white, cream and black enamel. *c.* 1885.

(*All from Cameo Corner*)

5. *Brooches and Pins*

(A) CORSAGE ORNAMENTS AND SHOULDER KNOTS

Diamond sprays.
Diamond birds perched on branches.
Diamond bow knots (*Fig.* 95).
Diamond stomacher in eighteenth-century style (*Fig.* 95).
Dragonflies with emerald bodies, ruby heads and diamond wings.
Orchid of diamonds, open-set in gold.
Stomacher of three diamond clusters against a background of foliage in open-
work, with three pendent pearls.
Diamond stomacher of girandole shape with scrollwork decoration and five
large pendent pearls, having a string of pearls ending in a clasp, to serve as
a safety-chain.

(B) BROOCHES HAND-MADE BY MEMBERS OF THE ARTS AND CRAFTS MOVEMENT, OR SHOWING THEIR INFLUENCE

Flower in silver set with turquoises. [1890–1900]
By C. R. Ashbee.
    Flower in silver, with amethyst centre (*Fig.* 110a).
    Star sapphire set in a cobweb of silver wire which is dotted with moonstones.
    Wild rose of hammered silver with pearl centre.
    Amethysts and silver (*Fig.* 108c).
    Convex brooch in gold and enamel set with a star sapphire (*Fig.* 110b).
    Peacock in gold, silver, diamonds and pearls (*Fig.* 110d).
By C. R. Ashbee & Hugh Seebohm.
    Silver brooch, set with opals, formed of two dragons (*Fig.* 111d).
Brooch in leaf and tendril pattern (*Fig.* 108d).
Butterfly in horn and jewels (*Fig.* 111a).

(C) LACE BROOCHES

1. IN JEWELS

(a) Carved moonstones with diamonds and pearls *c*.1890.
    Cherub (*Fig.* 111b).
    Jester.
    Man in the Moon.

(b) Diamonds, pearls or moonstones set in these shapes:

Arrows,

Bees,

Butterflies,

Caduceus (*Fig.* 109),

Chanticleer (*Fig.* 112),

Crescents (*Fig.* 109),

Crescent and star,

Dogs:
   Poodles,
   Terriers,
   Dachshunds,

Double circles,

Double crescents,

Doves,

Dragonflies (*Fig.* 112),

Ferns,

Fly,

Foxhead, and horseshoe,

Frogs,

Gamecocks,

Hooks and eyes,

Horseshoe (*Fig.* 112),

Kittens,

Larks,

Lizards,

Lyres,

Maidenhair sprays,

Merrythoughts, or wishbones,

Monkeys,

Moons (*Fig.* 110c),

Owls, flying or perched on crescents,

Pheasants,

Rabbit with carrot,

Shamrock,

Ships (*Fig.* 112),

Spider,

Stork drinking from vase,

Swallows,

Truelovers' knot,

Vases (*Fig.* 112),

Violin,

Wheel,

Wildrose.

(c) Pearls, as follows:
   Sprays of lily-of-the-valley,
   Bordering moonstone hearts,
   Horizontal flower sprays,
   In 'Antique' brooches, inspired by the Renaissance,
   Rosebuds with diamond leaves and stems,
   Mistletoe bough with a diamond robin (*Fig.* 109).

(d) Specially named Brooches:
   'Southern Cross' (*see* p. 196).
   'Turban', a circular brooch formed of twists radiating from the centre, resembling the twists of a turban. Usually in pearls and enamel,
   'Just Out', a diamond chicken emerging from an enamel egg-shell,
   'Comet', five single diamonds mounted on a bar, with the largest at one end and the smallest at the other,
   'Honeymoon', a jewelled bee perched on a crescent,
   'Coupling', two diamond hearts joined by a gold hook.

(e) Gold brooches:
   Etruscan patterns, now going out of fashion (*Fig.* 113, *Nos.* 12, 13, 15),

Curb and heart (*Fig.* 113, *No.* 10),
Curb and knot of riband (*Fig.* 109),
Twist and bead,
Bee (*Fig.* 113, *No.* 11),
Wish bone and mistletoe (*Fig.* 109),
Bird with a cherry in its mouth,
Fine gold wire twisted as tendrils into open hearts or circles, having a jewelled bird or flower in the centre,
Flowers modelled of gold.

(f) Bar brooches. Horizontal gold bars, having a small motif placed in the centre. The bar might be quite plain, or with a pearl or diamond at either end, or in the form of an arrow or a riding crop.

Some decorations of bar brooches:
Anchor (*Fig.* 112),
Bat, in diamonds,
Cat and Dog (*Fig.* 109),
Cat and Mouse,
Clover leaves in gold, with diamond dewdrops,
Crescents, pearls or diamonds,
Daisies, pearls or diamonds,
Diamonds, three single stones on bar,
Fly in pearls and diamonds,
Hearts,
Horseshoes (*Fig.* 112),
Shamrocks,
Snakes, in coils,
Sphinx heads in silver and opals,
Swallows, 2, 3 or 5.

2. IN ENAMEL

'Another pretty novelty is the brooch of coloured enamel, in the shape of some pretty flower, such as the violet, edelweiss, narcissus, snowdrop, blue cornflower, daisy, orchid, etc. These fancy jewels are great favourites with young ladies.' *Young Ladies' Journal*, 1890.

(D) LACE PINS AND SAFETY PINS

1. Pins, about two inches long, with pearl or diamond heads in the shapes of:

Birds (*Fig.* 109),
Clover leaves,
Chickens,
Clusters,
Crescents,

Foxheads,
Hearts,
Horseshoes,
Knots of various patterns,
Trefoils.

2. Safety Pins, of gold, set with any of the following in jewels:

Butterflies,

Horseshoes,

Clusters,

Lilies-of-the-valley,

Crescents,

Roses,

Daisies,

Single large diamonds,

Double hearts,

Swallows,

Flies,

Trefoils.

Hearts,

In 1890, a new safety brooch pin was patented. The pin was not soldered to a hinge; it passed through the hinge and was twisted round itself.

(E) SPORTING BROOCHES

[1885–1890]   Horseshoes in diamonds, pearls, paste, gold or silver (*Fig.* 113, *No.* 14).

Gold horseshoes with pearl or diamond nails.

In 1890. The *Queen* comments: 'The game of golf is ever growing in popularity, and a souvenir of it, which is now often given as a prize or a present, takes the form of a brooch, composed of two perfectly made miniature clubs, crossed, with the ball between them'. And again, 'Messrs Godwin's (of High Holborn) have pretty fanciful brooches, the most popular being a gold knot of ribbon and a device of golfing clubs entwined with the name of the club to which the recipient belongs'. (*see Fig.* 113, *Nos.* 7 *and* 9).

In 1901. 'Golf sticks' brooch (*Fig.* 109).

[1890–1900]   Brooches in the following shapes:

Foxheads (*Fig.* 113, *No.* 8),

Fox with horseshoe and riding-crop (*Fig.* 113, *No.* 4),

Horns (*Fig.* 113, *Nos.* 1 *and* 3),

Horseshoe and riding-crop (*Fig.* 113, *No.* 6),

Horseshoe and bow (*Fig.* 113, *No.* 2),

Hounds,

Running fox (*Fig.* 113, *Nos.* 4 *and* 5).

[1895]   The following motifs in diamonds were used on sporting jewellery:

Borzoi,

Flying goose,

Bull,

Flying partridge,

Cat,

Gamecock,

Cock's head,

Greyhound,

Dog pointing,

Grouse,

Duck,

Hound,

Eagle,

Macaw,

Falcon,

Owl head,

Fish,

Parrot,

Flying duck,

Parrot's head,

Partridge,
Pelican,
Rabbit,
Setter,
Squirrel,

Stork,
Terrier,
Whippet,
Wild boar,
Wild cat.

(F) NOVELTY BROOCHES

In 1890. Jeanne d'Arc brooches in all prices 'from the handsome enamel, round in form about the size of a half-crown, set in diamonds, representing the peasant heroine, clad in blue, waving a red oriflamme, to the cheaper effigies of Jeanne on horseback in oxidized silver, sometimes mounted on a coloured ground'.

In 1890. The Louis XVI clasp: 'a medallion in enamel representing a pow-dered belle. It is encircled with a gold rim and pearls, and headed with a lover's knot in brilliants. Especially effective in the folds of a Marie Antoinette fichu, or in the net strings of large lace bonnets'.

In 1890. Bridesmaids' presents: Watches pendent from a brooch which bears the bride's name written across in gold.

In 1897. For the Diamond Jubilee: Roses, shamrocks, and thistles in enamel (Plate VIII).

In 1901. The 'Century Brooch' in pearls and diamonds (*Fig.* 109).

In 1890. Cases containing the small coral, pearl or turquoise pins used to fasten back the narrow velvet strings of bonnets.

(G) HATPINS

(See *Fig.* 101 from the *Young Ladies' Journal* of April, 1890).   [1890]
'Hatpins are very fashionable at present, and are worn in every variety of form; they are sometimes of silver, gold, pearl, often very richly jewelled, others are of cut jet, garnets, or oxidized silver. In fact, they are seen in every possible form. A few of them are given in our illustration.

No. 1, round in form, is of old silver, richly embossed.

No. 2, in form of helmet and pike, is of oxidized silver.

No. 3, forming the Prince of Wales's feathers, is of gold.

No. 4, is of mother-of-pearl, lined with gold.

No. 5, in form like a Japanese fan, is of turquoise-blue enamel, with gold figures.

No. 6, the figure is of ivory and the spray of frosted gold.

No. 7, is a crescent in moonstone, with engraved flowers.

No. 8, is of gold, enamelled dark-blue, with a head in natural colours.

No. 9, is of jet, outlined with a thread of gold.

No. 10 is of gold, with medallion in the centre.

No. 11 is of garnets, in form like a crescent.'

In 1894. 'Ornamental hat or bonnet pins: No. 1 is of pale-blue enamel, studded with pearls set in gold. No. 2 is a moonstone, with a twist of gold, set with diamonds, and finished with a small arrow-head.' *Young Ladies' Journal*. (See drawing below.)

6. Bracelets

Worn in numbers, as many as four on each arm.

(A) BANGLES

1. JEWELLED BANGLES

Wide bangles still fashionable. [1885–1890]

Pearl and diamond daisy (*Fig.* 114a).

Pearl or diamond stars set into wide bangles.

Three diamonds, in star setting on bangle.

Three rows of pearls. } (*Fig.* 115).

Pearls set in floral pattern.

Pearls trimming bangle with pierced border.

Flat plain bangles with diamond crescent or pearl crescent and star.

Half-hoops of diamonds alone or with pearls, rubies, sapphires or emeralds. [1885–1900]

Three rows of jewels forming half-hoop.

Half-hoops of jewels set in a wavy line.

Pearl and diamond clusters in open setting.

Diamond flowers in open setting (*Fig.* 114c).

Pearls or diamonds in 'turban', or twisted pattern.

Pearl or diamond ivy leaves.

Diamond hearts (*Fig.* 116, *No.* 6).

Diamond cluster and bar (*Fig.* 116, *No.* 8).

Three-part bracelets, with the back of the bracelet composed of three fine wires [1890]
of gold.

Set with diamond detachable cluster to be worn as brooch or pendant, or
with any other fashionable motif.

Two-part bracelets, cut away in front, to give place to a diamond heart or
horseshoe (*Fig.* 116, *No.* 3).

Set with trefoils or clovers in diamonds (*Fig.* 116, *Nos.* 5 *and* 7).

Diamond cross-over patterns, geometrical or floral.

Single-stone diamonds set on narrow bangles.

Diamond snakes coiled round thin gold bangles.

Bangles set all round with a single row of pearls (*Fig.* 114b).

Three rows of pearls with diamond points.

[1890]   Very narrow bangles, having the gold wire twisted so that they spring shut, set with such jewelled motifs as the following:

In diamonds:

Cooing doves (*Fig.* 116, *No.* 1), Pearl and moonstone hearts.

Clusters (*Fig.* 116, *No.* 4),

Horseshoe and riding crop (*Fig.* 116, *No.* 2),

Trefoils,

Clover leaves,

Bow knots,

In pearls:

Bow and horseshoe,

Daisy,

Double heart,

Double horseshoe,

Knot,

Lily spray,

Turban,

Wave and bead.

2. Gold Bangles

In 1895, plain gold bangles were worn over gloves with afternoon dress. *Young Ladies' Journal* for May.

[1885–1890]   (a) Wide.

Round-edged, plain.

Square-edged, plain.

With ornamental patterns (*Fig.* 115, *Nos.* 1 *and* 3).

[1885–1900]   (b) Narrow. Several narrow plain gold bangles were often worn on each wrist during the day.

Bamboo pattern, imitating a circular bamboo stalk.

'Engagement' bangle, closing with padlock and key.

Fluted gold.

Knot decoration, the thin gold of the bangle being twisted on itself.

'Naval', resembling a rope and fastening with a hook.

Pencil case, attached to bangle.

'Turban', two thin bangles interlaced.

Twist and bead pattern.

'Yachting', in the shape of a life saver, with a fine gold rope attached at four points.

Open-ended bangles, which spring tight on the arm. Fluted or twisted gold with balls on either end.

(B) LINK BRACELETS

Curb chain bracelets, most popular, in various patterns: plain curb, Alma, French curb and double curb.

Set with gems (*Fig.* 109).

With padlock and key.

With charms (*see Fig.* 109).

Portes-bonheur, e.g. eyes, shamrocks,

Hearts (*Fig.* 109),

Coins,

Medallions.

In 1890, a pretty bracelet of two gold chains had as a fastening two little owls, with ruffled plumage in pearls, and diamond heads, their blinking eyes being a single ruby.

(C) FLEXIBLE BRACELETS

Serpents, large with many coils, in gold or jet.   [1885–1890]

Smaller, with one or two coils, studded with jewels or enamelled.   [1890–1900]

Jet ovals on elastic.   [1885–1890]

Bracelets made of bands of plaited gold.   [1885–1890]

(D) BEAD BRACELETS

Almost invariably pearls, several rows of them, held together with a jewelled clasp.

(E) RIBBON BRACELETS

Ribbon bracelets were worn to match dog-collars, in embroidered or beaded   [1885–1888]
velvet.

7. Rings

(A) DECORATIVE RINGS (*See* Plate IX, *Fig.* c)

New patterns:

    Cross-over (*see Fig.* 117, *Nos.* 19 *and* 20).

    Two part rings (*see Fig.* 117, *No.* 9).

    Three part rings (*see Fig.* 117, *No.* 21).

Rings with a piece cut away in the front, and a jewel occupying the space.

Single-stone diamonds are set on a very narrow band of gold, which does not become wider at the bezel.

Gypsy rings, with one or three stones, *Nos.* 12 *and* 18.

Half-hoop rings, *Nos.* 13 *and* 17.

Marquise rings, pavé-set.

Hearts, single and double, *No.* 16.

Clusters, *No.* 22.

Two rows of gems, *Nos.* 23 *and* 24.

Crowned heart.

All these may be seen in *Fig.* 117.

In 1890. Band ring: a wide gold band set with jewels in lozenges.

(B) GOLD RINGS

Wedding rings, which become narrow about 1890.

Serpents, with three or four coils.

Narrow bands of hammered or chased gold.

Strap and buckle pattern.

Curb pattern.

Rope pattern.

Twist and bead pattern.

Mizpah rings.

Magic rings, composed of two gold wires twisted in opposite directions, so that the stripes seemed to move.

(C) SIGNET RINGS

About 1890, the cartouches become very small.

8. *Miscellaneous*

(A) BELTS

Very wide, jewelled, or made of metal (*Fig.* 99, *No.* 1).
Gold woven ribbon set with turquoise.
Oxidized silver set with turquoise or paste.
Girdles with Egyptian motifs (*Fig.* 99, *No.* 9).
Medieval or chatelaine girdles, of metal.
In 1890. 'A beautiful example in oxidized silver tinsel cord, intermixed with
  huge pearls like bosses; united in front by an oxidized silver buckle, a copy
  of a Henry IV girdle.'

(B) BUCKLES

Chased or oxidized silver; sometimes gold.
Very high rectangular pronged buckles, to go on wide belts.
Coiled serpents.
Butterflies.
Portrait heads.
Large paste buckles, often worn at the back (*Fig.* 96).   [1897]

(C) CLASPS

Worn on dresses, but more often on coat or cloak collars.
In 1890. 'Neglected cameos are being exhumed from jewel-cases and mounted
  as clasps and snaps for gowns. Large rings of gold, plain or studded with diamonds, are provided for the same purpose with evening dresses.'
In 1890. C. R. Ashbee's cloak clasp in repoussé silver, with a portrait on one
  side and a flower on the other (*Fig.* 118a).
*c.*1895. C. R. Ashbee's clasps in silver, enamel and blister pearls (*Fig.* 118b).
  Jet was used for clasps, especially on black coats.

(D) LINKS AND STUDS

Sleeve links in fanciful patterns, e.g.
  Grapes of green and purple sardonyx.
  'The Academy Links, one being a gold palette studded with rubies, emeralds
  and sapphires; the other a sheaf of brushes.'
In 1894. 'A pretty novelty is the twin stud or double stud of gold, with a pearl,
  ruby or cat's-eye, joined together by a small gold chain. It is used to fashion
  a lace ruche collar or fichu round the neck, and double button holes are
  prepared on purpose. It is also worn on the sleeves and at the belt.'

[213]

(E) CHATELAINES

In 1893. C. R. Ashbee's chatelaine in silver openwork. The top is a horizontal
pattern, with in the centre a row of four cornflowers, and five silver chains
hanging from the bottom.

[1890-1900]   Chatelaine bags in velvet or soft leather with oxidized silver clasps as well.

(F) WATCH CHAINS, ETC

Ladies' 'Albert' watch chains, with bar, and tassels in several sorts of gold
chain patterns.

Brooches in the shape of a bow or safety pin were used in the nineties to
attach watches to the bodice.

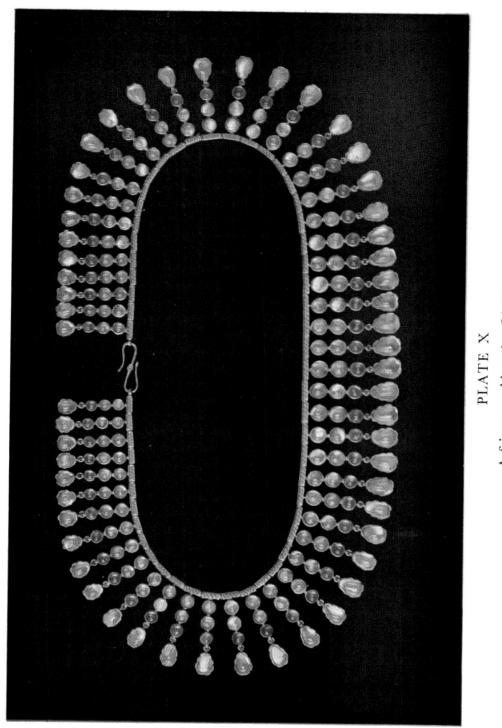

PLATE X

A fringe necklace by Giuliano

Of graduating moonstone and amethyst drops attached to a light-blue enamel collar.
c. 1890.

(Messrs Harvey and Gore)

Summary

(1885 – 1901)

I. MATERIALS CHIEFLY USED

FOR PRIMARY JEWELLERY

Amethysts.
Aquamarines.
Cat's Eyes.
Chrysoprase.
Diamonds.
Emeralds.
Enamel.
Gold.
Moonstones.
Opals.
Oxidized silver.
Pearls.
Peridots.
Platinum.
Rubies.
Sapphires.
Silver.
Topaz.
Turquoise.

FOR SECONDARY JEWELLERY

Coral.
Garnets.
Gilt.
Gold (real and imitation).
Horn.
Jet.
Mother-of-pearl.
Oxidized silver.
Paste.
Pearls.
Silver.
Turquoise.

II. MOTIFS MOST TYPICAL OF THIS PERIOD

Bows.
Clover leaf.
Crescent and star.
Cross-over.
Daisies.
Double heart with crown or knot.
Doves.
Dragonflies.
Egyptian.

Fuchsia.
Heart.
Horseshoe.
Kittens.
Knots.
Lily-of-the-valley.
Moons.
Owls.
Shamrock.

Star.

Swallow.

Turban.

Wild rose.

Art Nouveau.

Convolvulus.

Cornflower.

Heads of females.

Nasturtiums.

III. OTHER FEATURES CHARACTERISTIC OF THIS PERIOD

Bar brooches.

Carved moonstones.

Dog collars.

Invisible settings.

Narrow bangles.

Open-ended bangles.

Polished semi-precious stones.

Safety pins.

Sautoirs.

Spring bangles.

Square-set or star-set stones.

Stud earrings.

Three-part bracelets and rings.

Two-part bracelets and rings.

Fig. 95. Tiara, necklace with cross, stomacher and
shoulder-knots in diamonds. *c.* 1887

(From a photograph belonging to Mrs Doris Langley Moore)

Fig. 96. Toilettes de theatre
From the *Queen*, 1899. (*Mrs Doris Langley Moore*)

Fig. 97. Walking dress. c. 1901

(*From a fashion plate belonging to Mrs Doris Langley Moore*)

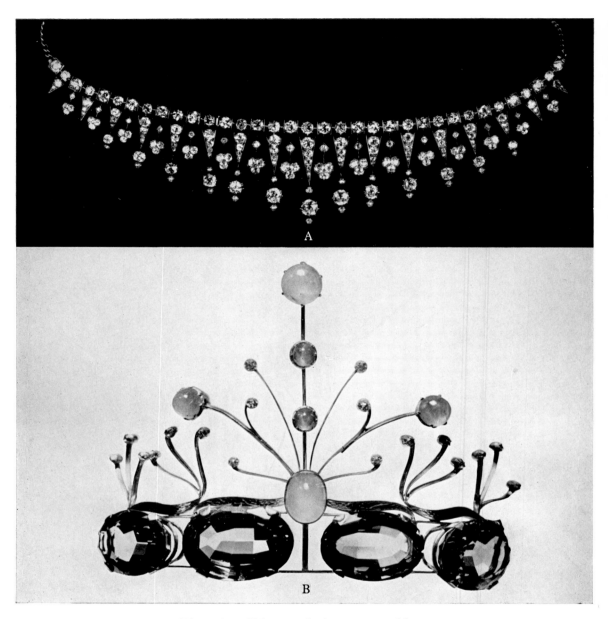

A

B

Fig. 98a. Diamond tiara or necklace

The diamonds are set in silver backed with gold. The graduated drops end in large brilliant-cut diamonds, alternating with shorter drops ending in diamond trefoils. *c.* 1895. (*Messrs Harvey and Gore*)

Fig. 98b. Tiara

with four large topazes, star sapphires, star rubies, and diamonds, decorated in green enamel. By Giuliano (marked C & A. G.). *c.* 1890. (*Mr Albert A. Julius*)

Fig. 99. 1. Belt of silver bands and butterfly clasp
2. Edema collarette in gold and pearls
3. Hair ornament in feathers, gauze and diamonds
4. Egyptian silver and *cloisonné* hair ornament with turquoise
  as centre-piece
5. Coiffure bow of spangled gauze bordered with tiny shells
6. Fan
7. Venetian hair net of shells
8. A wreath of tinselled leaves and berries
9. Egyptian silver chatelaine girdle

From the *Boudoir*

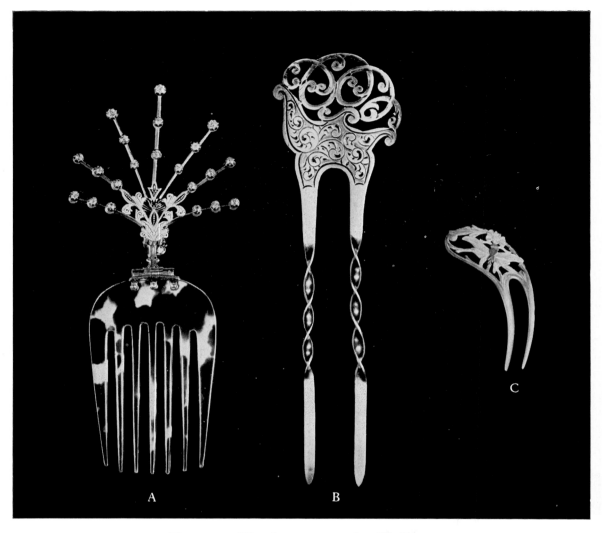

Fig. 100a. Head ornament by Giuliano

The aigrette, which is attached to a tortoiseshell comb, has a base of gold decorated with black and white enamel; from this radiate seven knife-edged bars of gold, each set with three diamonds. At the back of the base is an opening for the insertion of a tuft of ospreys. *c.* 1890.

(*Cameo Corner*)

Fig. 100b. Silver hair pin

with head of engraved scrollwork, some of it being openwork, showing the asymmetrical tendency of the nineties. (Hall-marked *Sheffield* 1897.)

(*Mrs Rita Smith*)

Fig. 100c. Hair ornament

in natural horn, carved and tinted. *c.* 1900.

(*H. Steiner*)

Fig. 101. Fashionable hatpins
From the *Young Ladies' Journal,* 1890.

1. Round in form, is of old-silver, richly embossed
2. In form of helmet and pike, is of oxidized silver
3. Forming the Prince of Wales's Feathers, is of gold
4. Is of mother-of-pearl, lined with gold
5. In form like a Japanese fan, is of turquoise-blue enamel, with gold figures
6. The figure is of ivory, and the spray of frosted gold
7. Is a crescent in moonstone, with engraved flowers
8. Is of gold, enamelled dark-blue, with a head in natural colours
9. Is of jet, outlined with a thread of gold
10. Is of gold, with medallion in the centre
11. Is of garnets, in form like a crescent

Fig. 102. Alexandra, Queen of Edward VII,
when Princess of Wales

Painted in 1894 by Sir Luke Fildes. She wears a pearl dog-
collar and long necklace of pearls, and several narrow bracelets.

(*National Portrait Gallery*)

Fig. 103a. Dog-collar

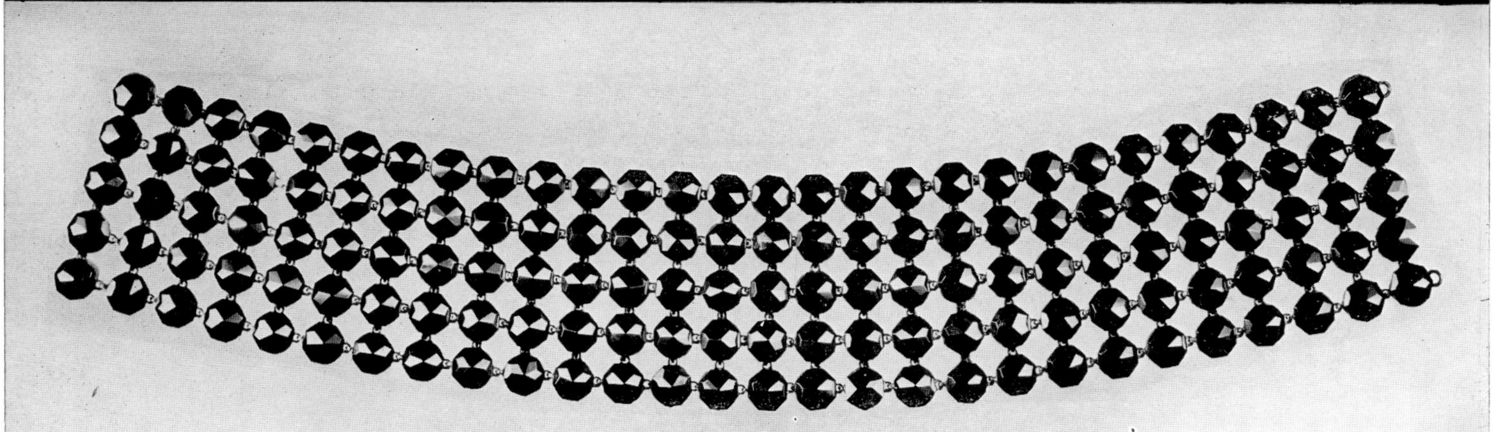

of eleven rows of artificial pearls, held upright by silver bars set with paste, and having a central openwork ornament of a daisy above a network pattern in silver and paste. *c.* 1900.

(*Mrs James Walker*)

Fig. 103b. Dog-collar of polished jet. *c.* 1890

(*The Author*)

Fig. 104a. Necklet in pearls and gold, and brooch in
gold, pearls and diamonds

The pearl daisies and the tiny three-petalled drops are particularly characteristic of their period. *c.* 1888.

(Mrs James Walker)

Fig. 104b. Necklet of seed pearls, gold and topaz
Indian work. *c.* 1885.

(The Author)

A

B

Fig. 105a. Necklet of moonstones, black and white enamel, gold and silver
(The moonstones are in an open silver setting ornamented with
enamel. The twisted wire links are gold.) By C. R. Ashbee from
a design by Hugh Seebohm. *c.* 1896.

Fig. 105b. Silver chain set with moonstones
By C. R. Ashbee from a design by Hugh Seebohm. *c.* 1896.
(*Both belonging to the Countess of Cranbrook*)

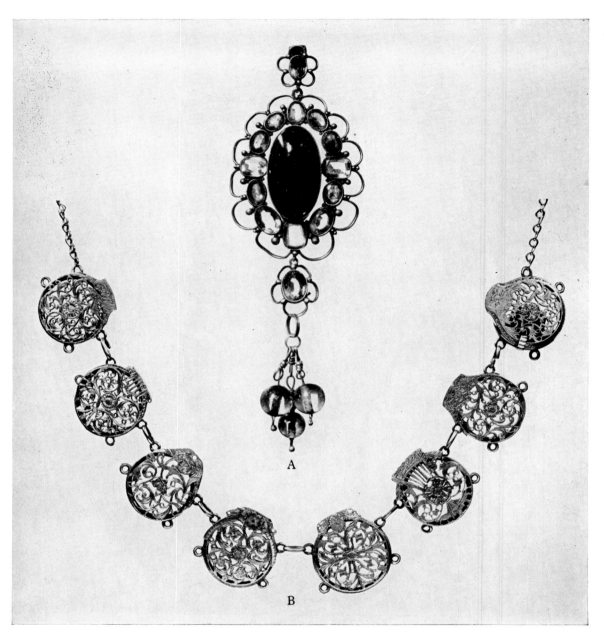

Fig. 106a. Pendant
composed of an oval carbuncle, surrounded by amethysts, the
whole set in silver. By C. R. Ashbee. *c.* 1897.   (*Mrs C. R. Ashbee*)

Fig. 106b. Necklace made of the gold escapement covers
of verge watches. *c.* 1885   (*Miss Elizabeth Edmondston*)

Fig. 107a. Pendant in green gold by Miault. *c.* 1901

(Mme Agazarian)

Fig. 107b. Cross in silver made by Henry Wilson
The cross hangs from a large baroque pearl, which in turn hangs
from a small silver crown. *c.* 1890.

(Mrs Hodson)

Fig. 108a. Pendant in silver, enamel and pearl blisters
By C. R. Ashbee. *c.* 1892.
(From a photograph belonging to Mrs C. R. Ashbee)

Fig. 108b. Locket
of enamelled gold, bearing the Egyptian hieroglyph *nefer*
(beautiful). Made by Giuliano. *c.* 1890. *(Victoria and Albert Museum)*

Fig. 108c. Brooch in silver, set with amethysts
By C. R. Ashbee. *c.* 1892.
(From a photograph belonging to Mrs C. R. Ashbee)

Fig. 108d. Brooch in 15-ct gold
set with pearls, diamonds and pink tourmalines. *c.* 1895.
(Mr Albert A. Julius)

Fig. 109. An advertisement for Christmas presents which appeared in December, 1901

[231]

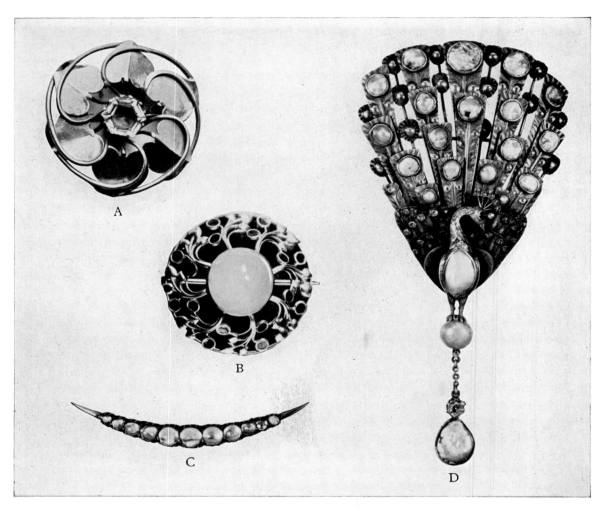

Fig. 110a. Brooch by C. R. Ashbee, silver set with amethyst. *c.* 1892

Fig. 110b. Brooch
in gold and enamel, set with a star sapphire; by C. R. Ashbee. *c.* 1892.
(*Both from photographs belonging to Mrs C. R. Ashbee*)

Fig. 110c. Brooch in the shape of a new moon
with eleven graduated moonstones in an open claw setting. *c.* 1890.
(*Mrs John Lawson*)

Fig. 110d. Brooch in the form of a peacock
the tail of silver and green gold, set with cabochon pearls and small diamonds;
the head and wings of gold, the body a large pearl; the eye a ruby, the crest
small diamonds. The bird stands on a nearly spherical pearl from which hang
on a gold chain a pearl and two diamonds. By C. R. Ashbee, executed by
Gebhardt, one of his craftsmen. *c.* 1900. (*Mrs Ames Lewis*)

Fig. 111a. Butterfly in horn
set with diamonds, emeralds, sapphires and rubies, decorated
with *plique-à-jour* and plain enamel. *c.* 1898.

(*Mr Albert A. Julius*)

Fig. 111b. Lace-brooch with cherubs' heads in carved moonstone
The gold wings are set with pearls. *c.* 1890.

(*Mrs James Walker*)

Fig. 111c. Bar brooch, with pearl and diamond cluster centre
and pearl ends. 1890–1900   (*Mr Albert A. Julius*)

Fig. 111d. Brooch of silver set with opals
By C. R. Ashbee from a design by Hugh Seebohm. *c.* 1896.

(*The Countess of Cranbrook*)

Fig. 112.   1. Chanticleer, in 18-ct. gold and diamonds with ruby
eye
2. Sailing boat in 15-ct. gold and enamel with diamond
sails and sapphire hull
3. Horseshoe in pearls and diamonds
4. Blister-pearl vase with diamond foliage
5. Dragonfly in pearls, rubies and sapphires
6. Hunting horn and crop in gold with double horseshoes in diamonds
7. Pointed bar-brooch with gold rope and pearl anchor

All 1890-1900

(*Mr Albert A. Julius*)

FINE GOLD BROOCHES.

In Best Morocco Cases, Lined Silk Velvet.

No. 11,787.—Fine Gold Horn.
£1 12 0

No. 11,788.—Fine Gold Bow and Horseshoe.
£1 5 0

No. 11,789.—Fine Gold Horn.
£2 0 0

No. 11,790.—Fine Gold Fox and Horseshoe.
£2 10 0

No. 11,791.—Fine Gold Horn and Fox.
£2 0 0

No. 11,792.—Fine Gold Horseshoe and Crop.
£2 0 0

No. 11,793.—Fine Gold Golfing Clubs
and Pearl Balls.
£2 10 0

No. 11,794.—Fine Gold and Platinum
Foxhead, Crop and Bit.
£2 10 0

No. 11,795.—Fine Gold Golfing Clubs
and Pearl Ball.
£2 0 0

No. 11,796.—Fine Gold Curb and Heart.
£1 5 0

No. 11,797.—Fine Gold Bee.
£1 10 0

No. 11,798.—Fine Gold Etruscan.
£2 5 0

No. 11,799.—Fine Gold Etruscan.
£1 15 0

No. 11,800.—Fine Gold Horseshoe.
£1 8 0

No. 11,801.—Fine Gold Etruscan.
£2 2 0

Fig. 113. A page of brooches
From the *Catalogue of The Goldsmiths & Silversmiths Company Ltd.* for 1895.

Fig. 114a. Pearl and diamond stiff bangle, daisy motif. *c.* 1885
(The Goldsmiths & Silversmiths Company Ltd)

Fig. 114b. Narrow gold bangle
decorated with a row of pearls in square settings. *c.* 1890.
(Cameo Corner)

Fig. 114c. Bracelet of fine gold
with three daisies and leaves in an openwork design, set with
diamonds. Six diamonds set in the back of the bracelet. *c.* 1890.
(Mr Fred Hurst)

FINE GOLD AND GEM BRACELETS.

In Best Morocco Cases, Lined Silk Velvet.

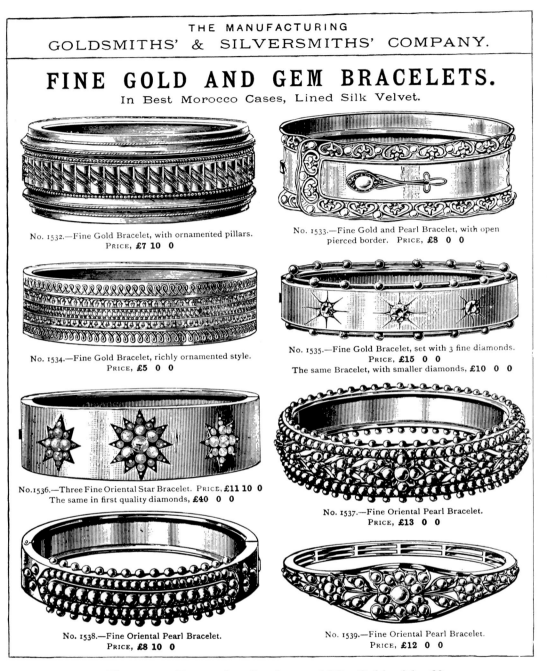

No. 1532.—Fine Gold Bracelet, with ornamented pillars.
PRICE, **£7 10 0**

No. 1533.—Fine Gold and Pearl Bracelet, with open pierced border. PRICE, **£8 0 0**

No. 1534.—Fine Gold Bracelet, richly ornamented style.
PRICE, **£5 0 0**

No. 1535.—Fine Gold Bracelet, set with 3 fine diamonds.
PRICE, **£15 0 0**
The same Bracelet, with smaller diamonds, **£10 0 0**

No. 1536.—Three Fine Oriental Star Bracelet. PRICE, **£11 10 0**
The same in first quality diamonds, **£40 0 0**

No. 1537.—Fine Oriental Pearl Bracelet.
PRICE, **£13 0 0**

No. 1538.—Fine Oriental Pearl Bracelet.
PRICE, **£8 10 0**

No. 1539.—Fine Oriental Pearl Bracelet.
PRICE, **£12 0 0**

Fig. 115. From the *Catalogue of The Goldsmiths &
Silversmiths Company Ltd.* for 1888
These bracelets were dropped from the catalogue in 1890.

[237]

FINE DIAMOND BRACELETS.

Of the Purest Water.

No. 10,305.—Fine Diamond " Cooing Doves."
£11 0 0

No. 10,306.—Fine Diamond Horseshoe and Crop.
£12 10 0

No. 10,307.—Fine Diamond Horseshoe.
£16 10 0

No. 10,308.—Fine Diamond Cluster.
£25 0 0

No. 10,309.—Fine Diamond Clover Leaf.
£25 0 0

No. 10,310.—Fine Diamond Heart.
£33 0 0

No. 10,311.—Fine Diamond Trefoil.
£35 0 0

No. 10,312.—Fine Diamond Cluster and Bar.
£35 0 0

Fig. 116. From the *Catalogue of The Goldsmiths &*
Silversmiths Company Ltd. for 1894

FINE GEM RINGS.

In Best Morocco Cases, Lined Silk Velvet.

No. 19,728.
Fine Pearl, "Turban" Pattern.
£1 7 6

No. 19,729.
Fine Pearl, 5-stone.
£2 0 0

No. 19,730.
Fine Pearl and Coral, 5-stone.
£2 0 0

No. 19,731.
Fine Pearl, 5-stone.
£2 0 0

No. 19,732.
Fine Pearl and Diamond, 5-stone.
£2 5 0

No. 19,733.
Fine Pearl and Diamond, 3-stone.
£2 10 0

No. 19,734.
Fine Diamond, 3-stone.
£3 10 0

No. 19,735.
Fine Pearl and Diamond, 5-stone.
£4 5 0

No. 19,736.
Fine Pearl and Diamond, 2-part.
£4 10 0

No. 19,737.
Fine Pearl and Diamond, 5-stone.
£5 0 0

No. 19,738.
Fine Pearl and Diamond, 5-stone.
£5 0 0

No. 19,739.
Fine Pearl and Diamond Gipsy.
£7 10 0

No. 19,740.
Fine Pearl Half-hoop, with Diamond Points.
£7 10 0
Other sizes from £4 to £25

No. 19,741.
Fine Pearl and Diamond 3-stone Coronet.
£20 0 0

No. 19,742.
Fine Ruby and Diamond, 2-part.
£22 10 0

No. 19,743.
Fine Pearl and Diamond Double Heart and Knot.
£17 10 0

No. 19,744.
Fine Pearl 3-stone Half-hoop, with Diamond Points.
£20 0 0

No. 19,745.
Fine Pearl Gipsy, 3-stone.
£4 0 0
Other sizes from £3 to £15

No. 19,746.
Fine Diamond and Pearl Cross-over.
£17 0 0

No. 19,747.
Fine Diamond and Pearl Cross-over.
£15 0 0

No. 19,748.
Fine Diamond and Pearl, 3-part.
£21 0 0

No. 19,749.
Fine Pearl and Diamond Cluster.
£23 0 0

No. 19,750.
Fine Pearl and Diamond Double-row.
£11 0 0

No. 19,751.
Fine Ruby and Diamond Double-row.
£11 0 0

Fig. 117. Rings in gold and jewels
From the *Catalogue of The Goldsmiths & Silversmiths Company Ltd.* for 1900.

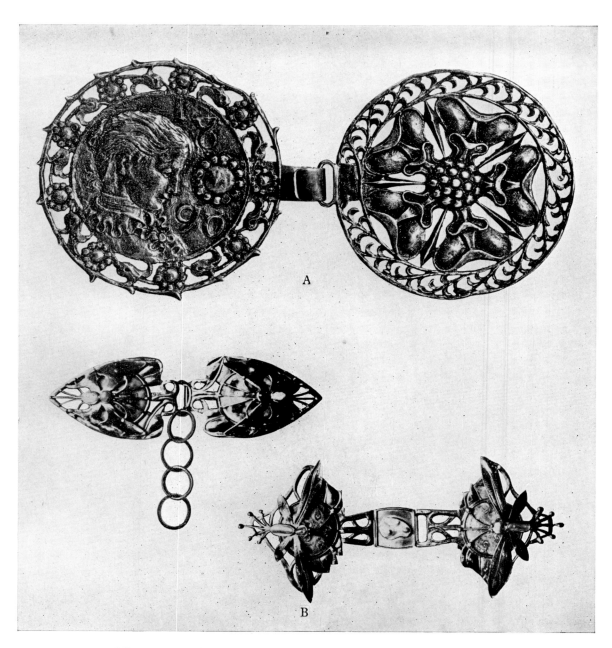

Fig. 118a. Cloak clasp in repoussé silver by C. R. Ashbee
On one side of the clasp is a portrait of the designer's mother. 1890.

(*Mrs C. R. Ashbee*)

Fig. 118b. Two clasps in silver, enamel and pearl blisters,
by C. R. Ashbee. *c.* 1896

(*From a photograph belonging to Mrs C. R. Ashbee*)

JEWELLERS

JEWELLERS

[As a possible convenience to readers in dating pieces of jewellery, I have listed here the names of as many jewellers and craftsmen as I have been able to discover who were in Britain during Queen Victoria's reign, with addresses and dates where they are known. The list is far from complete, and I should be very glad to receive any additional names or information.   M.F.]

J. J. ALLEN. Principal designer for the firm of W. & J. Randell.

JOSEPH ANGELL, manufacturing silversmith, at 10 Strand. Wholesale at 25 Panton Street, Haymarket. Showed jewellery at the 1862 Exhibition.

C. R. ASHBEE (1863-1942). *See* pp. 41-2, 201, 202, 203, 213, 214.

T. ASTON & SON, of Birmingham. Showed brooches at the 1862 Exhibition.

RICHARD ATTENBOROUGH. Founded 1796, and in business all through Queen Victoria's reign. In 1846, at 68 Oxford Street. In 1852, at 68 Oxford Street and 19 Piccadilly. In June 1898, called Jay, Richard Attenborough & Co., Ltd. Showed jewellery at the Exhibitions of 1851 and 1862.

W. BAKEWELL, of 25 Red Lion Street, Clerkenwell. Artist in hair. Showed specimens for lockets, brooches, etc. at the 1851 Exhibition.

JOHN BALLENY, of Birmingham. Showed brooches at the 1862 Exhibition.

J. & F. BIDEN, of 37 Cheapside. Showed gold seals and signet rings at the 1851 Exhibition.

T. and J. BRAGG, of Birmingham. Showed brooches at the 1862 Exhibition. In 1872, sponsored an exhibit showing processes in jewellery production.

BRIGHT & SONS, of Scarborough. Showed jewellery at the 1872 Exhibition.

JOHN BROGDEN. In 1846, a member of the firm Watherston & Bogden, 16 Henrietta Street, Covent Garden. In 1860, in business alone at the same address, where he continued until some time in the eighties. Medallist in the 1867 Exhibition. Castellani commended his work in the 1878 Exhibition.

W. CLEAL, of 53 Poland Street. Showed specimens of work in human hair at the 1851 Exhibition.

D. CONNELL, of 10 Nassau Street, Dublin. Showed brooches, bracelets etc. of Irish bog oak, mounted in Wicklow gold and Irish diamonds, at the 1851 Exhibition.

G. AND M. CRICHTON, of Edinburgh. Showed jewellery at the 1872 Exhibition.

ELLIS & SON, of Exeter. In 1851, exhibited their 'patent safety chain' brooches.

EMANUEL BROTHERS. In 1837, at 7 Bevis Market. In 1846, at 5 Hanover Square.

HARRY EMANUEL, F.R.G.S. In 1860, at 5 Hanover Square. In 1880, at 27 Old Bond Street. In 1890, at 40 Albemarle Street. Showed jewellery at Exhibitions of 1862 and 1867. Author of *Diamonds and Precious Stones*, 1865.

WILLIAM B. ESSEX, painter of enamel miniatures. In the fifties and sixties, at 3 Osnaburgh Street, Regent's Park.

W. B. FORD, painter in enamel. His best work was done 1884-7.

FORRER, of Hanover Street. Specialist in hair brooches, which he showed at the 1851 and 1862 Exhibitions.

FRANKLIN & HARE, of Taunton.

FRENCH & SONS, of 5 Newcastle Place, Clerkenwell Close. Showed jewellery at the 1851 Exhibition.

GARLAND & WATHERSTON. From 1837 to some time before 1846, at 16 Bridgewater Square.

R. & S. GARRARD, of Panton Street, Haymarket.

D. GASS & SONS. In 1837, at 166 Regent Street.

SAMUEL H. & DAVID GASS. In 1851, at the above address. In the 1851 Exhibition, showed the bracelet in Fig. 35a, also a silver gauntlet niello bracelet, designed by Maclise, and other jewellery.

CARLO GIULIANO (died c. 1912). See pp. 29, 131, 132, 137, 200, 202.

FEDERICO & FERDINANDO GIULIANO. In the nineties, at 47 Howland Street.

GEORGE A. GODWIN. In 1852, at 304 High Holborn. His copies of ancient jewellery mentioned in the Art Journal in 1875. His golfing brooches mentioned in the Queen in 1890.

RICHARD ANGELL GREEN. In 1860, at 82 Strand. In 1890, at 19 Cockspur Street. Sent jewellery to Exhibitions of 1862 and 1872. Won the prize for good taste in jewellery under £20 in 1868.

I. GREENBURY, of Whitby. Showed jet necklaces, bracelets, brooches and earrings at the 1851 Exhibition.

CHARLES FREDERICK HANCOCK. In 1851-60, at 39 Bruton Street and 152 New Bond Street.

HANCOCK & CO. At the same two addresses as the above, 1862-90. In 1890, at 204 Regent Street. Sent jewellery to the Exhibitions of 1862 and 1872.

THOMAS HANCOCK. From 1837 to 1852, at 17 New Bond Street.

J. HARDING, of St. David's, Exeter. Showed gold and silver bracelets, with secure snaps, at the 1851 Exhibition.

HARDMAN, of Birmingham. In 1851, executed jewellery designed by Pugin.

HARVEY & GORE, formerly Grayhurst, Harvey, Denton & Co. From 1832 to 1851 at 65 Strand, from where they moved to 126/7 Regent Street. Succeeded in 1870 by Harvey & Gore of Vigo Street.

HILLIARD & THOMASON, of Birmingham. Sent brooches, bracelets and corals to the 1851 Exhibition.

HOWELL & JAMES, at 5, 7 and 9 Regent Street, throughout Queen Victoria's reign. In 1837-46, described as linen drapers, silk workers and lacemen, as well as jewellers. In 1860, described as 'warehousemen'. Sent jewellery to the Exhibitions of 1862, 1867 and 1872.

HUNT & ROSKELL (See also Storr & Mortimer, and Mortimer & Hunt). In 1846, Hunt & Roskell (late Storr, Mortimer & Hunt) jewellers, goldsmiths and silversmiths to Her Majesty, were at 156 New Bond Street, with a manufactory at 26 Harrison Street. In 1890, they were at the same address.

B. LEE, of 41 Rathbone Place. Sent bracelets and brooches of human hair and gold, and hair guard chains to the 1851 Exhibition.

LISTER & SONS, of Newcastle-upon-Tyne. Showed jewellery and Highland ornaments at the 1851 Exhibition.

LONDON & RYDER. From c. 1855 to 1890, at 17 New Bond Street. Successors to Thomas Hancock. Received prize in the 1862 Exhibition.

CHARLES LYSTER & SON, of 84 Spencer Street, Birmingham. In 1872, they started a new piqué industry.

MARSHALL & SON, of Edinburgh. Showed Scotch jewellery at the Exhibitions of 1851 and 1878.

MARTIN, BASKETT & MARTIN, of Cheltenham. At the 1851 Exhibition, showed a bracelet and chatelaine, also pearls, ornaments, gold chains and jewellery, manufactured by C. Sparrow, London.

McKAY, CUNNINGHAM & CO., of Edinburgh. Showed jewellery at the 1872 Exhibition.

J. V. MOREL & CO., of 7 New Burlington Street. At the 1851 Exhibition, showed a bouquet of diamonds and rubies, the rubies being a unique collection.

MORTIMER & HUNT. From 1838 to 1848, at 156 New Bond Street. Succeeded by Hunt & Roskell.

MUIRHEAD, of Glasgow. Showed pebble jewellery at the 1862 Exhibition.

MRS. NEWMAN, of 10 Savile Row, W.

PASQUALE NOVISSIMO. Maker of pendant shown in Plate VII, *Fig.* a.

PARAVAGUA & CASELLA, of 3 Brabant Court, Philpot Lane. Showed carvings, bracelet, necklaces and cameos in coral at the 1851 Exhibition.

PARKER & STONE (*See also* Stone & Son). In 1860, at 7 Myddleton Street, Clerkenwell. Sent brooches to the 1862 Exhibition.

JAMES PARKES. From *c.* 1865 to after 1890, at 12 Vigo Street.

T. & J. PERRY, of 224 Regent Street, London, W.

ROBERT PHILLIPS (*d.* 1881). From 1846 to 1852, at Phillips Bros., 31 Cockspur Street. In 1860, the firm was at 23 Cockspur Street, at which address it remained until Robert Phillips's death. He sent work to all Exhibitions. Gold medal in 1867. Decorated by the King of Italy.

R. PRINGLE, of 21 Wilderness Row, London, E.C. Established 1835 and still in business.

W. AND J. RANDELL, of Birmingham. Showed jewellery at the 1867 Exhibition.

RETTIE & SON, of Aberdeen. Sent jewellery to the Exhibitions of 1851 and 1862.

C. & W. ROWLANDS, of 146 Regent Street. Showed bracelets and brooches in Holbein style at the 1851 Exhibition.

ROWLANDS & FRAZER. From *c.* 1870 to after 1890, at 146 Regent Street.

RUNDELL, BRIDGE & RUNDELL. Made Queen Victoria's crown. Also a finger-ring in the London Museum, commemorating the Queen's marriage, dated 1841.

C. T. SHAW, of Birmingham. Sent jewellery to the 1862 Exhibition.

ALFRED SHUFF, of 34 Great Marlborough Street. Maker of a gold-mounted hair bracelet, dated 1865, in the London Museum.

C. SPARROW, of London, (*See* Martin, Baskett & Martin).

STONE & SON, of 7 Myddleton Street, Clerkenwell. Sent chains, bracelets and rings to the 1851 Exhibition.

STORR & MORTIMER. In 1836, at 156 New Bond Street. In 1838, Storr, Mortimer and Hunt. Succeeded in 1846 by Hunt & Roskell.

EDWIN W. STREETER. In 1872, in Conduit Street. In May, 1875, moved to 18 New Bond Street. In 1880, had establishments also at 12 Clifford Street and at Colombo, Ceylon. In 1890, at the same three addresses. Sent jewellery to the 1872 Exhibition.

T. WALL, of Stokes Croft, Bristol. Sent original designs in hair work to the 1851 Exhibition.

WATHERSTON & BROGDEN (*See* Brogden). 1846-60, at 16 Henrietta Street, Covent Garden. Sent jewellery to the 1851 Exhibition.

WATHERSTON & SON. In 1867, at 112 Pall Mall East. Specialized in massive gold chains. Showed jewellery at the 1867 Exhibition.

HERMANN WEHFRITZ, of Clerkenwell. Two pieces made by him, one dated 1867, are in the London Museum.

J. WEST & SON, of Dublin. Showed jewellery embellished with Irish pearls and other gems, copied from antique Irish ornament, at the 1851 Exhibition.

G. & M. WHEELER, of 28 Bartlett's Buildings, Holborn. Sent jewellery and trinkets to the 1851 Exhibition.

WHITE & CAMPBELL, of New Bond Street. Sent jewellery to the 1872 Exhibition.

WILLIAM WHITELEY, of Westbourne Grove. Showed black glass jewellery at the 1872 Exhibition.

GLOSSARY

GLOSSARY

AGATE: Quartz with strata of different colours, or inclusions which resemble moss, or plain-coloured. Named for the river Achates.

AIGRETTE: A head ornament, of feathers or of jewels which are mounted in a shape resembling feathers.

AIGUILLETTE: A shoulder-knot, usually jewelled.

ALBERT: A fine gold chain with a bar at one end and a fitting to hold a watch at the other.

ALEXANDRITE: A variety of chrysoberyl which is green by natural and red by artificial light. Named after Alexander II of Russia because it first came to light on his birthday.

ALMA: The name of a chain with broad links, each link having a ribbed surface.

ALMANDINE: A violet-red variety of garnet.

AMAZONITE: Opaque green feldspar.

AMETHYST: A violet quartz. The so-called Oriental Amethyst is really a violet sapphire.

ANNEALING: Softening metal by means of heat so that all brittleness is removed.

ASTERISM: The name of the phenomenon characteristic of star-stones (called asterias). These stones, usually rubies or sapphires, have tube-like cavities regularly arranged at angles of 60° in planes at right angles to the crystallographical axis. When these stones are cut *en cabochon* perpendicular to that axis, a six-rayed star effect is perceived.

AVENTURINE QUARTZ: Quartz with glittering flakes of mica inside it.

BAGUETTES: Gems cut in the form of narrow rectangles; like baton-cut stones, but smaller.

BANDELETTES: Decorated ribbons worn in the hair, during the late sixties.

BANGLE: A bracelet which is not flexible.

BAROQUE (OR BARROK) PEARLS: Irregularly shaped pearls.

BASSE-TAILLE: A method of enamelling in which the surface of the metal is hollowed out to receive the enamel. Similar to champlevé.

BATON: Baton-cut stones are cut in the shape of a long, narrow rectangle.

BELCHER CHAIN: One in which the links are of equal size and of broad material.

BELCHER RING: A wide hoop through which a neckerchief was passed.

BENOITON CHAIN: A chain suspended from the bonnet or the coiffure encircling the face and making a loop on the bosom. *c.*1866.

BERYL: A species of precious stone embracing emerald, aquamarine, morganite, and stones of paler shades which jewellers term beryl.

BEZEL: Originally the part of a ring which holds the stone or other ornament. Now generally used to signify the salient or characteristic part of a ring, e.g. the setting, *including* the stone, or in a signet-ring the portion bearing the device.

BEZIL OR BEZEL Facets (Also called Top Main facets or Templates): The first four facets to be ground, immediately after the table, on the crown of a brilliant-cut stone.

BEZOAR: The stomach- or gall-stone of an animal set as a jewel and thought to be an antidote against poison.

BIJOUTERIE: The art of working in gold and enamel, as distinct from joaillerie, the art of mounting precious stones.

[249]

BLISTER PEARLS: A pearly deposit cut away from an oyster shell; irregularly-shaped and sometimes hollow.

BLUE JOHN: A blue variety of fluorspar.

BOART, OR BORT: Diamonds useless for cutting. Such pieces are crushed to powder and used for cutting or polishing.

BRILLIANT: A form of cutting introduced by Vincenzio Peruzzi at Venice in the late seventeenth century. Nearly all diamonds are now brilliant-cut and the word 'brilliant' commonly means a diamond cut in this way. In a perfect brilliant there are fifty-eight facets, thirty-three above, and twenty-five below the girdle.

BRIOLETTES: Oval or drop-shaped stones, facetted all over and often pierced at the top.

BRUTING: The first process in fashioning diamonds. The stone to be cut is ground into shape by rubbing it with another rough diamond.

BUGLES: Glass beads used in dress trimming.

CABOCHON: Cut in a curved shape, not facetted.

CAIRNGORM: A brownish variety of smoky quartz

CALIBRÉ-CUT: Small stones cut to special measurements.

CAMEO: A gem or shell carved in relief.

CARAT: The unit of weight for precious stones. The name comes from κεράτιον, the seed of the locust tree. These were once used to weigh jewels. A carat is one-fifth of a gram, and about $\frac{1}{142}$ of an ounce Avoirdupois.

CARBUNCLE: A garnet cut *en cabochon.*

CAT'S EYE: A variety of chrysoberyl showing chatoyancy.
     Quartz cat's eyes are also used for jewellery, but these are not the true cat's eyes.

CHALCEDONY: Greyish-blue quartz.

CHAMPLEVÉ: Enamel work in which a graving tool has been used to hollow out spaces for the enamel pastes in a metal background.

CHASING: Surface modelling of metal with hammer and punches.

CHATELAINE: A brooch or clasp from which hang on short chains a variety of objects, such as keys, a watch, scissors or trinkets.

CHATON: The central ornament of a ring.

CHATOYANCY: The characteristic displayed by some stones, notably chrysoberyl and some varieties of quartz, in which a single broadish band of light appears.

CHRYSOBERYL: A species of precious stone to which cat's eyes and alexandrites belong.

CHRYSOLITE: A pale yellowish-green stone, which is a variety of peridot.

CHRYSOPRASE: Light green quartz.

CLAW SETTING: *See* Coronet Setting.

CLOISONNÉ: Enamel work in which applied fillets of metal separate the coloured enamel pastes.

COCKTAIL RING: A name given about 1925 to heavy, elaborate rings of unusual design, thought to be suitable for wear at cocktail or dinner parties.

COLLET: A round of metal.

COLLET SETTING: A method of setting by which the precious stone is held in its place by enclosing it in a band of metal.

COLLIER: A wide necklet which encircles the neck from throat to chin.

CORBEILLE: Gifts made to a bride by the bridegroom.

CORDONNIÈRE: A girdle, twisted to resemble cord, tied in front, with long ends hanging down.

CORNELIAN: A clear red chalcedony.

CORONET OR CLAW SETTING: A method by which a precious stone is secured by means of claws projecting from the base of its setting. A coronet setting is always round, while a claw setting may be square.

CORUNDUM: A species of gem-stone next to diamond in hardness, doubly refractive, dichroic and variously coloured. Rubies and sapphires belong to this species.

COSTUME JEWELLERY: Ornaments made of non-precious material, and designed to suit the prevailing fashions in dress.

CREOLE EARRING: A hoop, in which the metal is thicker at the bottom than at the top.

CROSS FACET: Also called Break or Skill facets. The small facets which form the boundary of the girdle in a brilliant-cut stone. There are sixteen above and sixteen below the girdle.

CROSS-OVER: A type of ring, bracelet or brooch in which the decoration is composed of stones set at an angle to the main axis of the piece.

CROWN: That part of a brilliant-cut diamond which lies above the girdle. It contains thirty-three facets, including the table.

CROWN SETTING: An open setting with rebated points to hold the stone.

CULET: The point of a brilliant-cut diamond. It lies at the base of the stone and is ground to a blunt end, forming a minute horizontal facet.

CURB: The most common pattern for gold chain bracelets.

CYMOPHANE: The chrysoberyl cat's eye.

DAMASCENE: To incrust metals with other metals; an art once practised chiefly in Damascus.

DEMI-PARURE: A small parure, or matching set of jewellery. A demi-parure may be a brooch with earrings to match, a brooch with one or two bracelets, a necklace with earrings, and so on.

DICHROISM: A property possessed by certain doubly-refracting stones of showing two different colours when looked at from different directions.

DICHROSCOPE: An instrument through which dichroism can be observed.

DOUBLET: A thin piece of colourless or pale stone cut table fashion, to the lower side of which a coloured paste is cemented. The paste is hidden by the mount and the upper surface answers all the tests for hardness.

ENAMELLING: A kind of work in which a silicate of glass mixed with powdered metallic oxides, which produce the desired colour, is placed on metal in a prepared design and then fused until the enamel (powder or paste) adheres to the metal.

EN ESCLAVAGE: A necklace in which several strands start together and then separate, at an equal distance one from the other.

ETERNITY RINGS: Those in the form of a plain hoop, the circle being regarded as the symbol of eternity. The plain hoop of the wedding ring symbolizes eternal fidelity. Eternity rings are usually set with a continuous line of small stones.

FACET: One of the flat polished faces of a cut stone.

FEDE-RINGS: Those which bear two hands clasped in troth.

FERRONNIÈRE: Chain encircling the forehead and held by a jewel in the middle. (As in Leonardo da Vinci's portrait of 'La Belle Ferronnière'.)

FETTER CHAIN: One with long-shaped links.

FIBULA: (Ancient jewellery) A brooch or clasp.

FILIGREE: Lace-like ornament made in very fine wire.

GARNET: A variety of gem-stone which occurs in many colours. Some of the names given to garnets are:

    ALMANDINE, violet-red
    PYROPE, dark red
    RHODOLITE, pale violet
    SPESSARTITE, brownish-red
    GROSSULARITE, pale green
    HESSONITE, orange
    ANDRADITE, yellow or green
    DEMANTOID, olive green
    UVAROVITE, emerald green

GIPSY MOUNT: An even circular band of metal. Used in rings and earrings.

GIRANDOLE: A type of earring in which three pendent stones hang from a large central stone.

GIRDLE: The edge separating the upper and lower portions of a cut stone; also the edge which is fixed in the setting.

GRAIN: A small spherical bead of metal.

GRELOTS: Small elongated beads which hang as pendants from necklets or collars.

GUARD CHAIN: A long gold chain hung round the neck, originally used for keys and toilet necessities.

GUIPURE: A heavy, large-patterned decorative lace.

HELIOTROPE, OR BLOODSTONE: Dark green quartz with red spots.

INTAGLIO: A carving on a gem. The pattern is hollowed out below the surface, unlike the pattern on a cameo, which stands up in relief.

JASERON CHAIN: A fine gold neck-chain on which crosses and pendants are often hung.

JASPER: Opaque quartz, white, yellow, red, green or brown.

KEEPER RING: A heavy gold ring, with a chased pattern.

LABRET: A jewel worn in a perforation of the lip.

LACQUE or LASQUE DIAMONDS: Flat-topped irregularly shaped diamonds.

LEONTINE CHAIN: A long chain, like a guard chain, to which a watch was usually attached.

LIMOGES: Enamel work which resembles a painting.

MALACHITE: A bright green mineral with a variegated pattern, much used in pebble jewellery.

MANCHETTE: *Bracelet manchette*, or cuff-bracelet.

MARCASITE: Iron pyrites; a mineral of the colour of brass, with a metallic lustre.

MARQUISE: A pointed-oval shape used in rings or earrings.

MILLEGRAIN: A kind of setting in which the metal gripping the stone is decorated with a line of tiny grains or beads.

MOONSTONE: Whitish feldspar, with light blue wavy lines.

MORGANITE: The rose beryl.

NEPHRITE: Jade; usually the less valuable sort.

NICOLO: Onyx with a black ground and a thin upper layer of white, through which the black shines, making a bluish tint. Much used for cameos and intaglios.

NIELLO: A black material (sulphur, lead, silver and copper mixed) used to fill engraved work on silver or gold.

OBSIDIAN: A volcanic glass, or fused lava. Generally flecked bottle-green.

OLIVINE: A green stone, the peridot. Incorrect name for the green or demantoid garnet.

PARURE: A matching set of jewellery, consisting usually of necklace, brooch, earrings and bracelets.

PAVÉ SETTING: In this method the whole front of an ornament is covered or paved with stones. The arrangement should be clusters of seven stones touching each other from every position. The stones are held in position by grains of metal.

PAVILION: That part of a brilliant-cut stone which lies below the girdle. It contains twenty-five facets, including the culet.

PAVILION FACETS: The first four facets immediately after the culet, to be ground on the pavilion of a brilliant-cut stone.

PENDELOQUE: A drop-shaped stone often used for pendants. It is facetted all over, and differs from a briolette only in having a table.

PERIDOT: A bottle-green stone known to science as olivine or chrysolite.

PINCHBECK: An alloy, resembling gold, composed of about one part zinc to five parts copper. Invented by Christopher Pinchbeck in the early eighteenth century.

PLIQUE À JOUR: Enamel work in which the enamel has no background. The different colours are separated by wires, and the effect resembles that of a stained-glass window.

POINT CUTTING: An obsolete method of cutting diamonds. The stone tapered to a point, which could be used for writing on glass.

POSY-RINGS: Those which have a 'poesy' or motto engraved on the inner side.

QUOINS, or LOZENGES: Facets in a brilliant-cut diamond, coming between the templets or bezels.

REGARD RING: A ring set with a row of small stones of different kinds, the initial letters of which spell a word. For example, to spell 'regard', the stones could be:
Ruby
Emerald
Garnet
Amethyst
Ruby
Diamond

REPOUSSÉ WORK: The raising of a pattern in relief on metal, by beating from the back.

RESILLA: From *résille*, a network. A name applied to a type of ornamentation composed of small beads sewn in patterns.

RIVIÈRE: Long necklace of single stones, usually diamonds.

ROSE CUTTING: A method of cutting diamonds dating from the mid-seventeenth century. The stone has a flat base and rises to a point at the top. A Dutch Rose has twenty-four facets; the Rose Recoupée has thirty-six.

ROUGE: Peroxide of iron, used in the final polishing of precious metals.

RUBELLITE: The rose-pink tourmaline.

RUBY: The red corundum. Most fine rubies come from the famous mines near Mogok in Upper Burma.

SAUTOIR: A very long narrow necklace, often having a tassel or ornament at the bottom.

SHANK, or hoop of a ring: Circle of metal or other substance surrounding the finger.

SHOULDERS of a ring: Parts of the hoop approaching the bezel on either side.

SKILL FACET: *See* Cross Facet.

SPINEL: A precious stone, much like corundum, variously coloured. Its most prized variety is the rose-coloured gem incorrectly called the Balas-ruby.

STAR-FACET: One of eight triangular facets surrounding the table in a brilliant-cut stone.

STAR SETTING: When a gem is deeply set, with its table scarcely rising above the surface of the surrounding metal, rays are engraved as though coming from the gem, which then appears as a star. This method is used on gipsy rings and on plain gold lockets.

STOMACHER: An ornamental covering for the front of the upper body.

STRAPWORK: A kind of decoration composed of flat bands or straps which are folded, crossed or interlaced.

STRASS: A very brilliant type of paste. Stras, a Parisian jeweller, is said to have discovered the formula in the eighteenth century.

STUD EARRINGS: Those in which the gem is set on a short straight pin which goes through the ear and is held in place by a screw or spring fitting at the back. Thus the earring is held tight against the lobe of the ear.

SUITE: A matching set of jewellery. A parure.

EN SUITE: Matching. Forming a set.

SYNTHETIC GEMS: Those made by the fusion of the chemical constituents of the natural gem.

TABLE: The large horizontal facet on the top of a facetted stone.

TAILLE D' EPERGNE: a kind of enamelling, the reverse of *champlevé*, as the ornamentation is simply engraved and then filled with enamel, the colour of which is generally blue or black. It is mostly used for mourning rings, charms and similar jewellery. The designs are usually fine scroll ornaments, or interlaced lines.

TALLOW CUT: Rounded in shape like cabochon stones but with a flattish top.

TEMPLET: same as Bezil.

THREAD SETTING: One in which a thin thread of gold outlines the gem.

TOPAZ: A species of gem-stone doubly refractive and with perfect cleavage. Topazes of all colours are found. The precious, or Brazilian topaz, occurs in all colours, though yellow is the most usual. Brownish topazes, which are difficult to sell, can be given a heat treatment which makes them a fine rose-pink.

TRACE: The name of a chain pattern in which the links are oval and of equal size.

TOURMALINE: A variety of gem-stone having double refraction to a high degree and embracing all colours. Some tourmalines have chatoyancy.

TURQUOISE: A light-blue or light-green opaque gem, which received its name through being first brought from Turkey.

UNION PIN: A pin in two parts. On one part is a hole or socket into which the point of the actual pin fits, so that it is joined into one piece.

ZIRCON: A type of gem-stone appearing in all colours, and approaching a diamond in lustre.

BIBLIOGRAPHY

BIBLIOGRAPHY

I. JEWELLERY AND PRECIOUS STONES

ABBOTT, Mary: *Jewels of Romance and Renown*, 1933.
ASHBEE, C. R.: *Craftsmanship in Competitive Industry*, 1908.
BURGESS, Fred W.: *Antique Jewellery and Trinkets*, 1919.
CASTELLANI, Augusto: *Antique Jewellery and its Revival*, 1862.
       Della Orificeria Italiana, Rome, 1872.
CHURCH, Sir A. H.: *Precious Stones. A Guide to the Townshend Collection*, 1924.
DALTON, O. M.: Franks Bequest. *Catalogue of the Finger Rings*. British Museum, 1912.
DAVENPORT, Cyril: *Cameos*, 1900.
       Jewellery, 1905.
DAWSON, Nelson: *Goldsmiths' and Silversmiths' Work*, 1907.
DENT, Herbert C.: *Piqué*, 1923.
EMANUEL, Harry: *Diamonds and Precious Stones*, 1865.
FONTENAY, Eugène: *Les Bijoux Anciens et Modernes*, Paris, 1887.
HOLME, Charles, ed.: *Modern Design in Jewellery and Fans*, 1902.
KUNZ, G. F.: *Rings*, Philadelphia, 1917.
KUNZ & STEVENSON: *The Book of the Pearl*, 1908.
PACK, Greta: *Jewelry and Enameling*, New York, 1941.
ROCHE, J. C.: *The History, Development and Organization of the Birmingham Jewellery and Allied Trades*, 1927.
SELWYN, A.: *The Retail Jeweller's Handbook*, 1945.
SMITH, F. R.: *Small Jewellery*, 1931.
SMITH, G. F. Herbert: *Gem-Stones*, 1912.
SMITH, H. Clifford: *Jewellery*, 1908.
STOPFORD, Francis: *The Romance of the Jewel*, 1920.
STREETER, Edwin W.: *Precious Stones and Gems*, 1898.
VEVER, Henri: *Histoire de la Bijouterie Francaise au xix^e siecle*, 1908.
WEINSTEIN, Michael: *Precious and Semi-precious Stones*, 1929.
WIGLEY, Thomas B.: *The Art of the Goldsmith and Jeweller*, 1911.
WILSON, Henry: *Silverwork and Jewellery*, 1912.

II. FASHION AND COSTUME

BELL, Quentin: *Of Human Finery*, 1947.
BLANC, Charles: *Art in Ornament and Dress*, 1877.
BOEHN, Max von: *Modes and Manners. Ornaments*, 1929.
CUNNINGTON, C. Willett: *English Women's Clothing in the Nineteenth Century*, 1937.
       Feminine Attitudes in the Nineteenth Century, 1935.
HAWEIS, Mrs H. R.: *The Art of Beauty*, 1878.
LAVER, James: *Taste and Fashion*, 1945.
UZANNE, Octave: *Fashion in Paris*, 1898.
WALKER, Mrs A.: *Female Beauty*, 1837.
WOMEN'S MAGAZINES
 La Belle Assemblée
 Englishwoman's Domestic Magazine
 Le Follet

The Ladies' Cabinet
The Ladies' Treasury
Le Petit Courier de Dames
The Queen
Sylvia's Home Journal
World of Fashion
Young Ladies' Journal

III. EXHIBITIONS AND THE ARTS

Art Union, 1839–48.
Art Journal, 1849–1901.
Art Journal Catalogues of Exhibitions, 1851, 1855, 1862 and 1867.
CASTELLANI, Alessandro: *Esposizione Universale del 1878 in Parigi . . . Classe* xxxix.
  Gioielleria, Rome, 1879.
Journal of Design, 1849–51.
RIMMEL, Eugene: *Recollections of the Paris Exhibition of* 1867, 1868.
SALA, George Augustus: *Notes and Sketches of the Paris Exhibition*, 1868.
TALLIS: *History and Description of the Crystal Palace*, n.d.

INDEX

INDEX